H-POP

Praise for *H-Pop*

'We tend to think of music and poetry as art forms that entertain and elevate. Yet, as Kunal Purohit's powerful and compellingly original book shows, they can equally be used to foster division and hatred. This is a pioneering study, to my knowledge the first book to systematically investigate the use—and abuse—of popular culture by the Hindu right. Through closely reported profiles of performers, Purohit demonstrates how through their words and sentiments they seek to demonize and dehumanize religious minorities. A work of courage and clarity, this is an illuminating—and at times deeply disturbing—exploration into the paranoias and fantasies of an increasingly influential tendency in our public life.'

—Ramachandra Guha

'This is a very original and important book which shows that beyond politics, Hindutva is acquiring a societal dimension by penetrating the pillars of India's popular culture. Power may change hands, but these artistic genres are part of society. Kunal Purohit educates us on the long-term implications of what is not a saffron wave only.'

—Christophe Jaffrelot

'Like Klemperer in 1930s Dresden, Purohit documents the everyday brutality and degeneration being injected into the society we call New India. This vital work shows us the faces and makes us hear the voices of those on the frontline of the war this nation is waging against itself.'

—Aakar Patel

'Weaponizing pop culture in the service of Hindutva nationalism … Kunal Purohit uncovers a dark reality of what fuels the hate machine. Frighteningly real, this book is a must-read for anyone wishing to understand the cultural underpinnings of a religio-political movement. Based on solid ground reporting, this eye-opening book will awaken the reader to a "new" India that is being divided even by music, poetry, books.'

—Rajdeep Sardesai

H·POP

THE
SECRETIVE WORLD
OF HINDUTVA POP STARS

KUNAL PUROHIT

HarperCollins *Publishers* India

First published in India by HarperCollins *Publishers* 2023
4th Floor, Tower A, Building No. 10, DLF Cyber City,
DLF Phase II, Gurugram, Haryana – 122002
www.harpercollins.co.in

2 4 6 8 10 9 7 5 3

Copyright © Kunal Purohit 2023

P-ISBN: 978-93-5699-582-6
E-ISBN: 978-93-5699-583-3

Typeset in 11.5/15 Adobe Garamond Pro at
Manipal Technologies Limited, Manipal

Printed and bound in India by
Thomson Press India Ltd

To Papa and Ma, for getting us this far
And to my country, increasingly unrecognizable

The detailed notes pertaining to this book are available on the HarperCollins *Publishers* India website. Scan this QR code to access the same.

Contents

Author's Note

All the material in the book is based on interviews and references that have been included in the manuscript as endnotes. The viewpoints expressed by the interviewees are also in the public domain, through their work, interviews and social media posts. I have spent over three years interacting with the principal characters of this book, and it is their consent that has made this book possible. They were made aware of, both, my identity as a journalist and the purpose of those interactions, i.e., to write this book. All the conversations quoted here are on the record. To maintain accuracy, I have recorded the audio of all those interactions, with the consent of the interviewees, and have quoted the characters from those audio recordings.

Introduction

Some of the most important stories are often discovered accidentally. Journalists out reporting on one story, stumble upon another.

This book originates in one such accidental discovery. On a warm, dusty evening in March 2019, I found myself in Gumla, a town in southern Jharkhand.

Gumla does not make it to the news very often. Its narrow lanes are bustling with people, animals, blaring motorcycles and hand-pulled carts. Dust and oxygen get interspersed in the air, but you won't realize this because the noise—of people, animals, blaring motorcycles and hand-pulled carts—will drown out all other sensory perceptions.

It lulls you into believing that it's just another nondescript town, where nothing noteworthy happens. Until it does.

Exactly two years before my visit, in April 2017, the happenings of an evening had jolted this town into a stunned silence.

Over chai, locals told me the story. The story of a Ram Navami procession, thousands of men strong, that had slowly snaked its way peacefully through Gumla's labyrinthine lanes. Most of these processions consist of a caravan of open trucks with DJs, alongside powerful booming speakers, playing loud music to keep the crowds energized. Traditionally, the processions were a demonstration of a peaceful coexistence between the town's dominant Hindu population and its Muslim community. Each year, unfailingly, eminent Muslims would welcome the procession with sweets and garlands when it reached the town's biggest mosque in the heart of Gumla, the Jama Masjid.

That evening, the procession, suddenly and inexplicably, turned boisterous and ferocious, the moment it neared Jama Masjid.

No one seemed to know why the processionists had suddenly changed their attitude.

I couldn't understand either. How could a procession turn into a mob, I asked eyewitnesses to the incident.

I made them recount the sequence of events over and over again. Until in one re-telling, I caught one local summarily mention— more like dismiss—a single thing that changed as the procession got close: the music played by the revellers.

As the procession entered the lane housing the mosque, the music switched. The loud bass beats ensured not much was audible. But some words were: 'Toss the mullah's skull cap to the ground'.

And just like that, like a switch had been flicked somewhere, the crowds were suddenly electrified. They started chanting Hindu slogans, in ways that onlookers perceived were meant to be aggressive and deliberately provocative to Muslims.

The Muslims outside the mosque, waiting to welcome the revellers, suddenly felt threatened. Tensions were running high. It could have gotten worse. Thankfully, police officials swung into action and switched off the music.

A situation was averted. Till it wasn't.

A few hours later, some Hindu men from the same procession were returning home when they saw a Muslim man with a young Hindu woman in Soso village about 4 km away from Gumla. The man was twenty-year-old Gumla resident Mohamed Shalik; the woman was a local.

Many in the group knew Shalik, his father, MD Minhaj, told me.[1] But, bobbing with raw aggression and adrenaline in the wake of the procession, the men decided to forget they knew Shalik.

They tied him to an electric pole off the road and assaulted him with rods and sticks. By the time Minhaj reached there, Shalik was nearly dead. He died in Gumla's Sadar Hospital minutes later.[2]

I couldn't sleep that night.

That was also the night this book was born.

~

Back in my Rs 250-a-night lodging that night, I spent hours trawling the internet. What were these songs that were driving men into such mad frenzies? Who were the 'pop stars' of this world?

As I looked for answers, my curiosity soon dissolved into a mix of worry and shock.

I found this genre of music was thriving, with songs targeting everyone from Muslims to Pakistanis, from rival politicians to critics of Prime Minister Narendra Modi and his Bharatiya Janata Party (BJP). Across the internet, these songs had been viewed millions of times, shared and liked by tens of thousands of people and disseminated across social media platforms.

The more I dug in, the stronger my suspicion grew: What happened in Gumla had not been an isolated incident.

The nature of my trip changed after that night. For the next two weeks through Jharkhand, even as I tried to unspool the reasons that were driving hate crimes, I found myself investigating whether music had been a factor.

In district after district, I found a similar story unravelling: angry, hate-filled Hindu mobs were being goaded into violence by songs. Songs that echoed and amplified the hate inside them. Police officials confided in me off the record that they were now having to scrutinize the playlists in Ram Navami processions, afraid that provocative songs would stoke tensions. Music had been weaponized; its fundamental purpose to entertain and offer pleasure had been altered. Music was no longer meant to merely entertain but also indoctrinate.

This music was everywhere: on Jharkhand's streets, its concerts, its public buses, as phone ringtones. It got uncomfortably close— my driver on the trip, a young man with sympathies for the Hindu nationalist group Bajrang Dal had as his caller tune a song called 'Har Ghar Bhagwa Chhayega', Saffron will fly atop each home. The song made no bones about wanting to see India as a Hindu-first nation.

Such music, when fused with psychedelic beats and hypnotic rhythms, combined with the headiness that being in a group brings, can turn processions into bloodthirsty mobs, as Gumla showed.

Its threatening nature was clear to many in these regions: some, like local Hindu right-wing groups, vouched for it, others, like cops, minorities and activists, warned against it.

But beyond Jharkhand, not many knew this was happening. Most still don't.

I decided to dive in and find out more.

While investigating it, an entire ecosystem unfolded before my eyes—songwriters, singers, musicians, studios and production houses, all enmeshed in the process of producing songs to further the ideals of Hindu nationalism, of Hindutva.

En route I made another disturbing discovery—music was not the only form of popular culture to have been radically altered by the touch of Hindu nationalism. Like music, a new, Hindutva-fuelled genre had emerged in two other forms of mass consumption and entertainment: poetry and book publishing. Like music, each of these popular cultures has been weaponized in service of Hindutva ideals.

Since then, for nearly five years now, I have burrowed deep into this world of Hindutva-driven popular culture.

The book will attempt to tell the story of Hindutva's subversion of all three forms of popular culture, through the eyes of three protagonists—engaged in creating Hindutva music, Hindutva poetry and building a Hindutva publishing network, each. These three protagonists are nothing less than stars in their own rights—all of them enjoy fandom, and mass following; their work and words reaching and shaping millions of minds.

You might not have heard of any of them, but they are moulding their worlds in ways that have consequences for all our lives.

All of them are from diverse backgrounds, traversing different life trajectories and yet, all are united in their commitment to provoke, push their ideology, no matter how controversial, and to recruit more followers.

Set in north and central India, I travelled across countless villages spread across seven states, trying to understand what drove these pop stars and how ordinary Indians were drawn to their work.

Since that first night in Gumla, the story has lived with me. It is now ready to be shared.

This is the story of Hindutva pop, or H-Pop.

Popular culture, by its very definition, implies a form of culture and art enjoyed by large sections of society. Its reach and wide acceptance make it an enticing draw for those who seek wider audiences for their message—be it commercial advertisers or political actors.

Through the twentieth century, political propaganda has often masqueraded as pop culture.

For instance, the United States government has, for decades, cultivated pop culture to further its domestic and foreign policy objectives.

This has allowed it to shape public opinion in its favour and build a robust reputation for itself, no matter what it does. For instance, while the US government was contemplating entering the Second World War, a public poll in 1940 showed only 35 per cent of the respondents were in favour of the US joining the war.[3] The US government then masterfully crafted a comprehensive strategy to produce popular culture content to change this sentiment in favour of jumping into the war. One of the most significant ways it did so was by opening a liaisoning office in Hollywood and enlisting the likes of Walt Disney and the Warner Brothers through official contracts to create films with subtle but firm attempts at convincing citizens of the need to join the war.[4] The campaign worked, and the US joined the Allies' war effort.

Unsurprisingly, autocrats and fascists see great value in using popular culture to disseminate their political agenda. Disguising propaganda as pop culture sweetens the poison pill, packaging hate and anger towards the perceived enemy in easily consumable, seemingly trivial ways.

Even before the Americans saw the potential in tapping pop culture for their political goals, the Nazis in Germany and the Fascists in Italy had spent many years perfecting the practice. Soon after coming to power in Germany in the 1930s, the Nazi Party had established an unshakeable control over cultural production—books by critics and by Jewish authors were burnt and a new 'Reich Culture Chamber' was created to regulate and coordinate the party's control over film, music, theatre, press, literature, fine arts as well as the radio.[5]

In Italy, the Fascists funded theatre productions, while ensuring that these plays showcased qualities and ideals they were keen to promote, like 'faith, patriotism ... the theme of self-sacrifice' among others.[6] The state went out of its way to promote this brand of theatre—it even subsidized theatres so that they could lower ticket prices and allow more audiences to see this propaganda-disguised-as-theatre. The Fascists also funded the production of movies they approved of.

More recently, from Islamic fundamentalists like Al Qaeda to far-right white nationalists, extremists of various hues have relied heavily on creating their own, alternative cultural forms. These cultural pieces have allowed them to disseminate their ideology in ways that appeal to large sections, making themselves heard beyond their core audiences and luring new recruits into the fold.

There is extensive literature on all these subversions of popular culture globally. Not just academic, there are books, news features and documentaries that detail how these extremist groups disseminate their ideology. In contrast, the use of popular culture by the Hindu right-wing has been barely studied, even less understood.

This book hopes to lay the first brick in addressing this critical void.

~

At a time when Hindu nationalism has become the most dominant political ideology in the world's largest democracy, this study becomes even more important to undertake.

In my travels, I saw tectonic shifts in the way people were constructing their realities, conceiving their histories and imagining their futures. People's identities, complex and multilayered, were stripped down to their religion. Syncretic traditions and old relationships were breaking down. Communalism was being normalized, hatred for other religions was now acceptable.

The BJP, its ideological mothership the Rashtriya Swayamsevak Sangh (RSS), and their allied Hindutva outfits, have strived to ensure that these changes are not dependent on political victories—i.e., the genie is out of the bottle, whether the BJP is in power or not.

This new social order hasn't been built overnight. Helping the Hindu right-wing achieve this is an assembly line of dedicated workers, constantly striving to fulfil responsibilities they have either been allotted or have taken up voluntarily, purely out of their commitment to the cause or their rabid hatred for their 'enemies'. Unlike the politics of the past, these workers don't go door-to-door, nor do they hit the streets. Instead, they dominate social media platforms and drum up support for the party by drowning out all criticism, taking down critics and dissenters.

It is here, in this constant tug-of-war of narratives, that popular culture becomes important as yet another vehicle for narrative-setting.

Clothing propaganda in cultural forms like poetry, music and books makes it a lot more effective than undisguised political speech. By being insidious, it creeps up on unsuspecting victims, lodging itself deep inside their veins, eventually shaping their thoughts and beliefs.

A song with foot-tapping beats and a catchy rhythm might actually be warning you about an impending 'Islamic takeover' of India. Or a book that promises you the 'truth' behind the Partition of India is filled with conspiracy theories rather than historical facts, biases in place of evidence, all in line with the core beliefs of Hindu nationalists.

What makes propaganda-as-pop culture so effective is its everydayness, the easy access that it has to its prey. Its prey does not need to take the effort to visit a political public meeting, nor does it need to seek out passionately delivered political speeches. The prey just has to feel the need to be entertained. The prey needs to seek out a break from the routine—often, just a few clicks away. That's where propaganda-as-pop culture swoops in, locks the prey in a soft embrace on the pretext of delighting them, be it with beats, rhymes or easy prose. That's when it enters the veins, slowly, one moment at a time. Then with each repetition, it slowly builds up passions the prey didn't know existed before, passions of hate, anger and suspicion towards others around it.

These passions linger, biding for an opportune time, building up their strength, nonetheless. Then, be it a Ram Navami procession, a heady crowd full of men sharing similar passions or a minor dispute with that neighbour from a different religion—these passions get activated whenever they get a chance.

Having spent months investigating hate crimes, both their geneses as well as their afterlives, I saw how they came to be built, slowly, gradually, over time.

We, in the media, have often covered them as events—sudden, mindless outbursts of violence triggered by something immediate. The truth is, they are anything but that—lying at the core of these outbursts is a constant, unending supply of everyday communalism. Hindutva pop culture is custom-built to address this need for everyday communalism.

Instruments like music, poetry and books help in this slow radicalization, dripping bit by bit like a tap into a bucket, till the bucket overflows, eventually. Riots, hate speeches, public processions and rallies are passé—they are time-consuming, costly affairs and carry the risk of earning the perpetrators bad headlines. These events also don't reflect too well on the global statesman-like image that Modi has sought to craft for himself.

Hindutva pop solves some of these dilemmas. It provides ways to disseminate hate and stoke anger against minority groups and rivals each day, without ever becoming a tangible event, like a hate speech rally or a riot.

Instead, each time the cultural product is consumed—i.e., each time the song is heard or the poetry recited or the book read—Hindutva beliefs are pushed and reiterated, in a bid to provoke rage and fear for the 'enemy'.

It is time we take this slow, everyday communalism seriously. It is time we understand a rapidly changing India.

I hope this book makes you sit up and do that.

PART 1

Killer Beats, Poison-laced Words: Kavi Singh

An Introduction to Kavi Singh

Agar chhua mandir toh tujhe dikha denge,
Tujhko teri aukaad bata denge.

Don't you dare touch the temple,
Or else we will show you your place.

Much about Kavi Singh is difficult to believe. It is difficult to believe that she sang for the first time in her life only in 2019—and has since then recorded over eighty songs with tens more in the pipeline, recorded and waiting to be released.

It is also difficult to believe that she is just twenty-five years old. Her assured tone, her confidence, combined with her somewhat unusual dressing—she is always dressed in a kurta-pyjama set with a Nehru jacket to go and a pagdi, a turban, wrapped around her head—make her seem a lot older than she is.

What isn't difficult to believe is how seriously Kavi takes her work—she insists that she is on a mission. The mission is to spark

1

'deshbhakti', patriotism, among Indians who seem to have forgotten traditional values and 'desh prem', love for the country. For Kavi, an important part of that desh prem is to realize, like she has, the biggest threat that the country faces—that of an imminent Islamic demographic takeover. Kavi is convinced that the country's Muslim population is conspiring to execute a slow, silent coup against Hindus.

Kavi is a Hindutva pop star blazing her way through the country, creating songs that echo some of the core beliefs of Hindu nationalism.

In just four years, Kavi has delivered songs on almost every major talking point among Hindu right-wing circles—from the need to bring a law to control the population,[1] thinly veiled as an effort to halt the growth of Muslims in the country, or to warn Hindu girls against 'love jihad': an imagined Islamic strategy to lure them into Islam on the pretext of marriage.[2] Through her work, Kavi shapes narratives by presenting her take on all significant issues of the country's politics.

She does this without being affiliated to any Hindutva organizations, thereby creating the illusion of her independence from them. But her perspectives do little except push the Hindu nationalist thought further.

For instance, one of her most popular songs, 'Dhara 370', Article 370, hailed the controversial revocation of Jammu and Kashmir's special status and autonomy granted by the Indian Constitution, likening the occasion to Diwali. The song repeatedly referred to 'gaddars', traitors, and its video showed images of Kashmiri separatist leaders and politicians to coincide with the term.[3] Similarly, just weeks before the Supreme Court was slated to deliver its verdict on the issue, Kavi brought out a song that insisted that a new Ram Mandir, the temple to Lord Ram, would be built on the disputed land over which the Babri Masjid had stood till its demolition in December 1992.[4] This was precisely what the court was yet to decide on. For decades now, Hindus and Muslim petitioners in the court had been wrangling over a piece of land on which the Babri Masjid lay—the Hindus claimed the land was where Lord Ram was born, thereby claiming it to be fit for a temple in their God's honour. The dispute, bitterly contested by both sides, even spilled on the streets several times—most notably, when armed, violent Hindu nationalists climbed on to the mosque and brought it down in December 1992. Kavi, though, didn't want to wait for the court. Her song assured its listeners that the temple would be built at the very disputed spot.

This is why it is difficult to believe that Kavi sang her life's first-ever song days after her father, Ramkesh Jiwanpurwala, a popular Haryanvi singer, actor and director himself, had 'caught' her humming in the kitchen.

'That's when I knew she could sing,' Ramkesh told me, remembering that evening of January 2019.

'I took her to the studio immediately and asked her to record a song to understand how she sounds,' says Ramkesh. When he heard her sing, he knew his intuition was spot on. 'In that moment, I knew,' says Ramkesh, '*yeh toh ekdum fit hai*.' She's bang on the money.

From that moment on, Ramkesh became her manager, her lyricist, her director, her man Friday and her life coach—all rolled into one. Ramkesh decided to dedicate himself to becoming her shadow.

Days after his 'discovery' of her talent, just as suddenly, another unlikely event catapulted her to fame: On 14 February 2019, a suicide bomber in the Pulwama region of Jammu and Kashmir drove an explosive-laden car into a convoy of paramilitary soldiers, killing forty of them.[5]

It was one of the deadliest terror attacks in India's history. But when Ramkesh received a text from his friend and fellow Haryanvi poet and singer Azad Singh Khanda Kheri, he smelled an opportunity. The text contained a new poem that Kheri had written on the Pulwama attack.

The poem was controversial and polarizing. Ramkesh, nonetheless, decided that Kavi should sing it, even if just as an experiment. That evening, the father-daughter duo booked a local recording studio in Karnal, composed the tune within an hour and recorded Kavi's vocals over it. Before he slept, Ramkesh discreetly sent off the audio recording to a few friends. Maybe a couple of them would get back with comments, he thought to himself.

He wasn't prepared for what came his way the next morning. 'The song had gone viral on WhatsApp, ji,' Ramkesh told me when we met in March 2021. 'Within hours, the song had spread so far and wide that we started getting videos of people lip-syncing to the song,' he told me.

I investigated his claim and found this to be true. Days after the attack, many versions of this song found their way to the internet, including lip-synced videos, as Ramkesh had claimed. One factor was common to all these versions—no one seemed to know who the singer was.

Ramkesh raced to fix this—the day after the recording, Ramkesh hurriedly arranged for a cameraman to come and shoot a quick video of Kavi in a recording studio, lip-syncing to her own song. Overnight, the video was edited. By the next morning, it was online.

The video achieved virality almost immediately.

She might not have spelt it out, but it was clear to me that her song channelized the nation's grief and anger not towards the attacker, but instead towards local Kashmiris. '*Pulwama mein veeron ne jo jaan desh pe vaari hai*', 'The Sacrifices by Our Martyrs in Pulwama', attempted to lay the blame squarely on local Kashmiri Muslims for the attack. It questioned the focus on Pakistan as a source of terror in the region and called locals the 'real enemy' instead:

Dushman ghar mein baithe hai, tum kos te raho padosi ko,
Jo chuuri bagal mein rakhte hai, tum maar do na uss doshi ko.
Is dhoke ke hamle mein jo apno ka kaam nahi hota,
Pulwama mein un veeron ka yeh anjaam nahi hota.

The enemies are among us, but we blame the neighbour,
The one who is secretly carrying a knife, finish off that traitor.
If our own hadn't helped carry this attack,
Pulwama wouldn't have seen the blood of our bravehearts
    spilled.

Had the song gone viral despite these lyrics or precisely due to them? The answers followed in the days around the song's release—across the country, in state after state, Kashmiri Muslims were hounded, often assaulted and evicted from their homes by locals as retaliation against their perceived role in the Pulwama terror attack. The then governor of Meghalaya, Tathagata Roy, demanded a boycott of 'everything Kashmiri';[6] colleges started shutting doors on Kashmiri students.[7] There were outbursts of anger against Kashmiris in different parts of the country.[8] Many Indians blamed local Kashmiri Muslims for the attack. Just as Kavi's song had insinuated.[9]

In that moment of anger, outrage and violence, both Ramkesh and Kavi had a common realization—Kavi was now a star.

~

Hindutva pop music has become a little-recognized yet all-pervasive, a seemingly benign yet ingeniously insidious extension of the Hindutva campaign. These songs seek to normalize some of the most rabid, hardline elements of the Hindu nationalist ideology—often so hardline that even some of its most strident Hindutva votaries dither on backing such stances publicly. The lyrics are often aimed at dehumanizing the 'enemy', mostly Muslims, and are laced with threats of brutal violence and dispossession against them. This music often seeks to reinforce biases and stereotypes by creating inauthentic imageries around them.

Deep-rooted biases, fears and anger towards Muslims, combined with such songs that only accentuate these ill feelings, are increasingly becoming a dangerously combustible mix, driving mobs to violence and reprisals.

What makes music such a potent and insidious form of propaganda is its power to influence.

Scholars believe that while inflammatory lyrics are problematic, one major reason that makes music an impactful tool of propaganda are the beats and the tempo of the song. The more 'normal' they sound as songs, the more powerful they are. This normalcy 'dampens the extremity of the rhetoric' and makes the message of the lyrics 'more subversively palatable'.[10] Using an appealing form like music as propaganda also 'legitimizes' the rhetoric as well as the 'behaviour' that the propaganda calls for.[11]

For instance, the song '*Agar chhua mandir toh tujhe dikha denge*', 'Don't Dare Touch the Temple', a hugely popular song that is repeatedly played in Ram Navami celebrations across states, casts the Muslim as someone who is threatening the existence of Hindu temples. In response to these perceived threats, the song warns Muslims of brutal and dire consequences. On YouTube, dozens of videos show this song being played in Ram Navami processions,[12,13] including some where the song is being played in front of mosques[14] when the procession is passing by.

Agar chhua mandir toh tujhe dikha denge,
Tujhko teri aukaad bata denge.
Idhar utthi jo aankh tumhari,

Chamkegi talwaar kataari.
Khoon se is dharti ko nehla denge,
Hum tujhko teri aukaat bata denge.
Vande Mataram gaana hoga,
Warna yahaan se jaana hoga.
Nahi gaye toh jabran tujhe bhaga denge,
Hum tujhko teri aukaat bata denge.

Don't you dare touch the temple,
Or else we will show you your place.
Even if you as much as look at the temple,
My sword's edge will be ready.
We will bathe this earth red with blood,
We will show you your place.
Vande Mataram, you will have to chant,
Or you will have to leave this country.
If you don't, you'll be pushed out,
We will show you your place.

This is just one in over thousands of such songs that are churned out constantly by artistes and small-time studio productions across the country. The songs help articulate hardline stances on various topical and historical issues, thereby making it easier for listeners to grasp complex subjects through catchy lyrics and beats.

There is a song for everything: to push listeners to fight for a 'Hindu Rashtra'—a nation for Hindus; songs to defend and praise the Modi government by stoking naked nationalism and xenophobia after terror attacks; as well as songs hailing its controversial actions like stripping of Kashmir's constitutional autonomy overnight while placing thousands under house arrest. There are songs to demand a law to control the country's population as a way to defeat a secret Islamist demographic 'conspiracy' against Hindus, to warn against 'love jihad'. There are songs calling for temples to be built where mosques exist, songs that call for Pakistan to be obliterated, songs that target Muslims and threaten violence against them, songs that call for Hindus to 'wake up', asking them to take pride in their religion.

The subtext for most music in this genre is clear: Hindus are under attack, Hindus need to fight back and hit back hard at enemies within and outside the country's borders. As a result, the genre constantly creates enemies, demonizes them and asks its listeners to join in the project of retribution. All violence against such enemies is not just normalized but also justified and, possibly, welcomed.

This genre might be new to India, but several countries in the West have seen 'hate music' prosper for decades now. It is believed to have originated in the United Kingdom in the early 1980s with a band named Skrewdriver, which was found to be promoting neo-Nazi, anti-Semitic ideologies through their music.[15] The band gained popularity and was soon headlining concerts. The genre started getting recognized, and soon it spread to Europe, where similar bands sprouted in the same decade. By the end of the '80s, hate music spread to the United States, where it continues to remain a popular subculture to date. According to the Southern Poverty Law Center (SPLC), an Alabama-based nonprofit, there were at least eleven dedicated bands dishing out hate music in 2021.[16] Globally, hate music has many targets: from immigrants and asylum seekers to pro-abortion advocates to the LGBTQ+ community to Jews and Muslims, among others.[17]

It has now grown into a 'full-fledged multi-million dollar' business, according to the SPLC, with recording labels getting involved. Special concerts are now held in various parts of the world, which draw in audiences, leading to brisk sales of concert tickets as well as merchandise. In time, it has become 'perhaps the most important tool of the international neo-Nazi movement to gain revenue and new recruits'.[18]

Increasingly, links between hate music and real-life violence are becoming clearer. In the 1990s, in the run-up to the horrific Rwandan genocide of the minority Tutsi tribe by the majority Hutu tribe members, which led to over 800,000 deaths, two radio stations controlled by the Hutus, Radio Rwanda and the Radio Télévision Libre des Mille Collines, played songs that were inflammatory, polarizing and demonized the Tutsis.[19]

Such use of music in the lead-up to the killings was one way of successfully 'conditioning the psychological climate necessary for genocide', especially by setting these songs to popular American music templates.[20] Through this, the perpetrators were able to 'contextualize itself against a symbolically "Western" cultural backdrop, merging the local with the global, so that committing mass violence was viewed not as sociopathic and extremist but rather normative and socially acceptable'.[21]

This was not an exception. In neighbouring Myanmar, for decades now, Rohingya Muslims have been targeted with violence and displacement.[22] The violence perpetrated by state and non-state Buddhist actors against them has led to nearly a million Rohingyas fleeing their homes and taking refuge in neighbouring countries. There is evidence building up that shows that music has played a role in fomenting this hate against the dispossessed community.

Research has found how songs, containing hate-filled lyrics targeting the Rohingyas, has been commonly found on the internet and widely disseminated in Myanmar. These songs broadly reiterate four themes: they seek to reinforce the prejudice that Muslims do not belong to the Myanmar nation and that the nation is meant for one ethnic group, which is the Burman majority, and reiterate how to be Burman is to be Buddhist, linking citizenship to faith.[23] They insist that the majority Buddhism and Buddhist people are under threat from the minority Muslims and, hence, need to be protected, even if it requires force. The third theme that it reiterates is how

Muslims are engaged in a conspiracy for a demographic takeover of Myanmar and, hence, Buddhists must not marry Muslims and, in effect, try to ensure they do not get any marriage partners. Lastly, the songs call for an economic boycott of the Muslims as a way to disrupt the purported Islamic conspiracy to exploit Myanmar financially.[24]

The author of this research, Heather MacLachlan argues that 'these songs are inciting persecution of Muslim people in Myanmar, and that the creators and distributors of the songs are therefore complicit in the ethnic cleansing and genocidal violence perpetrated against Muslims during the past decade'.[25]

India's hate music is strikingly similar in its content and, increasingly, even in its intent.

∼

It's in this context that understanding the homegrown variety of such hate music becomes critical.

My travels through Jharkhand in March 2019, when I came across the death of Mohamed Shalik and the role of music in triggering tensions and violence, opened my eyes to this music and the real-world effect it was having. When my report was published on FactChecker.in and Scroll.in in June 2019, I wrote a long thread on Twitter focusing only on this 'Hindutva' music that I had discovered.[26] There had been scarce reporting on the issue, even less research into its existence, origins and impact. In my thread, I listed out some examples of the kinds of songs I had found. The comments and the messages I got in my inbox within days of it were overwhelming.

Many had heard of these songs, but not all of them saw these as an organized form of propaganda. When they heard these songs— most had only heard a song or two—they dismissed them as one-offs. The thread, they wrote to me, made them realize these were much more deep-rooted than that.

Trawling through all these songs, I soon realized that they merited serious attention and scholarship, both of which, till then, had been missing. One of the things that struck me was just how gendered this space of Hindutva pop music was: of the dozens of singers I saw singing this music, everyone was male, save two: Laxmi Dubey and Kavi. I gravitated towards wanting to understand the work of these two women better. The Hindutva music genre, much like its parent Hindu nationalist ideology, seemed a macho, masculine space with its constant references to aggressive nationalism and violence. Women have seldom played a visible role of leadership in the movement, barring exceptions.

I wanted to know what made them want to be part of this world and what drove their work.

Laxmi had produced one of the most popular songs in this genre, a song titled '*Har ghar bhagwa chhayega*', a song that fantasizes about India being turned into a Hindu nation. The song had been everywhere: from being sung in political rallies to viral videos to social functions. Laxmi had received some exposure from the media already—she had been interviewed a few times, and her work had been noticed. I found Laxmi's work to be limited in its scope and sporadic—while this particular song had gone viral and was a chartbuster, her overall work had been unspectacular.

On the other hand, Kavi, the only other female singer I could find in this genre, had a prolific body of work. Kavi was releasing songs frequently and on nearly every major issue that concerned the Hindu right-wing.

Since her first-ever song on the Pulwama terror attack, she had performed at concerts and had actively cultivated an internet personality for herself, as a strident Hindutva supporter.

The more I learned about her, the more I wanted to understand her better. Having spent time with her, travelling with her and watching her performances. I am convinced it is most fitting to tell the story of Hindutva pop music in India through Kavi Singh.

~

Kavi's career might be only four years old, but her belief in herself and the ideology underpinning her work feels unshakeable.

Take, for instance, her raison d'être—to 'shake' Hindus out of complacency against the existential threats that Islam poses.

Hindus are complacent, she says, because they are busy getting jobs and fighting to move ahead in their lives. 'But *they* don't do this. *They* just think, let's increase our population, kill the Hindus and all this will be ours,' she says, referring to Muslims. 'The only thing *they* believe in is to increase the country's jan sankhya, its population.'

Kavi's fears don't resonate with facts. Data from the Indian census study of 2011 showed that the rate of growth of the Muslim population had fallen by nearly 5 per cent over the last few decades, whereas the rate of growth among Hindus had fallen by just 3.1 per cent.[27] Various experts have dismissed the possibility of the country's Muslim population taking over its Hindu population, insisting that for it to happen, Hindus would have to 'stop producing babies entirely'.[28] A report by the Pew Research Center, in its estimates for 2050, said that Hindus were likely to remain an overwhelming majority, with a 77 per cent share of the population, while Muslims would grow to 18 per cent of the population, less than a quarter of the Hindu proportion.[29]

But Kavi believes in these fears, anyway.

In January 2020, while the country saw widespread street protests against the Modi government's introduction of the discriminatory Citizenship (Amendment) Act, which fast-tracked the citizenship of only non-Muslim refugees from neighbouring countries, Kavi made her fears known with a song named '*Sacche Hindustani—jansankhya kanoon lao, desh bachao*', 'True Indians—Usher In the Population Control Law and Save the Country'. The song vilified the protesters as anti-nationals, warned of anarchy and an Islamic takeover of the country, and pitched a bill to regulate the country's population as the answer to all this.

Her confidence is backed by her firm belief that she has been ordained by divine forces to carry out this mission. Her life hasn't occurred by accident. 'Somewhere, Bhagwan, God, planted these thoughts in my mind,' Kavi tells me.

Her family, some of her staunchest supporters, back this belief. Including Ramkesh, her father, and Prince Kumar, a fellow Haryanvi singer who Ramkesh got Kavi married to. Ramkesh told me Prince was his shishya, pupil. 'I have known him since he was a child, and thought the two would make a good pair,' Ramkesh said.

In the course of getting to know her better, I spent several days with Kavi and Ramkesh in March 2021. The two were heading to Rishikesh from Rohtak where they both live, to shoot videos for Kavi's songs. At the end of a long first evening in the temple town, while I probed them about their political affiliations and their backing for Modi and the BJP, Ramkesh suddenly turned to Kavi and, lovingly, told her that she reminded him of Modi. 'The shakti, strength, the energy that Modiji has, you have it too,' he said, at which she smiled.

Such assertions have ensured that Kavi takes herself seriously. Her styling is meant to ensure that others take her as seriously.

Kavi told me how her father and her husband planned her appearance in great detail, long before she was launched as a singer.

The deliberate choice of making her wear what is slightly unusual clothing for a woman singer—the Nehru jacket and the turban to go with her kurta-pyjama—is meant to instil a sense of respect in the audience, Kavi told me.

By mid-2021 though, Kavi had ditched her pyjamas and now sports a dhoti.

Her outfits are meant to be, both, an advertisement for her brand and a messenger of her beliefs.

They carry a deeper political messaging—through her songs and her public appearances, Kavi constantly reinforces the need for her audience to re-connect and embrace Rashtravaad aur dharm. Nationalism and religion. Both of these have become her calling cards, and what better way to signal her commitment to her own cause than by restricting herself to a costume that she believes straddles both ideas together. Kavi's outfits are meant to be an extension of her songs—an in-your-face demonstration of her beliefs.

In her head, Kavi is a 'character' when she dons her outfits. She is a different person outside of them—she also addresses herself in third person when referring to the jacket and turban-donning Kavi.

'Kavi will not touch anyone's feet, nor will she bend, because the pagdi, the turban, is a symbol of her heritage and she will not allow it to be lowered, no matter what,' she tells me.

The calculated persona has worked.

Her clothes, coupled with her confident stride, definitely make heads turn wherever she goes. Where they don't know her, people mistake her for a politician, a godwoman or an actor in costume. The clothes help her recall value immensely: many recognize her instantaneously whenever she is out.

In Rishikesh, while we waited on the banks of the Ganga River for the Ganga aarti to start, an activist of the Sangh Parivar from Maharashtra saw her from a distance and walked up to her. He admired her work immensely, he told her, and believed it to be of critical importance. Kavi smiled politely. What he says next stumps everyone around—he tells her he wants to wash her feet with the water of the Ganga, as a mark of his respect towards her. Kavi breaks out in a smile but fumbles in her response, before politely declining his offer.

'Only Kavi's father can wash her feet,' she later explained to me.

What makes this genre and Kavi's music critical to pay attention to is her reach—she isn't limited to releasing songs on the internet. Kavi also tours across the country, performing her songs in concerts and shows, peppered with her own take on everything from politics to religion. These performances get amplified on her social media handles, which she uses to not just push her songs but to offer her perspectives to her followers, who lap it up. She has a over million followers on her YouTube channel, where she releases all her songs and more than 800,000 on her Facebook and Instagram accounts, which she uses to post her views, often incendiary and polarizing, and gain a wider reach. Every update she posts fetches tens of thousands of likes, her videos get hundreds of thousands of views.

Like her video on 6 September 2022, where she describes how she got repeated calls threatening her, asking her to stop making polarizing songs and videos against Muslims.[30] She describes the callers as 'Muslims' who threatened to behead her. She asks her followers to ensure '*yeh log*', these people, are never '*hamare dost, hamare bhai, hamare grahak*', our friends, our brothers, our customers. These people, she says, will never change. That's why she has come to the realization that Hindus have to prepare themselves— not just with shaastra, ancient knowledge of Hindu scriptures, but also shastra, weapons. '*Yehi hamari sanskriti hai; yeh hamare sanatan dharam ki sanskriti hai.*' This is our culture; this is the culture of our Hindu religion.

The video gets 57,000 likes and over 250,000 views. More than 11,000 people write in, most of them supporting her. The comments reaffirm her stance, backing her call for boycotting Muslims.

Just over twenty-four hours later, the outrage among her followers about the 'threats' that Muslims pose still fresh, Kavi drops a poster of her new song—a song that she says is meant to *save* the country's mother tongue, Hindi.

In His Shadow

Khatre ka udgosh hua hai, ranbhoomi taiyyar karo,
Sahi waqt hai, chun chun kar ab gaddaaron par vaar karo.
Aatanki toh chaar maar kar tum hum khushi se phool gaye,
Sarhad ki chinta mein ghar ke bhediyon ko bhool gaye.

The battle cry has been made, get the battlefield ready,
The time is right to single out and punish the traitors.
We are content killing just a handful of terrorists,
Busy with the border, we forgot the enemies at home.

Two months after she debuted with her song on the Pulwama terror attack, Kavi found herself on stage, for her first-ever live performance.

It was April 2019, and the venue was the Shital Kund temple in Didwana, a city in Rajasthan around 150 km away from Jaipur. The temple, whose presiding deity is the Hindu God Balaji Hanuman, hosts massive celebrations annually to mark the birth of its deity.

Ramkesh had been invited, and so was Kavi, freshly minted with recent virality and fame.

Through grainy cellphone videos of the event, I could see Ramkesh finish his performance, then the video quickly cut to him handing over the microphone to Kavi, who was sitting on the stage along with the musicians. As soon as Kavi came center stage, Ramkesh took her place, in the middle of the musicians accompanying Kavi's singing.

Kavi was tentative, and she held the mic with both her hands, close to her face. She asked the audience to chant in honour of the temple's deity, but the response was feeble. She walked across the stage and went uncomfortably silent for a number of seconds, looking around at the audience.

Then, she told them she would present bhajans dedicated to Balaji, but before that, she wanted to add a disclaimer.

'*Aapki beti hoon, aapki bachi hoon. Agar koi bhool ho jaaye, koi galti ho jaaye, toh aap log mujhe maaf kar de,*' she said. I am your girl, your daughter. If there is a slip-up, if I make a mistake today, please forgive me.

'*Balaji maharaj toh maaf karenge hi.*' Lord Balaji will surely forgive me.

Respects paid, she tried to rouse her audience, asking them to chant slogans in the deity's honour. This time, the audience was louder in its response.

Kavi realized the truth of the audience before her—they are drawn to the event neither by her father nor her recent fame. The presiding deity is what draws them to sit here and listen to bhajans. So she defers her performance by a few minutes and, instead, sings paeans to Balaji Hanuman.

Her performance that day, she said, will just be her humble attempt to highlight his strength.

Even as Kavi navigated the anxieties of her first-ever performance, Ramkesh was constantly animated. In the videos, I could see

Ramkesh, seated right behind the spot where Kavi stood, being a bundle of nervous energy. Before he even sat down, he waved his arms towards someone off the stage and mimed holding a mic to his face. Even when Kavi was talking, he wanted a mic to himself. He sat down, and turned to the musician on his right, whispered something in his ear, turned to another musician on his left, whispered some more. Then he suddenly stood up and walked towards Kavi, even as she was speaking to the audience. Standing right behind her, Ramkesh waited for Kavi to look back. But she didn't, so, a few seconds later, he walked back and took his seat again.

He then faced the audience, and right in that moment, his face, suddenly, sported a wide grin. He wanted to switch roles from being the worried father to one who was pleased and proud. His actions, though, oscillated between the two roles. Whenever Kavi asked her audience to chant slogans, he chanted them into the microphone, overpowering whatever little response the audience offered. When Kavi asked her audience to raise their fists in the air, Ramkesh was the first one to do so. He looked at the gathering and asked them to follow suit, constantly gesturing with his hands. He then took the mic into his hands and took on the role of the lead chorus singer.

Even before Kavi completed her line, Ramkesh was ready with the chorus. I could see in the videos him goading the remaining musicians on the stage to join in, gesturing to them by drawing his mic closer to his face. Soon, at least three others got mics and joined him in the chorus.

Throughout the performance, he was animated. From signalling to Kavi his agreement over her choice of each song to prodding the audience to clap, Ramkesh was protective and anxious.

That protectiveness is part of a pattern.

In March 2021, nearly two years after that performance, we were in the car, meandering around the mighty Himalayan mountains outside Rishikesh, on the Char Dham route. Ramkesh was driving, while Kavi was sitting next to him. The father-daughter duo were hunting for locations where they could shoot Kavi's music videos.

Shooting days are critical for both, father and daughter. Her social media presence—from her YouTube music videos, to her Facebook Live videos shot on location—are the way that Kavi sustains and reinforces her popularity and gets to widen her base on the internet. They form the bulk of her interaction with her audience. This ever-widening audience base, then, translates to more popularity on the ground.

Over the years that I have followed her work for, her videos have retained the same format—the video will, almost always, feature only Kavi in her trademark outfits, staring into the camera and lip-syncing the words. She opens her arms up, sometimes closes her fist and occasionally, sways, while mouthing the words.

The colours are always bright and vibrant, the camera angles are always snazzy and swift and the production values, even for the simple format, are pretty decent. Though the format always remain the same, what changes are the locations.

Even the locations are varied—from the ramparts of ancient forts to lush green fields, to stunning river banks.

As I later discovered, hardly any of it is by design. Ramkesh told me they just keep driving till they stumble upon a fitting location.

That morning, Kavi was in a playful mood at the expense of Ramkesh. After Ramkesh drove the group to Rishikesh from Haridwar, where we were staying overnight, Kavi seized one such chance when at 7 a.m. Ramkesh approached a makeshift roadside stall selling chole bhature for breakfast.

Ramkesh approached the middle-aged woman running the stall and said, 'Mujhe soup de do', give me soup. The woman didn't understand what soup was. Ramkesh kept repeating the word soup. At one point, he even tried to make her understand how it's made. Even while that unfolded, Kavi was delirious in her laughter. Her laughter only got louder when the woman, having finally grasped what soup was, rejected Ramkesh's request with some disdain. *'Subah subah?'* Who has soup this early in the morning, she asked.

Kavi's loud laughter didn't embarrass Ramkesh. He smiled sheepishly and seemed happy that his awkward encounter had been a source of joy for his daughter.

For Ramkesh, Kavi was beyond reproach.

'If there is one person I am scared of, it is Kavi. Her and her mother, possibly. Bas,' he says. Such is the influence Kavi exerts at home that she turns the mediator each time her parents fight. Usually, Kavi is summoned by her mother during these disagreements. And usually, according to Ramkesh, Kavi has the last word.

This exalted status that Kavi enjoys has its reasons.

Kavi is Ramkesh's adopted daughter. She came into the family only eight years ago. He first met her when he was shooting for a Haryanvi movie at a school in Rewari, a city 50 km south-west of Gurugram, Haryana. Accompanying Ramkesh was Prince, a young aspiring Haryanvi singer who considered Ramkesh his guru. For Ramkesh, Prince was the son he didn't have.

Kavi was a student of that school in Rewari. Kavi was, then, Keshanta Singh, the daughter of Laxmi Devi and Tejaram, from Alwar in the north-western state of Rajasthan. Her older brother, Suresh, would always call her Kavi. The name stuck, and when she started a new life, it was with the name Kavi.

'When I saw her, I instantly felt like I had met my daughter,' Ramkesh says, 'I just can't explain that feeling.' Ramkesh remained in touch with Kavi, even met her family. Her father had died when Kavi was just seven. Her mother, a warden at a students' hostel near Rewari, was single-handedly raising Kavi and her brother. Kavi was deprived of a father's love and affection. Ramkesh wanted to step in.

'I told her she should think of me as her father.'

Family relations grew. Slowly, Kavi's closeness to Prince grew, and both fell in love with each other.

Kavi, then fourteen years old, moved to Rohtak to pursue her studies. That way, she could spend more time with Prince, who also lived there.

Their affection for Prince meant that Ramkesh's own family, his wife Bhateri Devi and their two children, opened their arms to Kavi. Kavi says they never made her feel like she was an outsider. Kavi started spending more time with Ramkesh's family than her own. In 2021, Ramkesh decided to adopt her officially.

In our conversations, Ramkesh said he often sought to over-compensate Kavi by letting her know that the family would always back her and defer to her. She would be consulted on all major decisions; her judgement would always be respected. Kavi, on her part, embraced this.

From the mischievous girl in Alwar, carefree in her role as the youngest child in the family, she stepped into her new family aware that she was now suddenly the oldest and, hence, expected to be the most responsible sibling.

~

Kavi's adopted status has remained a closely guarded secret within the Haryanvi entertainment industry.

But there are other whispers around the father-daughter duo. Whispers around the influence that Ramkesh exerts on Kavi's life, how he orchestrates every move she makes, how Ramkesh is the puppeteer holding the strings to Kavi's career and her life.

Ramkesh is Kavi's shadow—he pervades and controls almost every aspect of her life as an artiste. From the clothes she wears to the songs she sings, from the man she marries to what she says in interviews—Ramkesh delivers the stamp of approval.

It is a criticism that Ramkesh has often had to face, he admits. *'Mere aas paas ke logon ko lagta hai ki usko main direction de raha hoon',* Ramkesh tells me. People around me say that she acts on my directions.

He doesn't dispute that. He admits that he gives her directions, but insists he has limited success. 'It is not easy to create such pressure on her,' he adds.

Instead of dismissing the allegations outrightly, he absorbs them with a sense of confidence. 'These people, who believe that I am controlling her ... that I am orchestrating everything in her life, are people who know us personally,' he says. 'But, others don't care. It's only those who know us and are around us who say all this.'

It's not difficult to see why the father-daughter duo face this criticism.

Up until a few years before she made her singing debut in 2019, Kavi's heart was set on becoming a cosmetic expert and an authority on skincare and beauty treatments. She even did a month-long course in administering cosmetic treatments, and after the course, almost immediately started getting contacted by clients.

'The others were struggling for work and took several months to learn what Kavi learnt in a month,' says Ramkesh.

Her career as a beautician was slowly taking off. This was her first professional experience, and she was already enjoying it. Soon after, she also took to stitching dresses. In 2018, when Kavi was getting married, she designed and stitched her own wedding gown from scratch. She even stitched the dress her mother wore at the wedding.

A year later, in 2019, even as she was slowly making inroads into her newly found professional interests, Ramkesh came up with a proposition that startled Kavi—why doesn't she become a singer?

This seemed sudden and rather random to Kavi. Especially when she was doing something she was thoroughly interested in.

But Ramkesh had his reasons. In that moment, Ramkesh convinced Kavi that her humming was not meant merely for the kitchen. It was meant for greater things, like shaping the nation's politics and earning popularity and fame.

Kavi's recollection of this episode—of her father's insistence that she leave the career of her choice to become an overnight pop star—

is only a confirmation of her belief. The belief that her father knows what is best for her.

'Even before I knew I could sing, my father already did.'

Looking back, Kavi has no regrets about the dramatic turn her life took in that moment. Within a few days, the father-daughter duo would go on to record what would become Kavi's most popular song and catapult her to instant fame and virality—her song around the Pulwama suicide bomb attack.

Ramkesh's own journey into fame and popularity, much of it sudden and unexpected even for him, had something to do with his decision to abruptly anoint Kavi as his successor.

~

Ramkesh was born in the Jiwanpur village of Haryana's Jind district, 150 km away from New Delhi.

Born in a family of farmers, Ramkesh would attend performances of ragini, a form of folk music popular in Haryana, in which performers sing on everyday themes and perform to rudimentary musical instruments like pots and the chimta, musical tongs. The words of these songs touched his heart and slowly, he found himself writing lyrics for these songs. Very soon, he was performing them in local events. His songs found many takers, and his popularity grew. Convinced that he could get bigger, he moved to Rohtak in 2006 to explore the Haryanvi entertainment industry.

His career took off. His big break came with a song he wrote called 'Pehli aali hawa', a Haryanvi number that was a nostalgic ode to a simpler past. The song catapulted Ramkesh into fame. He went from one hit to another. Slowly, he even started getting offers to act in Haryanvi films, and he was only too eager to grab them.

In his music, Ramkesh tries to retain the earthiness from his ragini days. His songs range from inspirational to reflective to even romantic. But they are never political. Ramkesh has carefully side-stepped any reference to politics or his ideological leanings. His songs are ideology-agnostic and, instead, end up reinforcing good morals and family values. His latest, a song called 'Struggle', talks about his journey to becoming a pop star, extensively mentioning his humble origins. Another, called 'Safalta' (success), features Ramkesh delivering a speech to the camera before the song starts. In the fifty-five-second-long speech, he says the song is meant to motivate and inspire people and make them realize that sangharsh, struggle, is the only way to become truly successful in life.

Jo bhi karte kaam, usmein dhyaan lagana padta hai,
Confidence, positive thought, junoon jagana padta hai,
Aate hai galat vichar, unko door bhagana padta hai.

Whatever work you do, you must focus on it,
You have to have the confidence, positive thoughts and a passion to do it,
If you have stray thoughts, you must drive them away.

Ramkesh often breaks into his songs mid-conversation. Once, while explaining to Kavi the importance of having a good work ethic, he pauses and says poetically:

Yahaan koi kisi ke liye kuch nahi karta hai,
Khud hi jeena padta hai, khud hi marna padta hai.

No one does anything for anyone here,
One must live and die, all alone.

Ramkesh has internalized the song. The key to understanding his role in Kavi's career lies in these lines of his.

'The truth is, we are all always acting in our self-interest,' he says one night in March 2021, sitting in the room of an ashram in Haridwar where we are staying.

His decision to continue his role as an apolitical entertainer, even as he silently drives Kavi's career as a politically polarizing figure, is a part of this epiphany. By controlling the strings of Kavi's career—from writing most of her songs to the words she mouths publicly to curating her appearances—Ramkesh gets to partake and be identified with the ruling political ideology of the day, without having to jeopardize his profile as a bipartisan entertainer and a conscience-keeper with moral values and Haryanvi ethos.

A cynical calculation of their actions shows that this way, the family gets to build their popularity up by appealing to distinct sets of people at all times—Kavi can cover those who are driven by politics and Hindutva; her husband, Prince Kumar, with his snazzy videos of love and dance numbers can appeal to a young audience; whereas Ramkesh can appeal to those who yearn for the past and want entertainment that is more rooted and rural in its appeal.

Ramkesh admits that his decision to stay apolitical while driving Kavi's career is a calculated one. 'Somewhere, I am doing all this for Kavi because I know that she becoming famous will also make me famous.'

Already some of his ambitions are taking fruit.

Over the last two years, Ramkesh's proximity to power has been growing increasingly, boosted by Kavi's work. The duo has been invited by different Hindu nationalist groups and figures to perform at events and concerts. Many of them want to tap into Kavi's popularity in a bid to boost their own. In Uttar Pradesh, Kavi has performed for leaders of the BJP in their constituencies. Ramkesh said he had been invited at least twice by the Haryana Chief Minister and BJP leader, M.L. Khattar, in the last two years.

On one of those occasions, Ramkesh's double life, both as a conscientious entertainer and as a Hindutva songwriter, got rewarded.

Khattar, formerly a full-time missionary with the Hindu nationalist RSS, was appointed as the Haryana CM in 2014, after the BJP won the state election.[1] News reports, then, said his proximity to the RSS top brass helped him clinch the post.[2] Two years ago, Khattar was meeting different entertainers from the state. The meeting, Kavi says, had at least forty to fifty artistes.

Ramkesh recalls how Khattar was asking the artistes to introduce themselves. 'There was this disc jockey (DJ) who introduced himself and mentioned how he had composed many popular dance numbers,' Ramkesh says. But Khattar was visibly unimpressed by this introduction, in Ramkesh's retelling. Instead, he pointed to Ramkesh.

'He said, *"Woh sab toh theek hai, par vicchar kya hai?"* and then pointed at me,' Ramkesh says. All that is okay, but what is the thought behind it?

'Jaise Ramkesh ji ke gaano mein vicchar hote hai, unki beti ke gaano mein vicchar hote hai,' Ramkesh recalls Khattar telling the suddenly beleaguered DJ. The way Ramkesh and his daughter's songs always have a thought behind them.

Kavi lights up while recalling the meeting. She always had immense respect for Khattar and was intimidated at the prospect of meeting him. But what Khattar said left Kavi grinning ear-to-ear.

'He told us he only listens to Papa and my songs,' Kavi says, recounting the meeting. The chief minister, she says, even pointed out songs he enjoyed the most. 'He said, "You've made such good songs on Article 370 and on the Ram Mandir." I was elated that he knew of and even remembered my songs,' says Kavi.

Ramkesh had a crucial role to play in both those songs, but especially with the song that hailed the abrogation of Article 370, which propelled Kavi to the status of a Hindutva pop star who seemed to have an inside connection to the BJP.

~

In 2019, after the popularity that her song around the Pulwama suicide bomb attack brought her, Kavi's newly born singing career reached a crossroads.

Her almost overnight initiation into singing meant that there was no clear path for her and Ramkesh to take, following Pulwama's success. What had started as just an experiment to gauge her singing capabilities through the WhatsApp-circulated voice note had to suddenly transform into a full-fledged dive into the world of music and entertainment, resulting in a hurriedly shot music video. What was to be done next? The question plagued Kavi as well as Ramkesh.

Kavi was just one song old. She needed to do a lot more to be established and known for, before she could be, say, invited for concerts and shows. The only way for her to do that was the internet. For singers like Kavi who want to be effective content creators online, time is of the essence. With so much content waiting to be devoured at all times, a long absence online can hurt. While there is no authoritative prescription, digital marketing strategies advise YouTube creators like Kavi to post at least once to multiple times a week, for the platform to boost their growth and promote their content organically.

Kavi's work reflected the confusion between the need to figure out her plan ahead and the pressure to be visible online. Soon after the Pulwama number, she brought out a string of songs, experimenting with various themes. About twenty days after the Pulwama song, Kavi brought out her next, a deshbhakti (patriotic) song about India becoming a vishwaguru (world leader) by reforming its social evils—from female foeticide to illiteracy and casteism. It cast subtle digs at the Muslim community without any explicit mention, by saying those who refuse to sing 'Vande Mataram' must not be allowed to live in India.³ Beyond that one reference, it had no political overtones.

A fortnight later, with an eye on the upcoming Lok Sabha polls, Kavi released her next single, a song to boost voter enthusiasm. The song, titled 'Matdan', or voting, exhorted citizens to come out and vote in large numbers. The song did not show any political leaning, instead it listed general qualities that citizens should look at, while making their electoral choice:

Jiske chaal chalan mein na ho kisi kisam ka khot,
Jo nahi maarta kisi janata ki bhavna pe chot

The one whose conduct is unimpeachable,
The one who will never harm people's sentiments

Another fortnight later came Kavi's third song, *'Jai jawan, jai kisan'*, Hail the soldier, hail the farmer. The song paid plaudits to farmers and soldiers for contributing to the nation. That same month, in April, came another song, *'Abhiman'*, Pride, hailing Lord Ram and professing a more ethical conduct in life.

But none of them matched up to Pulwama's success. The instant virality that Pulwama had found, the overnight sensation of being a celebrity it had lent Kavi, and the chord it had touched with a grieving nation was nowhere close to what the subsequent three songs offered. The songs barely registered among her audience.

The Pulwama song had stood out for its brazenness—it was clear to me that it sought to target Kashmiri Muslims for 'aiding' the suicide bomber, reaching a conclusion that even the government hadn't come to then. Instead of asking hard questions around the government's security strategies, it had directed the anger of its audience elsewhere— to the 'traitors' who had helped carry out the attack.

All that was missing in her other four songs. What was also missing was Ramkesh.

None of those four songs were written by Ramkesh. Three different poets had written them. Although the Pulwama song was not written by Ramkesh, its lyricist, poet Azad Singh Khanda Kheri, was a close friend of his, allowing Ramkesh a greater say in the way the song shaped up.

Ramkesh could see Kavi's career was floundering and decided to take matters into his own hands.

The duo slowed down. From releasing a song every fortnight, the two did not release any songs for a month. Finally, at the end of May 2019, Kavi brought out a new song, written by Ramkesh this time. It was called '*Bharat ki gaurav gatha*', the proud tales of India, an eight-minute number that sought to highlight events and persons who occupy a place of pride in India's social consciousness. It looked extensively at Hindu mythological figures—brothers like Bharat and Lakshman from the Ramayana, warriors like Bheem in the Mahabharata, among others.

The song was a slow ode to India's Hindu mythological tales. But it didn't click with her audience. It pushed the father-daughter duo down into more of a slump.

In the next two months, Kavi released two more songs, both focused on similar themes, highlighting Hindu religious and mythological figures like Lord Shiva and Lord Krishna. But they met the same fate as the five songs that preceded them.

Before she knew it, Kavi's fledgling career was flailing. The father-daughter duo was not going to stop making songs, but somehow the two could not recreate the high that the Pulwama song had gotten them.

Yet, they decided to continue trying. On 4 August 2019, Ramkesh, Kavi and a cameraperson left Rohtak and headed towards Jaipur, Rajasthan, six hours away. On the agenda was shooting several videos for some of their upcoming songs. Ramkesh had written the songs and composed the tunes.

Midway through the day, when the group took a break, a flash of news on his phone caught Ramkesh's eye. There was a buzz that the Narendra Modi government was slated to take a major decision on an issue related to Jammu and Kashmir. News reports were not sure what it was going to be. There were rumours of various kinds.

Ramkesh knew what this was going to be. He gathered his group, told them that he was calling off the shoot and that they would need to head back to Rohtak immediately. A song had to be written, recorded and shot within the next twenty-four hours.

Their lives were going to change forever.

That night, Ramkesh stayed up till late, glued to the news for updates. His suspicions only strengthened when the authorities in Jammu and Kashmir placed severe restrictions on public movement, by shutting down educational institutes and restricting public mobility in the capital city of Srinagar.[4] Imposing a lockdown, authorities started enforcing curbs on activists and political leaders, placing hundreds under house arrest starting midnight of 4 August.[5]

The next morning, his suspicions were proved correct. In the Rajya Sabha at 11 a.m., Union Home Minister Amit Shah announced that the government was abrogating Article 370 and Article 35-A of the Indian Constitution, both of which effectively granted a special status to the state of Jammu and Kashmir and, thereby, greater autonomy for the region and special rights for its residents.[6]

The decision was momentous, especially since it came on the backs of a decades-old demand by the Hindu right-wing to scrap these special powers to Jammu and Kashmir and 'integrate' the region better into mainland India.

Ramkesh got to work quickly—he knew that an event as big as this was likely to remain a talking point for days. Hungry for news, updates and opinions, Indians were likely to log on to the internet and look for it all. And when they do that, they were very likely to use video platforms like YouTube, rather than search and read through other text formats.[7]

Ramkesh knew he had to be quick. He started writing a song on this massive announcement for Kavi to perform. Within minutes, he was ready with the verse.

In the next hour, Kavi got ready, memorized her lines and was all set to record the song. At 4 p.m., she went into a studio and was done recording in an hour, with just a few re-takes.

Then, she started getting ready for the shoot. She donned a soft pink kurta with a white pyjama and an orange Nehru jacket. Her pagdi for the occasion reflected her sentiment— tricoloured, with broad strokes of orange, white and green running through it. They didn't have time for an elaborate shoot, so Ramkesh and Kavi decided that the video would just have to be Kavi standing before a green screen. With that, the video editor, during post-production, would have the option of adding a different backdrop behind Kavi, instead of making it look like they've shot the video at home.

They rushed to the studio and got started on the shoot. It didn't take much time, just some shots of Kavi swinging her arms, pointing her fingers towards the camera while lip-syncing the words. Within hours, the shoot was done, and the video was sent to Bhurra, the editor, in his studio in Karnal.

Bhurra worked through the night, while Kavi spent a sleepless one. At 6 a.m., she rushed to the studio. The video was yet to be edited completely—but she kept pushing Bhurra. Finally, the edit was over, and the song was uploaded on YouTube.

By then, Kavi was so exhausted that she fell asleep even before the song was finally uploaded.

The song turned out to be an uncritical, unabashed backing of the government's move to scrap the two constitutional Articles. It likened the occasion to a 'sacchi Diwali', the real Diwali, for India and Indians and billed the occasion to be heralding a new era for both the region and the country.

70 saal se lagi bimari, aaj uska ilaaj hua
Hua andhera door desh ka, aaj hai roshan Taj hua.
Na ab patthar barse na Khushi ki raah ko mundenge,
Ab Kashmir ki ghaati mein Shri Ram ke naare goonjenge.

A 70-year-old illness, has finally found a cure,
The country's darkness dispelled, the Taj now shines bright.
Nor will stones be hurled anymore, nor will happiness escape,
In the Kashmir Valley, chants of Shri Ram will now be heard.

Apart from praising the Modi government's actions—'*Saari duniya dekh rahi aaj bharat ka jalwa hai*', the whole world is watching India in its full splendour today—the song insidiously weaponizes the event to attack any criticism that might emerge against it. Even before the Modi government, the BJP and the Hindu right-wing could possibly respond, it labelled all criticism of the decision as treasonous and all critics as traitors.

The song drew harsh, bold lines between those who backed the decision, by calling them nationalists, and those who opposed it, by calling them traitors. Lines like '*Desh bhakht hai jhoom rahe, gaddaaron ki aankh mein paani hai*', true patriots are delirious, but traitors are shedding tears, and '*Jo desh mitana chahte the, woh aaj baith kar royenge*', those who wanted to obliterate us, will sit today and bawl, were meant to do just that: delegitimize any criticism of the move pre-emptively.

Kavi woke up to a call from her father. Within just a couple of hours, the song had racked up 850,000 views on YouTube, with over ten thousand comments from people.

Kavi was a star, again.

I Wonder Why

Kuch logo ki toh saazish hai,
Hum bacche khub banayenge.
Jab sankhya hui humse zyaada,
Fir apni baat manayenge.

Some people are conspiring,
That we will produce many children.
When their numbers go past ours,
They will make us dance to their tune.

Growing up in Alwar, Kavi was never quite far from the Hindu right-wing.

Alwar has had a history of communal tensions and violence. The region was known for the patronage its royalty provided to Hindu organizations in pre-colonial India.[1] Thousands of Muslims were killed there in communal violence that occurred while India was being divided into two in 1947.

But growing up, Kavi was far, far away from politics. Their fragile financial health and the early loss of her father, the sole male member in the household never allowed the family to think beyond their daily existence. Dabbling in politics was a luxury they could not afford.

Her political ideology as she knows it today, came from experiences early in life—experiences that she tied simplistic explanations around.

Not far from her home in Alwar was a Muslim neighbourhood. As a child, Kavi never witnessed any tensions between Hindus and Muslims around her. The Muslim neighbourhood was never off-limits for Kavi, and she never faced any discomfort or prejudice.

But she had been told that, unlike her family, the Muslims were a community of meat-eaters. The othering of the community had taken seed inside her.

On visits to the neighbourhood, Kavi spotted carcasses of animals being hung at meat shops. 'I was left disgusted at the sight. I started feeling scared of them.'

In school, among her friends were Salma and Shabnam (names changed), two Muslims from Alwar. Kavi would spend much of her time outside school with them. They would be regulars at each other's houses, even share meals, play and study together. Their friendship was cut short when Shabnam's family married her off at fifteen when they were in Class Seven.

But in their time together, Kavi says she noticed something that didn't fit right with her—their ostensible lack support for the Indian team during cricket matches.

'I never enjoyed cricket, but whenever India won, I was happy nonetheless. *Apna desh toh apna hota hai na?* We love our country no matter what, right?

But neither Salma nor Shabnam, recalls Kavi, would ever be happy when the Indian team won.

'I even told them you stay in Hindustan; the country gives you everything.' But they didn't agree. Kavi says the girls told her that their loyalty lay with Pakistan instead. 'They told me, "All our people are in Pakistan. We are just staying here temporarily. One day, we will move to Pakistan too."'

Kavi says she felt that was strange. She didn't understand why they would say that. '*Pata nahi kyun,*' I wonder why.

For questions like these, Kavi found an answer in an unlikely event—the release of the popular film *Gadar*. The Hindi potboiler told the story of a Sikh man and his Muslim wife, set around the Partition. The wife's Pakistani parents forcefully try and separate the two after the Sikh man refuses to settle in Pakistan and embrace Islam. The 2001 film stood out for its jingoism and hyper-nationalism, commodities that sold well in an India fresh out of its war with Pakistan in the Himalayan region of Kargil just two years before. The climax features thousands of Pakistan Muslims lining up outside a mosque with cannons, asking the Sikh protagonist if he wants to convert to Islam, pushing him to chant '*Hindustan Murdabad*', death to India. The hero is enraged at the demand and uproots a handpump from the earth to fight off the mob of thousands.

It won numerous awards and remains one of the highest-grossing Hindi feature films ever.

The film was already half a decade old when Kavi watched it. But it left a deep imprint on her. The film became a benchmark of patriotism for her. She loved it, but Salma and Shabnam didn't.

'*Pata nahin kyun,*' she says again. I wonder why.

'*Pata nahin kyun,*' repeats Ramkesh after her and breaks into laughter.

Gradually, Kavi says, she realized the problem was not with Salma or Shabnam. They were emblematic of their community being very 'different' from the other people she had grown up with—mostly Hindus.

I asked her if she'd ever had any other Muslim friends after Salma and Shabnam.

'*Unke kisse hi itne mahaan hote hai, ke soch ke hi ...*' she trails off. Their tales are so legendary, that just the thought of them is enough to ...

But these prejudices have not stopped Kavi from cultivating beneficial relationships with Muslims.

Many years after her viewing of *Gadar* and her experiences with Salma and Shabnam, when Kavi wanted to learn photography, she went to a Muslim man she calls 'Khan sir', because he was supposed to be the best photography teacher in Rohtak. For months, she learnt under the watchful gaze of Khan sir, who even selected her for a photography assignment in Goa.

Kavi's family in Alwar, which includes her brother Rajendra, mother and the daughter of Kavi's sister, live in a flat owned by a Muslim man. He is a family friend who refuses to charge rent.

The friend, aware of the family's delicate financial health, has never asked for rent, says Kavi, and the family is indebted to him for what he does.

Kavi tells me that the friend, though, runs a grouse against her: 'Why does she vilify us Muslims? Not all of us are the same, not all of us are bad,' he tells Kavi's family.

Kavi laughs when I ask her what she thinks. 'I know they feel bad [about her work],' she says. 'But I tell them that my criticism is not about people like you.'

She believes that the Muslims she has met are 'the good ones'.

'And sometimes, these good ones end up spilling the beans about the others,' Kavi says. She tells me of Ramkesh's Muslim friend, who was helping them buy a plot of land. The friend's family had a plot of land they wanted to sell, so he got the two parties in contact with each other. But secretly, he warned Ramkesh against buying his family's land. 'He told us, "*Yeh log mere jaise nahi hai. Raat mein kaat ke khaa jaayenge, patta bhi nahi chalega.*" These people are not like me. They will kill you before you know it.

For Kavi, the Muslim friend was good because he snitched on his family and because he was a *Mahadev ka bhakt*, a devotee of Shiva.

Kavi's simplistic explanations and her preconceptions around Muslims were vindicated when she met Ramkesh.

Ramkesh, consumed by his own experiences and preconceived notions, combined them with confidence and became her political guru. Over long drives that the two would take for shoots, Kavi would ask him questions and Ramkesh would offer all the answers he had. These answers, Kavi later told me, would go on to form the foundation for all her political beliefs.

Both would take their observations from the past and present, dip them in anti-Muslim biases and personal prejudices and back each other.

Except, Ramkesh's political evolution had been driven by sudden turns and knee-jerk responses.

~

Ramkesh was three years old when Rajiv Gandhi took over as the Prime Minister in 1984. He doesn't remember the event, but he distinctly remembers seeing Gandhi all over the handful of television sets that his village then had. Gandhi was the youngest PM the country had ever seen, and a young Ramkesh was captivated by what he had to offer—his oratory, his personality, the promise of a modern, foreign-educated pilot transforming politics.

Ramkesh was in awe of the way Gandhi carried himself: a stylish, suave man keen to bring about a technological transformation in the country.

'*Main deewana ho gaya tha unka.*' I was crazy about him, Ramkesh tells me.

One time, when Gandhi visited Jind district, Ramkesh travelled for an hour just to catch a glimpse of him. The visit was partially successful: Ramkesh couldn't spot Gandhi, but he spotted a group of people that he assumed was the crowd assembled around Gandhi.

Ramkesh remembers bawling for days and refusing to eat as a ten-year-old when Gandhi was assassinated on 21 May 1991. His family did not have a television set then, so he went to his neighbour's and cried while watching Gandhi's funeral procession. Over a decade later, when his children, Rahul and Priyanka, started emerging on the political horizon, Ramkesh was firmly with them. He felt like he had a personal connection with the two of them.

'I adored the two of them. I used to be very fond of them,' he said. But all this changed in 2014, in the run-up to the general elections in the country, when Modi, the aspiring PM, crisscrossed the country, mounting stinging attacks against the Congress.

Those speeches roused Ramkesh, and within a few months, he realized how wrong he had been his entire life.

Phir Modi aaya, aur maine jab uske bhashaan sunne, toh laga yeh log hamare dushman hai,' Ramkesh says, laughing. Then Modi came along, and when I heard his speeches, I realized that these people were in fact our enemies.

For three decades, Ramkesh had backed one generation of the Gandhi family after another. He had welcomed Rahul's entry into politics. But listening to Modi's attacks on parivaarwaad, dynastic politics in the Congress, Ramkesh suddenly felt a sense of cognitive dissonance. He didn't know which way to swing. He had never had any objection to the Gandhi dynasty being in India's politics; he had, if at all, only welcomed it eagerly. But when the BJP, under Modi, rolled in and mounted a campaign to paint the Congress and the Gandhis as anti-Hindu Muslim appeasers,[2] the dissonance cleared up.[3] The campaign was appealing to Hindus like Ramkesh to not fall for the party that never cared about Hindus.

That hit home. Suddenly, Ramkesh saw his favourite political family and their party in a new light. 'This was true, I realized. The Gandhis were Hindus, but the party had always been two-faced and leaned towards Muslims,' Ramkesh says.

Ramkesh was sold. His allegiance had shifted to the BJP, and it was not going back.

~

From then on, like Kavi, Ramkesh started looking for validation for his political views from all kinds of sources.

Two years ago, a man from Pakistan, purportedly a fan of his work, started following him on various social media platforms and ultimately messaged him on WhatsApp. Ramkesh says he treated him like he would treat any other fan—he acknowledged the fan's praise and thanked him politely. But the man continued to communicate. He would message, comment on every update that Ramkesh and Kavi posted. He would never call; the two would only talk over messages.

He even made a video montage out of all the photos that Ramkesh and Kavi had posted online recently. Ramkesh was touched by this attention and would routinely respond, communicate with him. The acquaintanceship grew, and he invited Ramkesh and Kavi to Pakistan. His brother was a politician there, and they would be treated with respect and adulation, he assured Ramkesh.

The bonhomie was growing. But one day, Ramkesh received a text message that left him fuming. 'He told me, "You guys are such good people, you should become Muslims,"' Ramkesh recalls.

'I said, "What is this? What are you saying?"'

The man, though, continued. 'He said, "Become Muslims, and you will get jannat. Heaven."'

Ramkesh could not bear to hear him anymore. In that moment, he wished the man wasn't separated by an international border and thousands of kilometres. He wished the man was sitting across the table from him, so he could beat him to pulp. Ramkesh did the next best thing.

'I called him up and told him, I will come down to Pakistan and beat you up,' he says. Ramkesh, prone to using colourful language in moments of passion, offered an earful and hung up.

For both father and daughter, these brushes were not isolated, exceptional instances. Both see it as a glimpse into the religion and the community of its followers.

Ramkesh, for instance, has concluded that Hindus and Muslims cannot ever coexist peacefully. The gulf that separates their 'cultures' and their 'ways of life' is too vast to be bridged now, he insists.

He illustrates this with an example. 'For us Hindu men, every girl in the village is our sister. But Muslim men even marry their sisters, so they obviously won't look at village women as their sisters.'

He goes on. Hindus eat *saatvik khaana,* vegetarian food sanctioned under the yogic philosophy. Muslims only eat *masahari khaana,* non-vegetarian food.

For the father-daughter duo, their life's core beliefs are peppered with such simplistic and, often, factually incorrect generalizations made from their own, often, singular and coloured experiences.

In March 2021, while we drove northwards from Haridwar, in search of a picturesque shoot location, Kavi told me about her recent trip to Jaisalmer, where she came across a community of Muslim families living in penury. All the families lived in tarpaulin huts and could barely eke out enough to feed themselves. They had no money to fund their children's education. Kavi reacted to the situation with disgust, instead of compassion, and felt angry at their sheer deprivation.

For Kavi, this was a reiteration of what she already believed to be true. 'They don't want to be educated; they don't want jobs. They don't do any work. All they want to do is increase their population, and one day, they will take over the country.'

For Kavi, Muslims were poor because they chose to be poor, that poverty was a choice they had consciously made. Her father confirmed that and went one-up: poverty was not just a choice, but a conspiracy.

Ramkesh, driving the car towards Haridwar from Karnal in Haryana, chimes in. *'Islam shuru hua 1,400 saal pehle, aur aaj woh log sattavan desho ko control karte hai.'* Islam originated only 1,400 years ago, but they are now already controlling fifty-seven countries across the world.

A United States Commission on International Religious Freedom report of 2012 analysing the text of the constitutions of Muslim-majority countries found that there were only 46 nations in the world where Islam was the dominant religion.[4] Of these, 23 nations had Islam as the official religion of the state, while 22 nations mention Islamic principles or law as a source of legislation.

Yet, like much of the Hindu right-wing, Ramkesh believes that the growth of Islam has been facilitated by a worldwide conspiracy among Muslims to grow their tribe. He is most animated each time the country's growing population is mentioned. For him, the burgeoning growth only points to one fear—the takeover of Hindustan by Islam.

Much of this, as the book has mentioned before, is without basis—the Muslim rate of growth has slowed down, and declined more than the Hindu rate of growth of population. Population estimates also underline the fact that such conspiracies within the Hindutva networks are just that: conspiracies.

Yet, many like Ramkesh continue to ignore facts. For Ramkesh, this Islamic conspiracy first took root by strengthening Muslim demography around some of Hinduism's most revered, holiest places of worship.

'Wherever we had our *dharmic sthals*, our places of worship, be it Kashi, Mathura or Ayodhya, they strategically increased their population. Mandirs were broken down, and masjids were made,' Ramkesh explains.

Data does not demonstrate any such conspiracy through a 'strategic increase' in Muslim population in any of these areas. In Kashi, officially known as Varanasi, the population of Muslims has been stable for centuries now—from 28.4 per cent in 1827[5] to 28.8 per cent in 2011, as per the latest Census.[6] Similarly, in Mathura, the Muslim population increased only marginally from 7 per cent in 1961[7] to 8.5 per cent in 2011.[8] In the erstwhile Faizabad district, under which Ayodhya fell, the Muslim population increased ever so slightly, from 13.3 per cent in 1991[9] to 14.8 per cent in 2011.[10]

Yet, it is in history that Ramkesh believes lies a rational, logical understanding of the community.

'All the Muslim rulers that came to India, they came to power only after killing their fathers and brothers,' Ramkesh says. 'So it is very clear to them—you can grow or come to power only by killing others.'

~

What makes Kavi potent are not these prejudices and beliefs, but her ability as an influencer to propagate them, reiterate them as facts, help normalize them and radicalize her listeners.

This is precisely what makes her a vital cog in the Hindutva ecosystem: a non-politician and a seemingly unbiased singer who reiterates the most hardline elements of Hindu nationalism and helps popularize it among unsuspecting listeners.

I witnessed this in April 2022, a year after our Haridwar trip. Kavi had garnered a formidable following of nearly 700,000 followers on Facebook by then.

In early April that year, a clash between Hindus and Muslims had broken out in Karauli town of Rajasthan. This, after a bike rally by Hindus to celebrate the community's new year, entered Atwara, a Muslim-dominated locality in the area, and the encounter turned into a full-blown communal clash.[11] The clash left at least forty-two people injured and many shops charred.[12]

Kavi was enraged. '*Aap maun hi rahiyega. Secular bane rahiyega.*' Stay silent and remain secular, she said in the video she posted on her Facebook account.[13] There were so many atrocities committed against Kashmiri Pandits, but Hindus did not speak up for them, she said. 'At least now, speak now.'

Kavi soon abandons dog-whistling in the video and launches into an unhinged diatribe against Muslims. If they can, she tells her audience, they will kill every Hindu in India. The day isn't far away, she warns them.

She told her followers to not believe that 'they' were 'just 15-20 per cent' of the population; she referred to the Muslim community without naming it. That 'they' were much more.

The government of India, under Modi, had released the Census 2011 data by religious communities. That data had revealed that Muslims were only 14.2 per cent of the population, while Hindus were 79.8 per cent. But Kavi did not believe the data. 'They are somewhere around 50 per cent of our population,' she says.

The basis for such a big assertion, yet again, is personal experience. 'I used to believe that there are hardly any of them around me. But when I started asking people their names, I realized they were all Muslims,' she says, astonished.

Her experience, Kavi says, comes from visits to the local Rohtak market. She started asking the vegetable and fruit vendors, as well as those who ran the market's roadside eateries, their names. 'Initially, they would tell me their names were Sonu, Monu and the likes,' she says. 'But when I pressed them further, they revealed their *real* Muslim names.'

That anecdote is enough for Kavi to authoritatively dismiss data that might run contrary to her belief.

Such experiences, combined with beliefs, have coalesced into an unbridled backing of Hindutva. Kavi's work now seeks to propagate her own fears and hatred born out of these beliefs.

In late 2019, the country was swept by protests against the Citizenship (Amendment) Act passed by the Parliament. The Act, along with the proposed National Register of Citizens, were the Modi government's ways of fast-tracking citizenship applications from non-Muslim refugees, followed by a nationwide exercise to determine and expel all 'illegal immigrants' within the country.[14] It was widely feared that its discriminatory provisions would be targeted at Muslims in the country, leading to protests from various sections of society, across the country.

The longest and the most significant symbol for these protests came from a Muslim locality in Delhi, Shaheen Bagh, where local Muslim women started a peaceful sit-in protest that, over time, attracted tens of thousands of protesters from across the country, drawing in support from political parties as well as artistes and celebrities.

The protests roiled the BJP, with even Modi calling the Shaheen Bagh protests a 'political conspiracy' and an 'experiment' to disturb the peace and harmony in the capital.[15]

For Kavi and Ramkesh, though, the protests became a way to channel their anger and reiterate what they have always known—that a growing Muslim population was going lead to such 'anarchy', as Modi had described the protests.

On 31 January 2020, Kavi brought out a new song titled '*Sache Hindustani*', the real Indians. The song attacked the protesters, singled out Shaheen Bagh and, without naming it, stoked anger against the Muslim community.

She warned her followers of the threats from these protests. She flagged the protests as being conducted to divide the nation into smaller pieces—*tukde tukde*—and said the protesters, with a tiranga, tricolour, in their hand and danga, riot, on their mind, were carrying out nothing but jihad. They weren't just protesting, Kavi said in her song, but were standing against the nation, *desh ke viprit*, and hence, they were *Jinnah ki aulaad*, or Jinnah's descendants, a thinly veiled, derogatory reference often hurled at Muslims.

For all these threats, the song presented one solution—curbing the growth of 'their' population through a population control law.

Justifying that, Kavi, in Ramkesh's, words, harked back to her own beliefs and fears, of an Islamic takeover of the country.

Kuch logo ki toh saazish hai,
Hum bacche khub banayenge.
Jab sankhya hui humse zyaada,
Fir apni baat manayenge.
Kavi Singh bas apna desh, dharam bachana chahti hai
Mera Hindustan ho vishwaguru, bas yehi khwaab sajati hai.
Inko bahar nikaalo tum, apna desh bachalo tum.

Some people are conspiring,
That we will produce many children.
When their numbers go past ours,
They will make us dance to their tune.
Kavi Singh wants to save our nation, our religion.
My country becomes a world leader, that's the only dream she
harbours.

Throw these people out, save our nation.

The song ended with a grim warning if the advice wasn't followed.

Agar abhi yeh nahi hua,
Toh fir intezaam nahi hoga.
Is duniya mein fir yeh apna,
Hindustan nahi hoga.

If this doesn't happen now,
Nothing else can save us.
In this world no more,
Will Hindustan exist.

~

Such polarized rhetoric, normalized and repeatedly injected into the veins of a gullible audience, can often result in grim circumstances.

There are growing links between consuming hate music and tendencies towards violence and aggressive behaviour. Academic studies, as well as analyses of real-life violence, have shown that hate-filled music might have been a contributing factor in inciting violence, even if a direct link between music and violence has not been established yet.[16]

Arno Michaelis, founder of Life After Hate, a support group for former violent far-right extremists, said 'hate music' did a lot more than entertain.[17] 'If you are playing white power music [...] you are learning how to hate people and you are practicing emotional violence against them.' While Michaelis referred to music meant for white supremacists, the analyses stand true for all such music meant to indoctrinate and act as political propaganda.

In his book, *Sound Targets: American Soldiers and Music in the Iraq War*, author Jonathan Pieslak details how American soldiers would listen to heavy metal and rap music as some sort of an 'inspiration for combat'. Such music, Pieslak wrote, facilitated a state of mind that was 'necessary for killing'.[18]

Experts tracking far-right extremist groups believe that music can be a major factor in motivating people towards action; it can end up inducing pride in people about their actions and the cause they represent, while driving up their anger and resentment levels.[19]

Nothing illustrates this better than the experience of the Rwandan genocide, one of the worst-such the world has seen.

For over three months in 1994, members of the majority Hutu community, especially its police, militia and army, went on a genocidal spree against the minority Tutsi community members. They targeted every Tutsi, from top leaders to common citizens, using weapons like machetes. More than 800,000 people were killed in that wave of genocidal killings during those three months.[20]

The United Nations Security Council established the International Criminal Tribunal for Rwanda to examine serious violations of international law in Rwanda and prosecute those responsible for the genocide. It functioned for twenty-one years and ended up indicting ninety-three people for their role in the massacres,[21] including the Prime Minister of the interim Rwandan government, Jean Kambanda.[22]

But an unlikely inclusion in the list of indicted figures was the singer and songwriter Simon Bikindi. In pre-genocide Rwanda, Bikindi was so popular that he would often be known as 'Rwanda's Michael Jackson', and 'probably the most talented artiste of the generation'.[23]

But Bikindi's music played an active role in stoking anger against the Tutsis. He had composed three political songs that were played repeatedly, several times a day, on the Radio Télévision Libre des Mille Collines, the Hutu-run radio station known to have played a key role in the genocide.[24] His songs valourized historical Hutu heroes while demonizing the Tutsi monarchy of the past, stoking fears of Hutus being killed by Tutsis.

The singer was charged with six counts: genocide, conspiracy to commit genocide, complicity in genocide, direct and public enticement to commit genocide, murder as a crime against humanity and persecution as a crime against humanity.[25]

Apart from being a popular Rwandan musician, Bikindi was also an official in the Rwandan government's Ministry of Youth and Sports as well as a part of the ruling party. Under the count of direct and public incitement to commit genocide, Bikindi was accused of having:

> … composed, performed, recorded or disseminated musical compositions extolling Hutu solidarity and characterising Tutsi as enslavers of the Hutu … these compositions were subsequently deployed to target Tutsi as the enemy or enemy accomplices and to instigate, incite and encourage the Hutu population to separate themselves from the Tutsi and kill them.

In addition, the charges added how Bikindi's

> … lyrics manipulated the politics and history of Rwanda to promote Hutu solidarity … Calls for attacks on the enemy in these RTLM broadcasts were often preceded or followed by these songs composed and performed by Simon Bikindi.

To help with their case, the prosecution during the trial relied on a report prepared by Gamariel Mbonimana, a history professor at the National University of Rwanda, and Jean de Dieu Karangwa, a

Rwandan linguist at the National Institute of Eastern Civilizations and Languages in Paris. An excerpt from the report says,[26]

> [Bikindi's] songs are a true combat weapon and the RTLM managed to make the most of this. Well composed ... they could replace the lengthy and sometimes boring speeches and effectively complement the radio presenter. As a musical symbol they elicit an enthusiasm which words alone or any other declamation cannot convey.

Three decades later, India's Hindu right-wing is realizing and milking the power of such emotionally charged music.

~

India has among the cheapest rates in the world for mobile internet data. One direct result of that has been the boom in the consumption of online videos on mobile screens across the country.[27] From 266 million in 2018, India's online video viewer base has grown to over 350 million in 2020 at nearly double the speed at which markets like China and Indonesia have grown.[28]

Of the average five hours that smartphone users spend on their phones, over an hour is spent watching only videos, data show.[29] As a result of this cheap data boom, more and more Indians are now looking increasingly towards YouTube as their preferred search engine, where they go when looking for new information.

Each time a news event occurs, more people are likely to go to YouTube and Facebook to search for content online to inform themselves.[30] As the news cycle and online conversations revolve around the event, Indians, hungry for video content, are skipping past long pieces and television news and heading straight for online videos to understand and shape their responses better.

Ramkesh and Kavi realize this. In their heads, they believe they are not very different from journalists.

'It makes sense to run these songs the same day the event happens. *Agle din koi nahi sunta*,' nobody is interested in it the next morning, Ramkesh tells me.

In early October 2020, an Indian jewellery brand, Tanishq, released a forty-five-second advertisement promoting a new jewellery line. The ad showed a Muslim family organizing a traditional Hindu baby shower for their expectant Hindu daughter-in-law. Within a few hours, the ad was attacked by Hindu right-wing social media influencers and sympathizers for promoting love jihad, a term often splayed by Hindu fundamentalists for denoting an inter-faith union involving a Hindu woman and a Muslim man.[31] Four days later, the brand was forced to take down the advertisement and even issue an apology for the 'inadvertent stirring of emotions' through the ad.[32]

Even as the dust settled on it, a twenty-year-old Hindu woman, Nikita Tomar, was shot to death moments after she stepped out of her college in Ballabhgarh, a town in Haryana.[33] The assailants turned out to be two Muslim men, one of whom was Tomar's spurned lover, dejected at her refusal to marry him.[34] Amidst the outrage the case generated, there were allegations that Tomar was killed allegedly because she had refused to convert to Islam.

Almost overnight, an issue firmly pursued for decades by the Hindu right-wing became a top governance priority for BJP governments.

Within days of the killing, Uttar Pradesh Chief Minister Yogi Adityanath announced that his government would soon bring a new law to curb love jihad and threatened to bump off all those who forcefully convert 'our sisters and daughters'.[35] Following suit swiftly, seven other states—Karnataka, Assam, Haryana, Uttarakhand, Himachal Pradesh, Madhya Pradesh and Gujarat—promised similar laws.[36]

The father-daughter duo sensed an opportunity and moved in swiftly.

Within a day of Yogi's announcement, Ramkesh penned down the lyrics. Kavi took a day to memorize and record the song. Two days after Yogi's big announcement, a new song was out.[37] It was called 'Love Jihad'.

The song starts with Kavi loudly chanting 'Vande Mataram' twice and diving straight into the issue. Without naming Muslims, the song targets an enemy and lashes out at them. Through the song, she only addresses the community as a distant 'they/them', but she doesn't leave any doubt about who she means.

The first four lines spell out the intent.

In desh drohi, makaaron ko
Karo bahar gadaaron ko.
Manavta ke hathyaaron ko,
Karo bahar gadaaron ko.

These anti-nationals, their ingrateful wretches,
Throw these traitors out.
These destroyers of humanity,
Throw these traitors out.

The song calls all 'these' people terrorists and paints an existential threat to Hindus from them, the kind that Kavi and Ramkesh have come to deeply believe in.

Leaving no doubt about the song's inspiration and its intent, Kavi even displays an image of the spot where Tomar was killed.

Desh ka kanoon nahi maante,
Beech sadak par maara hai.
Fir yeh kaise kehte hai,
Ki bharat desh hamara hai.

These people don't believe in laws,
They've killed on a street,
How can they, then, say,
That India is their country.

The song ends with a dire warning—of the impending end for all
Hindus, if they don't 'wake up'.

Inki mansa ka ab,
Pata chal gaya hi hoga.
Jab ghar mein ghus kar maarenge,
Kya tab ehsaas tumhe hoga?
Tum ab bhi jaag na paaoge,
Toh sote hi reh jaaoge.

Now, at least, you know
Their real intent.
Will you realize the truth,
Only when they get into your homes and kill?
If you can't wake up now,
You will sleep forever.

Immediately after the song ends, with Kavi sporting a slight smile
and her hands joined in prayer, the screen dissolves and instead
appears a poster that reads *Hindu bhaiyon se appeal,* an appeal to
Hindu brothers.

This is the first time Kavi has such text to follow her songs. The
poster sports the visual of a young woman in a salwar kameez riding
pillion with a bearded young man wearing a green T-shirt. The
backdrop is a temple.

The poster, in Hindi, warns how Muslim men were now sporting
sacred Hindu threads on their wrists or using Hindu names to lure

young Hindu women with false promises of love, converting them to Islam, only to exploit them sexually before dumping them. The poster also offers examples.

Udaharan ke taur par, Bollywood abhineta Saif Ali Khan vah Aamir Khan ne Hindu ladkiyon se shaadi kar, bacche paida kar, unhe chod diya.

For instance, Bollywood actors Saif Ali Khan and Aamir Khan married Hindu women, produced kids with them and then dumped them.

The poster lays out the warning.

Agla shikar tum ho.

You will be the next victim.

A Sudden End

Jo Ram Ko laaye hai, hum unko laayenge
UP mein phir se hum bhagwa lehrayenge.

Those who brought Ram back, we'll get them back
In UP, we'll unfurl the saffron flag again.

The year 2021 had been a dream run for Kavi. Since the Covid-19 pandemic had ended up cancelling events and concerts, Kavi had focused on releasing her songs online and working on her social media presence. By the end of that year, Kavi had released a whopping twenty-one songs on her YouTube channel. The consistent presence on the platform meant that Kavi garnered nearly 200,000 new subscribers throughout the year.[1]

Her online presence was peaking at the right time for her, professionally. Early next year, in 2022, the state of Uttar Pradesh was going to polls. Yogi Adityanath's re-election was an important landmark for the Hindutva ecosystem. While Kavi had never publicly campaigned for Yogi, she admired him immensely, a sentiment widespread within the ecosystem.

Like with most things, her reasons for liking him were based on individual experiences, supplied helpfully by Ramkesh.

He told me the biggest difference that he saw after Yogi came to power was the fear among Muslims in UP. During his many road trips, Ramkesh would frequently crisscross across UP. Till a few years ago, those trips would scare him, he said.

'Each time I would pass through a Muslim locality, it used to be so dangerous,' Ramkesh said. 'They could stop your car and do whatever they wanted,' he told me. I pressed him for specifics. Did he ever encounter any untoward incident himself? He had not. 'It used to be so dangerous to drive through these [Muslim-populated] areas that people used to warn against night-time driving in UP,' he added. But this had changed. 'Yogi has made the state so safe, you can now drive here anytime you want.' He also mentioned that the Yogi government had cleaned up crime syndicates and had conducted 'more than 12,000 encounters'.

The figure was not factually accurate. By August 2021, which was five months after Ramkesh had told me this, the UP police under Yogi's tenure had conducted 8,742 encounters, injuring 3,302 alleged criminals and killing 146.[2]

However, such stories were enough to convince Kavi. She was a Yogi fan. The pace at which her online presence had been growing, she would have been an asset for the Hindu right-wing ecosystem to drum up support for Yogi, the Hindutva mascot and, as a result, for the BJP.

It was a prospect that Kavi would not be particularly averse to— Ramkesh told me that he was close to numerous BJP leaders and the two of them had even performed in a concert organized by a senior BJP leader in UP, who he was on great terms with.

But as 2021 was drawing to an end, I started observing a discernible downtick in Kavi's social media activities. Throughout the year, she had been bringing out an average of two songs a month—sometimes even within days of each other. Every few days, especially around the time her songs released, Kavi would upload social media posts and even appear 'Live' on Facebook, where she would offer her take on political and social happenings, served with a dollop of Hindutva.

All this, though, had dwindled as the year wound down. From releasing three songs in August and two in September, I barely saw any activity from her in October. By the end of October, she finally released a new song: '*Desh Prem*', 'patriotism'. The song was written by Kavi herself, and is pretty much about her:

Desh par mit jaane ko maine janam liya,
Apne dharam par hi gaane ko maine janam liya.
Yaad karu jab qurbani, toh khoon khaulne lagta hai,
Tujhe bhi kuch kar jaana hai, hriday bolne lagta hai.
Main mar jaau is dharti pe jalakar sach ka diya,
Apne dharam par hi gaane ko maine janam liya.

To be spent on my nation, is why I was born
To sing for my religion, is why I was born
My blood boils, reliving those sacrifices,
My heart cries, I must do the same.
I will sacrifice myself, upholding the flame of truth,
To sing for my religion, is why I was born

This was to be her last song for the year.

I called her after, asking her if she was well. She told me that she had faced a series of health troubles. But just when she had recovered, her mother in Alwar had taken ill.

With one health emergency after another to attend, Kavi told me she was weak and had not yet recovered her vigour. Singing will have to wait, and so will canvassing, albeit indirectly, for the BJP in the upcoming polls in Uttar Pradesh.

~

In early February 2022, even while the seven-phased elections in UP were slowly unfolding, I visited Uttar Pradesh and ventured deep into the state, into small towns and villages that had been sites of religious violence in the last five years or so. Since 2014, the country has been witness to a string of instances of religion-driven violence—from clashes to assaults and even lynchings. I had been tracking such instances across various Indian states for a few years, going to the ground, speaking to the various actors involved in them, including the perpetrators and the victims, and reporting on the implications of such violence on the social fabric.

As the UP elections were coming closer, I wanted to understand how the Yogi government's tenure had shaped these precarious communal relations in places where such hate crimes had occurred. So, in February 2022, I found myself travelling across five districts of UP, traversing over 1,800 km in eight days, in search of some of these answers.

I didn't realize that, unwittingly, this trip would end up revealing how pop culture was silently driving voters towards the BJP.

One of the first places I visited was the village of Purbaliyan in Muzaffarnagar district, in western Uttar Pradesh. The village had seen violence even during the 2013 communal riots in the region, which had left over 40,000 people displaced from their homes and at least sixty dead. Five years after the violence in August 2018, a cricket match among local boys spiralled out of control and turned into a communal clash, with Hindu and Muslim families of the boys trading charges of assault.[3]

At the centre of the clash was Sumit Kumar Pal, a nineteen-year-old Hindu, who told the police that he was assaulted by Muslims twice in a span of three days after his cousin got caught up in the fight at the match. When I first visited him a year after the clash, in 2019, just weeks before the general elections, Sumit seemed content that he had exacted revenge.[4] He had filed two separate First Information Reports (FIR), alleging how he and members of his family had been assaulted by local Muslims. The local BJP Member of Parliament (MP) and a minister in the Modi government, Sanjeev Balyan, had visited the village just a day after the second assault and publicly sided with Sumit's family.[5] Balyan had even declared that the offenders—all Muslims—would be charged under the National Security Act (NSA), 1980.[6,7]

Soon after, the police swung into action. They arrested twenty-seven men—all Muslim—and even charged three of them under the NSA, an act that allows for preventive detention extending up to twelve months, without reasons offered.[8]

While Sumit had seemed content with police action, the Muslims in the village were anguished at the excesses of the police— they complained about the police breaking into Muslim homes and wrongfully detaining locals.[9]

In 2022, I decided to go back to Purbaliyan to understand the impact of this violence on the village's social fabric, and the changes it had brought into social relations between the communities.

I sat in Sumit's home, waiting for him. His uncle tried to call him, as I sat on the single settee in their living room. The Pals had a small business of distributing milk in the local villages, so most of the space on the ground floor of the house was occupied by buffaloes.

When we dialled Sumit, his phone rang to a tune that was catchy and loud—a man with a heavy voice crooned the words. The lyrics caught my attention immediately:

Jo Ram ko laaye hai, hum unko laayenge
UP mein phir se hum Bhagwa lehrayenge.

Those who brought Ram back, we'll get them back
In UP, we'll unfurl the saffron flag again.

The thirty-second dialler only allowed for these two lines to fit in, but each time we dialled Sumit, these lines kept playing, like on loop.

Even before I had reached UP, I had been tracking political developments in the state closely, what with such a tantalizing electoral contest on the cards. But I had never heard this song before, nor known of its existence. Now that I was travelling across mofussil Uttar Pradesh, it felt omnipresent.

Wherever I went, I would find someone who either had this song as their caller tune like Sumit did or as their ringtone or would be playing it loudly in their shops, car or on their phones.

I soon found out that the clip was from a longer song, whose lyrics hid little about who it backed:

Bhagwa hai chola jinka, bas Ram ki baat karein
Hindu hai Hindu hum, bas Ram ki baat karein.
Upar se nahi hai Ram, andar se Ram ke hai
Bas isi liye Yogi, bande kamaal ke hai.

Those donning saffron robes speak only of Ram,
Like us Hindus, who speak only of Ram.
Not just on the outside, he carries Ram deep within,
That's just why, Yogi is a man to reckon.

The song ends on a strikingly confident note.

Yogiji aaye hai, Yogi hi aayenge
Santon ki nagri ko, Babaji chalayenge.
UP mein phir se hum, Bhagwa lehrayenge.

Yogi has won once, Yogi will win again.
The land of saints, will be run by another saint.
In UP, we'll unfurl the saffron flag again.

~

The song had been written and sung by a man named Kanhiya Mittal—well-known for his devotional songs, especially in northern India. Till this song, Kanhiya was best known in the region for his songs devoted to Khatushyam, who Hindus believe was a warrior when the Mahabharata had unfolded.[10] Kanhiya's bhajans were devoted to Khatushyam and the Khatushyam temple in Rajasthan's Sikar district.

But with the all-important election coming closer, Kanhiya was not reluctant to promote Hindutva as an almost organic extension of his devotional music.

Apart from '*Jo Ram ko laaye hai*', Kanhiya also sang a duet with the BJP MP and its former Delhi chief, Manoj Tiwari. Titled '*Bhagwa rang chadne laga hai*', the saffron is getting deeper.[11] The song hails the construction of the Ram mandir. It asks the listener to envision the day when the temple will be ready, insisting that the country will turn glorious the day it happens. Similarly, it also campaigns for temples in Kashi and Mathura, two cities where the Hindu right-wing has claimed existing mosques were built on land where originally temples stood.

Kanhiya had a sizeable presence on social media—across YouTube, Instagram and Facebook, Kanhiya had over four-and-a-half million followers. But he had rarely received any media coverage, especially in mainstream media organizations that operate out of Delhi and Mumbai.

In the digital world, he seemed immensely popular. His posts on Facebook and Instagram received thousands of reactions from his followers; his bhajan performances routinely received millions of views on YouTube. The thumbnails of his YouTube videos would often sport the number of views. His video descriptions carried a phone number, a move common among artistes, especially in smaller centres, keen to increase their presence and exposure to all possible growth opportunities.

I decided to try to meet him and understand how the song came about, all while getting a glimpse into his politics.

Getting in touch with him was difficult. The number advertised was Kanhiya's own, but he refused to answer calls. Text messages to him went unanswered. Finally, Kanhiya responded via text and told me he wasn't well. On social media, though, I could see why he didn't have time to respond: the song's popularity had catapulted Kanhiya into becoming one of the most popular campaigners for the BJP. Latching on to the song's virality, the BJP was showing him off as a powerful endorser of its politics. Kanhiya made for an attractive package for the party: he could be presented as someone who was ostensibly independent and not affiliated to the BJP, a figure steeped in Hindu religiosity and a popular artiste who backed the BJP's politics.

The election campaign was getting heated: apart from UP, elections were being held simultaneously in Uttarakhand as well as Punjab. Uttarakhand was especially significant for the BJP, considered the fountainhead of Hinduism, with several destinations and temples venerated by religious Hindus located within the state.

Every day, Kanhiya was in a different city—sometimes, he was even touring multiple cities in a day across UP and Uttarakhand. Even though Kanhiya hadn't yet agreed to meet me, his social media feed kept me informed: he would chronicle his journeys in private jets and chartered aircraft unfailingly. In one video that he posted on social media on 11 February 2022, he referred to these journeys crisscrossing the country.[12] He was in Kichha, a town in Uttarakhand, at noon. In the evening, he was expected to perform in Bathinda, a city in Punjab that was a ten-hour drive away. In a live video on Facebook, he said he had been receiving queries from his followers about how he would make it to Bathinda in time for the show. As a response, he showed off the private jet he was travelling in, a small jet that had only a handful of seats. He didn't reveal who had funded the trip; instead, he said his deity, Khatushyam, had 'arranged' the trip.

Ten days later, Kanhiya finally agreed to meet me in Delhi, where he had a performance. He invited me to his four-star hotel in Pitampura, where he was spending the night, before taking off for a BJP rally in UP the next morning.

Kanhiya is a short, bearded man with broad shoulders and a loud voice. He has been singing since he was seven, he told me. Growing up in Chandigarh, where his family had migrated to from Sri Ganganagar in Rajasthan when he was a child, Kanhiya joined a local bhajan group that performed devotional songs and hymns in the homes of believers and continued performing through his young adulthood. His long years of experience as a bhajan singer had, over the years, helped him consolidate his following among the believers of Khatushyam.

Religion helped Kanhiya earn a name for himself, gain fame and followers. From performing in people's homes, Kanhiya started getting invited for devotional shows that resembled rock concerts.

On the way, though, he saw how easily religion mixed with politics. He was born in 1990, at a time when the country's politics was in the throes of tectonic changes: the political movement conceptualized and executed by the Sangh Parivar demanding the construction of a temple for Ram in Ayodhya was gaining steam furiously. Religion was becoming an increasingly important factor in the country's political discourse.

But the ten years of the Congress-headed UPA government had left Kanhiya angry and disillusioned. According to Kanhiya, in that decade, the country 'only saw rapes, corruption, inflation, dynastic politics and how only the lady controlled the Prime Minister.' Religion had taken a backseat in the country's politics, and Kanhiya didn't like that.

In 2014, when the BJP stormed to power, all that started to change for Kanhiya. Religion now mattered, and religiosity became a matter of pride for people.

This sentiment reached its zenith for Kanhiya when the Supreme Court cleared the way in November 2019 for the Ram temple to be constructed in Ayodhya.

But for Kanhiya, the SC's role in the issue was negligible. Instead, it was Modi who had made the temple possible. Kanhiya said having Modi at the helm made ordinary Hindus believe that the temple would be constructed. For him, this belief in Modi is what, finally, caused the SC also to deliver its verdict in favour of Hindu groups. 'No one is denying that the court exists … but it also operates on people's perception,' he said.

This belief in Modi's extra-constitutional abilities led Kanhiya to write his song, '*Jo Ram Ko Laye Hai*'.

The song, instantly, became a massive hit.

When the results were declared on 10 March 2022, Kanhiya was vindicated. Adityanath was back with a full majority, and the Hindutva project had just gotten a massive fillip.

Within days of Yogi's victory, Kanhiya received an award from Yogi and a cash prize of Rs 51,000. Kanhiya returned the money, saying he wanted to donate it so that the UP government could buy a new bulldozer with it.[13]

~

Kavi's inactivity continued through most of 2022. We remained in infrequent contact; the few times that we spoke on the phone, Kavi told me how her health issues had refused to subside fully, that things were getting better but not quite.

In January 2023, I finally decided to make the 1,500-km-long journey from Mumbai to Rohtak to see her.

That was when I found out that for a year and a half, Kavi had been giving me a very distorted picture of her life. In these eighteen months, her life had changed completely.

Just months after I had last met Kavi in March 2021, she and her husband, Prince, had decided to file for a divorce. Prince, Kavi told me, was her childhood sweetheart, the reason for her to move from Alwar to Rohtak.

But as Kavi's career grew more and more successful, while her husband's plummeted, relations between them turned sour. When we met, Kavi told me how they had lost respect for each other.

Respect, for Kavi, was everything. Her life's trajectory—from the decision to sing songs of patriotism to the attire she would don, to the way she would conduct herself publicly—had been shaped by the pursuit of respect. But closest to her, she told me, she struggled to earn her husband's respect.

The relationship had to end. The two had agreed to get a divorce.

But this tumult had also caused deep fissures in a bond that felt unshakeable—the one Kavi shared with Ramkesh.

When I met Kavi, she told me Ramkesh was no longer a part of her life. I was stunned. The father-daughter duo was so deeply enmeshed in each other's lives that it felt nearly impossible that something like this could ever happen.

According to Kavi, as her marriage began disintegrating, Ramkesh started to take some blame on himself. Had he maybe gotten himself entangled in the private affairs of his daughter and her husband? Should he have drawn some lines? Kavi told me Ramkesh had started asking these questions of himself and had slowly started withdrawing. The calls dried up, so did the visits. Even working together was now out-of-bounds.

Suddenly, Kavi found herself without either of the two pillars she had rested on throughout her career.

Her career was now floundering, and so was her mental health.

Prince, Kavi said, was not just her husband but her best friend, manager, guide and even her father, all rolled into one. I asked her why she called him fatherly, an unusual term to describe your partner.

'Because he was like my father. I met him when I was still in school, and he had guided me since then,' Kavi told me. From choosing a college for her to the field to pursue, to guiding her life's choices, Prince was everywhere. Till Ramkesh took over some of these roles as Kavi's career grew. Kavi had lost her father when she was a child. In some ways, Kavi felt Prince's presence fill the years-old vacuum.

Losing him had left Kavi rudderless.

I decided to meet Ramkesh, but Kavi warned me that he might not want to be a part of the book any longer, now that their ties had ruptured. My fingers firmly crossed, I called Ramkesh and told him I was in Rohtak and wanted to see him.

I sensed the slightest sense of reluctance. Seconds later, he had agreed to meet me the next morning at 11. There was a lot that I needed to ask him, and I couldn't wait.

~

Through the past year and a half, since our last meeting in March 2021, Ramkesh and I had not been in contact. I was wary of not letting him control my access to Kavi and her interactions with me, and hence, I would meticulously circumvent him while trying to reach Kavi.

But in those months, I had received a steady stream of WhatsApp messages from him, from links to his new songs to photos of the album art announcing a new song or a movie, as well as short clips.

Most of those messages were not conversations but instructions:

On one YouTube link to a song of his, he had said, '*Paanch paanch comment karein, aapka dhanyavaad*', post five comments each, thank you, followed by emojis of folded hands and a red rose.

On a thirty-second video clip of his song: '*Apne status par lagaye*', make this your status. A message with a link to an Instagram reel featuring an attractive young woman, possibly in her twenties and dressed in Western outfits that changed every three seconds, and in the background, Ramkesh's song playing: '*Iss par zyaada se zyaada reel banaye. Dhanyavaad*', Make as many reels on this as you can. Thank you.

As always, Ramkesh's songs were everything from motivational like '*Taaliyan milo chahe gaaliyan milo*', you get brickbats or bouquets, to out-and-out romantic ones where Ramkesh is romancing women who seem like they are half his age.[14]

I called him five minutes before he was supposed to arrive at my hotel to pick me up. I was ready, my memory of his famed punctuality still fresh. A groggy voice answered my call. Ramkesh was fast asleep, in his home, a thirty-minute drive from my hotel.

Memories of my Haridwar trip with him came flooding back when he had threatened to leave all late-risers back, only for me to wake up in terror at 5 a.m., get ready hurriedly and then see him wake up after our designated call time. Ignoring the strong sense of déjà vu, I asked him when he thought he could meet me by. An hour, he promised. Seventy-five minutes later, he reached.

When he stepped out of a swanky white SUV, I almost did not recognize Ramkesh.

When I had seen him last, Ramkesh had looked perpetually exhausted, his facial skin sagging and with baggy dark circles. That was combined with his receding hairline and his visible balding pate. But the man now standing before me looked nothing like him. His skin was shining, his face chiselled, with a beard that was blacker than jet black and manicured finely along his jawline. The balding pate had disappeared; in its place was silky black hair overflowing off his head. Sporting a blazer with a red-and-white striped turtleneck, Ramkesh stepped out to greet me

I asked him about his makeover. He laughed and said he had been trying to get fitter. '*Main race karta hoon, har din, har dusre din,* 1,200 m, 1,600 m,' I try to sprint every day, anywhere from 1,200 m to 1,600 m. He wanted a new look, so he decided to grow a beard too. I shamelessly asked him about his now-invisible balding pate. He laughed some more.

'*Baal lagaye hai maine,*' he admits. I've worn a wig. '*Har 1.5 mahine mein servicing karni padti hai, bas.*' It just needs to be serviced every 1.5 months.

We head to Rohtak's famous Maharshi Dayanand University (MDU), spread across a sprawling green campus with neatly laid-out buildings and open spaces aplenty.

Ramkesh takes me to a students' canteen on campus. There's an empty table with just one chair, so his aide, an aspiring singer named Manmohan who also works as his man Friday, swings a chair from an adjoining table. Except the adjoining table already has a college student sitting, and the empty chair Manmohan had swiftly taken away was for her companion, who was getting coffee. She has her sandwich in her mouth, so she starts mumbling loudly, protesting Manmohan's unannounced move.

Manmohan sheepishly smiles at her, folds his hands, and puts the chair back on her table even before she can finish chewing.

'The more I got involved with her, sir, the worse it got,' Ramkesh tells me, even before I ask him, wanting to address the elephant in the room.

Ramkesh told me that he was conscious of the fact that he had chosen to get enmeshed in his daughter's life, to an extent that had left him feeling uncomfortable.

'*Meri limit se bahar pyaar tha, inn par. Kahin na kahin, thodi limit hoti hai pyaar karne ki.*' My love for her was limitless, boundless. Somewhere, love has to have some limits.

'If someone calls me five times a day and asks about me at all times, a third person would wonder why she is calling him five times. I felt like I wanted to teach her everything in one day. Whatever knowledge I had, I wanted to pass it on to her.

'In some ways, I had become Kavi Singh. I had stopped thinking of anything else. Kavi Singh was all I could think of—how I could further Kavi Singh, how I could make her grow, how I could make her more popular, that's all I would spend my time on,' he said.

Ramkesh's obsession with Kavi Singh started clashing with Kavi's own ambitions, her own priorities.

Much of that, I realized, had to do with the genesis of Kavi's singing career.

~

The first pop song Ramkesh had ever written way back in 2008, the nostalgic ode named '*Hatt jaa tau*', had become a runaway success as soon as it was released. It had marked Ramkesh's debut in the most spectacular way possible. According to the Haryanvi artistes I spoke to, the song was a blockbuster single, a fun, foot-tapping number. It got so popular that was it later used in a Hindi film, *Veerey Ki Wedding*, that released in 2018. The success notwithstanding, Ramkesh was not happy. He had written the song, but the song's success almost entirely went to its singer. Ramkesh barely got any fame coming his way. The misery pushed him into a slump. His first song had been a fantastic hit, but no one really associated him with it.

One night, he went to his father and cried his heart out. His father offered him a perspective that Ramkesh carries in his heart, even now, years later. 'He told me, "Ramkesh, *you* have created the singer. No one knew him before this, but now everyone knows him,"' Ramkesh recalled. 'What he said next stuck with me. He said, "That means, Ramkesh, you have the talent to make anyone go from *zero to hero*." I was blown away by his words,' Ramkesh told me.

Ramkesh took his father's words to heart. Since that day, he started believing in his ability to *make* people, their careers, their lives. 'I am not bragging about it, but I know that if I want to make someone big, they will become big,' he said.

'Like, if I decide that I want to make Manmohan big,' he says, pointing to his man Friday seated to his left, 'I can make him big.' Manmohan, sitting uncomfortably on a stool, offers a hopeful smile.

Convinced in his belief, Ramkesh decided to kick-start his own singing career. The self-belief propelled him to cut across streams, take to acting, even directing and, later, producing.

In his mind, Ramkesh's own legend grew. His growing stature had convinced him of the power his father had made him discover. So, he decided that his closest must also be the benefactors of his power. That's when he turned to Kavi, his simpleton daughter, content in her life with her role as a wife and beautician.

Ramkesh had seen early signs of a possibly rocky marriage, he told me. A medical situation meant that Kavi would never be able to conceive, and this worried him. Kavi had made peace with it, but Ramkesh could not.

'I felt that she was all right at the time, but in a few years, she would feel that vacuum immensely. What will she do then?' he said. *'Kiske liye jiyegi woh? Bahut tension rehti thi mujhe.'* Who will she live for? I used to be constantly worried about it.

So, he brandished his power and made a decision that would change all their lives forever—he was going to *make* his daughter a singer. Never mind that she had never sung in her life. He knew he had the power to make her a singer anyway.

'Suddenly, I had a brainwave: why not push her into singing, so she gets a purpose in life and knows that there are people who love her, her fans?' Ramkesh recounted the moment. 'Somewhere, her happiness and her fame would fill her life's vacuum.'

That's when he decided to *create* Kavi Singh, a persona who could make up for Kavi's weaknesses and drawbacks.

That's when he, along with her husband Prince, started drawing up the contours of what Kavi Singh would be like—what she would wear, what she would perform, what her identity would be. Kavi went along; she told me she didn't mind them deciding these details for her. She just wanted to wear a pagdi.

Everything started falling into place, slowly. The idea of *Kavi Singh* was getting finalized; he had even got Kavi to attend classes to improve her singing. Her career as a singer was all set to take off.

But her first song as Kavi Singh changed everything for Ramkesh.

When he saw just how wildly successful the song had been, blending patriotism with nationalism, spiced with a topping of Hindutva, he decided to recalibrate his plans.

He decided that singing was a temporary stop—Kavi Singh's destination was going to be politics.

Neither Ramkesh nor Kavi had ever told me any of this in the past two years that I had known them. In fact, during our trip to

Haridwar, when I had asked them if they ever saw Kavi joining politics, the two had been shy to offer answers.

Neither of them had ever dismissed the possibility of being in politics, but neither ever spelt their intent out so clearly. Nor had Ramkesh ever been as candid about his role in the making of Kavi Singh.

Ramkesh's revelations, now, I realized, had been driven by his ambitions being smashed. Of realizing that he could no longer pull the strings of his daughter's life. It meant a serious reversal of Ramkesh's plans for Kavi, which he had many and charted in great detail.

$$\sim$$

Ramkesh's role in Kavi's life had remained undiminished from the moment he had initiated her into her singing career, through both, the dizzying highs he had reached as well as the crushing lows she had found herself in.

When Kavi started experiencing troubles in her marriage, Ramkesh stood by her. He also stood by her when the couple decided to file for divorce. But after the divorce, Kavi and Prince had started living together again.

Kavi had told me that the two had decided to give their relationship another shot, the divorce be damned. It was going to be a new start—a start without the burden of the relationship getting a label.

But that didn't go down well with Ramkesh and his wife. That was when he drew the line.

Ramkesh told me that he had even started planning for Kavi to be re-married. He wanted to start looking at prospective grooms, start planning the way she would navigate this part of her life.

So, when Kavi and Prince started living together, Ramkesh was shocked. He objected to it, only for his objections to be cast aside by

Kavi. The Kavi that he believed was entirely malleable and supple to his instructions, suddenly was not.

'It was a rude shock to me. That day, I thought to myself, "Who the hell do you think you are?" That's the day I walked away.'

That was also the day when Kavi's proposed political journey went into disarray. In the blueprint that Ramkesh had created for Kavi, 2024 was going to be the year she was going to be launched in electoral politics. Ramkesh had not planned on aiming low—he had wanted her to make her electoral debut fighting to become an MP.

'I had a lot of dreams [for her]. I had full confidence that I could bring her into 2024 politics,' he said, ruefully.

The blueprint had a detailed roadmap of just how that was going to happen: Kavi's political launch was to be announced in style, with a yatra across the country, from Rameshwaram, the country's southern-most tip, to Srinagar, in the heart of Jammu and Kashmir, much like the Congress's Bharat Jodo Yatra. Except, Kavi's yatra was to be antithetical to the Congress version—her yatra would seek to popularize Hindutva, drum up support for hard-line Hindutva positions and while doing so, pitch her as a leading voice of the cause. She would rake up issues she had raised in her work and tell her audiences about the worries and fears the father-daughter duo harboured—an Islamic takeover of the country, a love jihad conspiracy against Hindus, protecting Hindu temples and pushing for a Hindu rashtra.

'Along the way, we would involve local like-minded groups to join in; we would hold small public meetings en route and create buzz about Kavi. Hindutva-vaadi leaders would have also joined in,' Ramkesh told me, laying out his plans.

Ramkesh had it all planned—the yatra would last for five to six months, he would hire a vanity van that would serve as their rath, chariot, and the whole exercise would cost Rs 15–20 crore, he had estimated.

'I would have created such buzz that the BJP would have given her a ticket. I would have exhausted myself in every way possible if that was what it took. But I would have made it happen,' Ramkesh said.

Ramkesh told me how he had access to multiple leaders of the BJP, including ministers in the Union government, chief ministers and members of the RSS.

For Ramkesh, Kavi becoming an MP would be just the beginning of her political journey. 'My dream was to see her as the Prime Minister. But I would have at least made her a mantri, minister,' Ramkesh revealed. 'The opportunity was there. I had planned everything.'

All of Kavi's work—her Hindutva-filled songs, her live videos, her public persona as a Hindutva crusader—had all been carefully manicured to lead her to that 2024 launch.

By this point, I was surprised not by his revelations per se but by his admittance of them. I decided to prod further. In this cleverly manicured exercise, why had Ramkesh chosen Hindutva to be Kavi Singh's ideology? What not something else?

His answer was unsurprising. Ramkesh said the choice of Hindutva, as her ideology, was also a calculated one.

'Hindutva is the right thing to say in this mahaul, political climate,' snap comes Ramkesh's response, before quickly insisting that it wasn't just in keeping with the political environment.

The choice of Hindutva, he said, was not a wrong one by any measure. Leave the cynicism aside for a minute, and even then, Hindutva was the right choice for them to make, Ramkesh tries to convince me.

'What is wrong in talking about our religion and our country?' The country's politics, Ramkesh said, had changed. There was no future for any politician if he/she wasn't going to be a Hindutva cheerleader.

'I am giving you a guarantee—those who do not talk of Hindutva will be destroyed in our politics in the future,' he said. '*Likhwa lo aap mere se parchi pe*,' I can write that down for you.

Hindutva was going to get increasingly relevant, by the day. Ramkesh saw a grim, dark future for the country. 'This is only going to get bigger. Believe me, there will be bloodshed. There will be a massive riot. Trust me. And it will be so big, much, much bigger than 1947.'

~

For Kavi, too, the unexpected parting from her father had disrupted her life and her career, equally. Suddenly, the destination her father had pinned for her had vanished off the map.

During our conversations in February 2023, Kavi told me she had given up on the 2024 dream. With just about a year to go for the elections, she knew she was not going to be picked for a parliament ticket.

But, hurt at having lost her father's support, she was now raring to go and wanted to prove a point. She told me she had made it her mission to 'fulfil her father's dream of seeing her in politics'.

She was ready to make sacrifices if that was what it took. The first such sacrifice was that she was likely to move out of Rohtak, away from Haryana and back to her home state of Rajasthan.

YouTube analytics told her she was not as popular in Haryana as she was in UP, Madhya Pradesh, Bihar and Rajasthan. But of all the four states, Rajasthan was where she had another advantage, that of being a local.

She had already spoken to an MP of the BJP from Rajasthan about wanting to join him. The MP had been aggressively campaigning against the Congress government in the state and had strong links to Hindutva forces in and outside Rajasthan.

Kavi had received positive feelers from him and his aides, and she was keen to join in as he travelled across the state, taking out yatras attacking the rival Congress and popularizing Hindutva.

The prospect had enthused Kavi. The yatra that Ramkesh had planned for her may not have worked out. But for now, in the run-up to the 2024 elections, Kavi Singh had found a new yatra to embark on.

PART 2

Weaponizing Poetry: Kamal Agney

An Introduction to Kamal Agney

Hindu armaano ki jalti ek chitaah they Gandhi ji
Kaurav ka saath nibhaane waale Bhismapitah they Gandhi ji.

The burning pyre of Hindu aspirations, that was Gandhi
The Bhismapitah who decided to back the Kauravas, that was
    Gandhi.

I t is 2017, and the venue for the *kavi sammelan*, a poetry recital by professional poets, in Ghaziabad is packed to the gills.[1] Even the stage is teeming with poets and organizers, seated on the ground over thinly cushioned mattresses.

The youngest poet in the gathering takes the stage. Dressed in a blazing saffron kurta and a matching gamcha around his neck, Kamal Agney, originally Kamal Varma, walks up to the standing mic. He pulls up his right sleeve to his elbow.

He has been working on a kavita, poem, for two years now, he tells his audience. It is about a man who is a forgotten shaheed, martyr. 'But I just haven't been able to find the right audience for it.' Till today,' he adds after a deliberate pause.

The event has been organized by a hard-line Hindu nationalist, Yati Narsinghanand, the head of a temple in the northern Indian town of Dasna, popular among its devotees.[2]

A year before this performance, Yati had announced that he was setting up a religious army of Hindus to fight the Islamic State and would be establishing up to fifty centres to train Hindu boys and men.[3]

His reputation in the Hindutva ecosystem only got stronger after that. Narsinghanand is known for his vitriolic hate speeches targeting Muslims, calling them 'demons' and promising to make India 'Islam-free'.[4] His comments proved so hot for even the BJP to handle that Narsinghanand was arrested and spent a month in the Haridwar district jail before being granted bail in February 2022.[5,6]

His temple in Dasna has a notice outside, barring Muslims from entering it.[7]

On stage that day, Kamal says, pointing to the banner behind him, 'That shaheed's photo, is not featured even on the banner.' That's how controversial this poem is.

The martyr in question is Nathuram Godse, Mahatma Gandhi's assassin. As soon as Kamal announces Godse's name (always carefully adding a 'Pandit' before his name), applause breaks out spontaneously. Narsinghanand walks onto the stage immediately with a garland of orange marigold flowers. Kamal breaks into a pleased smile upon seeing him and bows down with his hands folded to let Narsinghnanand garland him.

For the next thirteen minutes, Kamal, through his poem on Gandhi and Godse, launches into what is, simultaneously, a searing indictment of Gandhi's role in the freedom struggle as well as a justification and glorification for Godse's action. The poem blames Gandhi for everything—from 'betraying' India by not stopping the executions of the three revolutionaries, Bhagat Singh, Sukhdev and Rajguru, to wrongly backing Nehru, instead of other, ostensibly more deserving, leaders, for the post of the Prime Minister of independent India. But the subtext, through the poem, was clear: killing Gandhi was justified and necessary. The reason? Gandhi cared only about appeasing Muslims, and Hindus had suffered gravely because of his actions. Here is a line from his poem:

Gandhi ji ka prem amar tha, kewal chand-sitaare se.
Gandhi had eternal love, but only for the crescent and star.

Kamal's poem paints Gandhi as being hurt by the suffering of the Muslims while looking away as the Hindus suffered when India was partitioned, and Pakistan was carved out as a separate nation.

Railon me Hindu kaat-kaar kar, bhej rahe the Pakistani
Topi ke liye dukhi they, par choti ki ek nahi maani.
Satya-ahimsa ka yeh naatak bas kewal Hindu par tha.

Pakistanis were sending back butchered bodies of Hindus on
 trains,
His heart felt nothing for the shikha, but for the skullcap it
 felt pain.
His truth and non-violence were only for the Hindus.

Kamal then goes on to recreate the moment of Gandhi's assassination. He steps into Godse's mind and takes the listener along:

Uss din Nathu ke maha-krodh ka paani sar se upar tha,
Gaya prarthana sabha mein karne Gandhi ko pranam,
Aisi goli maari unko ki yaad aa gaye Shri Ram.

Nathu had had enough of all this, he could take no more
He went to Gandhi's prayer meeting to bid his final adieu,

And pumped a bullet so hard that Gandhi finally remembered
Lord Ram.

The audience breaks into a rapturous applause, enough for Kamal
to pause his recital. He folds his hands and repeatedly looks around
the room. The clapping, the hooting and cheering continue for a
few more seconds. Audience members rush up to the stage with
marigold garlands; some others on the stage join in. The garlands
form a turtleneck around Kamal's neck.

But Kamal isn't done yet. He has one final flourish left, one that
will ensure his audience is certain that Godse's actions were not just
correct but also deeply necessary.

Agar Godse ki goli utri na hoti seene mein
Toh har Hindu padhta namaz, Mecca aur Medine mein.
Mook ahimsa ke kaaran Bharat ka aanchal phat jaata,
Gandhi jivit hote toh phir desh dobaara batt jaata.

Had Godse not pumped that bullet into Gandhi,
Every Hindu would have been praying at Mecca and Medina
today.
Meek non-violence would have torn India apart,
Had Gandhi lived, the country would have been splintered
into more parts.

~

Kamal was born exactly forty-three years after the day Gandhi was
assassinated. Thanks to his viral poem, however, that moment of
Gandhi's assassination has now been made to come alive, several
million times over, at just a click.

Kamal is one of the few Hindi poets in the country whose poetry
revolves almost exclusively around the cause of Hindutva. His

poetry furthers Hindutva in innumerable ways: he will find ways to emphasize some of the core elements of the ideology. He will clearly delineate the 'enemies' of Hindus, he will stoke anger and hate towards them, dehumanize them using his rhetoric and won't shy away from creating new foes.

In doing so, Kamal, at twenty-eight, is reinventing how both poetry and digital platforms can be used for political propaganda.

He will tell his audiences of imagined enemies the nation, and the Hindus, face—from the Muslim community[8] to a bunch of students[9], from political critics of the BJP[10] to protesting farmers demanding the scrapping of controversial farming laws—and stoke anger against them. He will also stoke fears—of India becoming an Islamic nation, of Pakistan eating away into Indian territories if Modi's rivals come to power, of Hindus being decimated in their own land.

Kamal urgently wants to rewrite history in a way that benefits Hindu nationalists. He does this by reinventing the past and recasting inglorious events that painted Hindu nationalists in a poor light, by pitting historical figures against each other and urging his audience to discard icons who were critical of Hindu nationalism.

Travelling to smaller cities, mofussil towns and villages, Kamal carries the message of Hindutva through his craft. He helps to spread the ideology in areas where most mainstream forms of popular culture might not have the reach and, as a result, the same impact as his poetry could. Addressing dozens of such events each year since he started in 2017, Kamal has traversed across the northern, western and eastern parts of the country many times over, incidentally, the regions where the BJP gets the bulk of its electoral backing.

Through his work, Kamal makes his message simple to understand: conjuring up vivid imagery of a glorious past, painting the present to be abhorrent and stoking fears in his audience about a grim future.

He will ask seemingly straightforward questions. One of his most popular works focuses on the revolutionary Chandrashekhar Azad, titled '*Chandra Shekhar Ko Kya Mila?*', 'What Did Chandra Shekhar Get'. In it, he juxtaposes how Azad died and has since been forgotten while Jawaharlal Nehru was rewarded with the Prime Minister's chair. Between these selective, conveniently chosen comparisons lies his politics and its aims: such comparisons hide more than they reveal. His rhetoric, coupled with his powerful oratory in packed kavi sammelans, urges the listener to suspend reason and rationale and, instead, consume the emotion.

Kamal tells his listener how Azad was shot dead at the age of twenty-four by the British colonial police in the then-Alfred Park of Allahabad city. Azad had spent ten years in the country's freedom struggle, starting with Gandhi's Non-Cooperation movement and later joining the Hindustan Republican Association, an outfit formed by revolutionaries.

While he rightfully extolls Azad's contributions, Kamal wilfully and carefully neglects any mention of Gandhi and Nehru's contributions. He doesn't mention anything that Nehru and Gandhi have done, none of their struggles, nor their time in prison during their decades-long involvement in the freedom movement.

Such poetry reduces complex historical issues, nuances and debates to binaries: pro-Hindu vs anti-Hindu, good vs evil. Such binaries are easy for audiences to grasp since they don't require any contextual knowledge of these events or personalities and, instead, appeal to their innermost emotional fears and the deeply submerged prejudices and stereotypes that they harbour.

Even the issues Kamal flags are taken out of the BJP and the Hindu right-wing's playbook: from decrying the growth of Muslim population in India to stoking fears of threats to the existence of Hindus and Hinduism, to attacking liberal arts institutes like the Jawaharlal Nehru University (JNU) to targeting Muslim film actors with malicious propaganda. Without declaring his allegiance openly, Kamal attacks all of the BJP's rivals, from critics in the media to the Opposition political parties and leaders.

For Hindutva to survive and flourish, it seeks enemies, and hence, needs to constantly produce newer enemies. Kamal reinforces the old enemies, helps single out new ones and also helps the Hindutva ecosystem sustain both, the villainization of these enemies and the glorification of 'real' heroes, like Godse.

In doing so, Kamal, through his work, normalizes some of the most rabid, hard-line elements of Hindutva by presenting hate-filled, prejudiced viewpoints to be pronouncements of a popular *desh bhakt,* patriotic poet. In effect, Hindutva poets like Kamal end up peddling political propaganda in the guise of entertainment to audiences that attend these cultural events.

By repeating the core ideological narratives of Hindutva from the platforms of the various kavi sammelan events he performs at, Kamal is lending his weight to these narratives and legitimizing them. As a result, repeating incendiary propaganda about other communities or engaging in disinformation around historical events gets normalized.

All of this, ultimately, ends up helping the BJP and the RSS in furthering its dominance and pushing its narratives. For instance, Kamal's poems against Nehru seamlessly sync in with similar efforts by the BJP, and its sympathizers online, to peddle narratives around Nehru that paint him in a poor light.[11,12,13]

~

The role of poetry in political and religious mobilization is, often, overlooked. Poetry is seldom seen as a powerful tool for indoctrination, even though evidence is stacked in favour of this proposition.

One of the most popular religious texts in Hinduism is the Ramcharitmanas, a sixteenth-century poetic retelling of the epic Ramayana. It is possibly 'the most influential religious text of the Hindi-speaking heartland' with influence 'far beyond' this heartland.[14] The poet and saint Goswami Tulsidas wrote it to serve as possibly the first written text that tells the story of Lord Ram; until then, the story was largely transmitted among people orally.[15] The Ramcharitmanas changed that; it gave Hindus a document that 'took the story of Lord Ram to every household in north and central India, creating an emotional connect between an average Hindu household and Lord Ram'.[16]

Even before the Ramcharitmanas, the Bhakti movement, a campaign to reform and challenge the caste hierarchy by 'emphasizing the individual's direct connection to god',[17] spread on the backs of poetry and the works of poet-reformers, from Guru Nanak and Kabir to Meerabai, Surdas and Chaitanya.

If these texts spurred religious mobilization, other poetic works helped political mobilization.

In the mid-to-late nineteenth century, poetry became a key carrier and disseminator of nationalism in the country as poets started expressing nationalistic sentiments by combining them with religious motifs to awaken consciousness among citizens. In 1870, poet Hemchandra Bandyopadhyay wrote a poem in Bengali titled 'Bharat Sangeet', Song of Bharat, which asked Hindus to 'become experts in the deployment of weapons, go mad in the rasa of warfare' against colonial forces.[18] The poem gained wild popularity and became 'the next great landmark in the nationalist literature of modern Bengal'.[19]

Similarly, in the period immediately after the First World War, when the Khilafat movement, a pan-India movement among the Muslim community demanding the restoration of the Islamic Caliphate, gathered momentum, political poetry in Urdu was used to mobilize masses and spread political messaging about the movement.[20]

Later in the twentieth century, when Prime Minister Indira Gandhi imposed the Emergency between 1975 and '77, blanking out free press and placing drastic curbs on free speech and freedom of expression, thousands of poems by poets across the country circulated underground, many of which were ultimately published after the Emergency was lifted.[21]

But not all mobilization done through poetry was for just causes like the overthrow of colonial rule or religious mobilization to end caste hierarchies. The Hindu nationalist movement also started eyeing the influence of poetry among the masses.

Academic Rosinka Chaudhuri found that Hindu nationalist poetry like Bhagat's might have laid the foundation for the emergence of an organized Hindu nationalist force like the RSS, five decades later, in 1925:[22]

> The Hindu Nationalist Movement in India, for instance, takes as its starting point the year 1925, when the Rashtriya Swayamsevak Sangh was first formed. The ideological developments in the nineteenth century that made it possible for such political formations to come into being, however, were operating, at least in Bengal, from the 1830s onward, when the idea of the Indian nation was still in its early stages of construction. It is my contention that certain influential ideas and images of the nation were envisaged in poetical practice long before such conceptions found currency in historical or political discourse in India.

Much later, poetic rhymes were also used to a powerful effect by the Hindu right-wing during the Ram Janmabhoomi agitation, starting in the late 1980s. One slogan, especially, went on to become an impactful clarion call during the agitation:

Ram lalla hum aayenge,
Mandir wahi banayenge.

Dear Ram, we will come, do not fear,
To build the temple right there.

This slogan, coined at a Hindu right-wing rally during the movement in 1986, remains popular even now, inspiring scores of similar poems and songs.[23]

Globally, too, poetry has been a potent tool in indoctrinating people with extremist ideologies. It remains little known, but the Islamist militancy has often relied on using poetry for propaganda purposes.

Some of the top leaders of Al Qaida, the terror outfit that was born in Afghanistan in 1988 and subsequently spread globally to attract members from various countries, including the West, were known to use poetry extensively in their speeches.[24] A few, from Osama Bin Laden to Ayman al-Zawahiri and Abu Musab al-Zarqawi, even penned poetry themselves.[25]

Researchers following this use of poetry in extremist indoctrination believe that the art form is well-suited for such use.

'The power of poetry to move Arab listeners and readers emotionally, to infiltrate the psyche and to create an aura of tradition, authenticity and legitimacy around the ideologies it enshrines make it a perfect weapon for militant jihadist causes,' writes academic Elisabeth Kendall.[26]

'In the practical function of argument, poetry has the added advantage of papering over cracks in logic or avoiding the necessity of providing evidence by guiding an argument into an emotional rather than intellectual crescendo,' she adds.[27]

Much of poetry's power to be used as an effective tool of propaganda to further such extremist ideologies comes from its ability to be able to construct 'an enemy' through its words and the imagery it conjures. To quote Kendall:[28]

There is no clear original jihadist identity, only a constantly repeated imitation of the idea of the original. Poetry helps to create this, for example, by referencing heroic figures from Islamic history, employing well-known tropes (such as referring to jihadists as lions and warriors), employing hyperbole when mentioning contemporary jihadist acts, eulogising martyrs and mythologising their virtues. Constructing a coherent enemy 'other' helps to produce a sense of identity and common global cause for jihadist struggles that may in fact be fuelled in large part by local and regional concerns.

Much of this rings true, even in the case of poets sprouting Hindutva poetry, like Kamal.

~

For Kamal, constructing 'enemies' through the telling of real and imagined injustices is an essential part of his craft. The 'enemies' that he creates are in line with critics and dissenters who find themselves in the crosshairs of the BJP.

Such alignment with the country's dominant Hindutva ideology and the Modi government's policies has tangible benefits.

Kamal has often been recruited by BJP leaders to campaign for them in their individual constituencies during elections across UP and Madhya Pradesh. In these rallies, Kamal uses his craft and his oratory to pitch these candidates before audiences, attack rivals and sprinkle Hindutva as and when required to push the candidate over the victory line. In these performances, Kamal often becomes the person mouthing words that the official candidate might want to say but won't be able to, lest they attract charges of delivering hate speeches.

Kamal tells me he dials up or down the Hindutva quotient in these speeches on the request of the candidates and the needs of the party in that constituency. If the candidate wants polarization, Kamal will deliver. If the candidate wants a performance high on nationalism, without any communally charged remarks, Kamal will deliver that as well, no problem.

He has also been at ease performing at BJP-backed kavi sammelans during elections, where the poetry has mostly focused on attacking the party's rivals or talking up its own achievements.

In January 2020, in the run-up to the Delhi assembly elections, when the city was hit by protests against the Citizenship (Amendment) Act and the proposed National Register of Citizens, Kamal performed in a sammelan organized by the BJP as part of their electoral campaign.

Sharing the stage with the then Delhi BJP Chief, Manoj Tiwari, and the controversial BJP leader Kapil Mishra, known for his inflammatory remarks against Muslims, Kamal attacked rival parties, the Congress and the Aam Aadmi Party, in acerbic fashion. He launched a series of blistering attacks: he insinuated that the former Congress Chief Rahul Gandhi takes 'massages by the sea in Bangkok' to a rousing applause, demanded Pakistan's nuclear obliteration, expressed gratitude for the changes in the citizenship laws, justified police brutalities against protesters opposing those laws and recommended pouring 'the acid of Gangajal into the eyes' of protesting students, a reference to incidents of Bihari police officials pouring acid into the eyes of petty criminals in the 1980s in an operation titled 'Gangajal'.[29,30]

Kamal frequently ends up getting invited for sammelans that might not be entirely political in nature but are backed by BJP leaders or governments in BJP-ruled states.

Kamal has also made an insidious entry into the covert political machinery that works for the BJP on social media platforms and messaging apps like WhatsApp. Sitting in his three-bedroom rented home in Greater Noida that he shares with two others, which also functions as an editing suite and a makeshift studio for shoots, Kamal can often be found tweaking the kind of anonymously created videos that circulate on WhatsApp, attacking BJP's rivals viciously. In March 2021, weeks before the West Bengal election, where the BJP was making an all-out bid to wrestle power away from the Mamata Banerjee-led Trinamool Congress, as I sat watching, Kamal supervised a video being edited, which alleged how Bengal was turning into an Islamic republic. With visuals of burning tyres, violent mobs wearing skull caps, carrying sticks, the video was overlaid with loud, grim music and an angry voiceover.

Kamal's craft is malleable. He knows it, as does the Hindu nationalist ecosystem he is a part of.

~

Yet, Kamal, at heart, is most at ease when he is on stage at a kavi sammelan. The changing nature of kavi sammelans, their growing digitization and their reliance on virality have only acted as an impetus for Hindutva poets like Kamal.

Academic Francesca Orsini, in her book *The Hindi Public Sphere 1920–1940*, says that Hindi language kavi sammelans, mostly in northern India, took off first in the 1920s as formal poetic readings to elite audience, before expanding into events of entertainment for mass audiences.[31] Soon, though, they became events drawing in large crowds, so much so that they became popular social gatherings at schools, colleges, student hostels and even the sessions of the Indian National Congress, no matter what the occasion.[32]

So popular were these that often, these sammelans would turn unruly with Orsini reporting that many of them descended into mass 'bawdy gatherings', with uncontrolled crowds and chaotic settings.[33]

Much of this has changed. Old-timers in the industry insist that the sammelans are now, often, struggling for resources—neither are patrons willing to fund it, nor are audiences, willing to flock to it anymore, like they did in the past. Hyper-sensitive politicians are another reason why these kavi sammelans struggle. In the past, many sammelans would depend on local politicians and governments for funding. For politicians and governments, such events were a win-win: they could associate their names with some of the most popular poets and in the process also facilitate a free mode of entertainment for locals. The poets, especially if their material was comic or nationalistic, were bound to comment on the state of affairs, even take pot-shots at politicians, especially those in power. Politicians would tolerate much of it, even enjoy the tongue-in-cheek potshots. This, old-timers say, has changed. Over time, politicians have grown increasingly intolerant of satire and criticism, resulting in the drying up of patronage towards these sammelans.[34]

Yet, sammelans remain a popular mode of entertainment, especially as one moves away from the metros. Estimates from industry watchers say approximately 70 per cent of the sammelans that take place, happen in rural and semi-rural areas.

These sammelans continue to draw crowds, anywhere from a few hundred to a few thousand—still sizeable numbers. The National Capital Region sees a regular stream of these sammelans being held, either backed by government bodies or politicians or private organizers. As a result, those like Kamal enjoy a near-continuous stream of work.

The internet has been a shot in the arm for the craft. Social media has added a new dimension to these sammelans by way of YouTube channels dedicated to airing them, helping poets reach millions digitally. These channels have hundreds of thousands of followers, enabling poets to get a much wider audience than they ever would otherwise.

A channel named 'Kavi Sammelan' has over 720,000 followers and its videos have got over 105 million views so far. Another channel named 'HiTech Kavi Sammelan' has over 367,000 followers and has garnered over 62 million views so far.[35]

The largest of them all is a channel run from a two-bedroom home in east Delhi's Laxmi Nagar: 'Namokaar Channels Pvt Ltd' with over 1.93 million followers. Its posts have travelled far and wide, having garnered 175 million views.[36] Namokaar has been covering poetry recitals since 2016 and has had a major part to play in the virality that poets have achieved online. Kamal's poem on Godse, for instance, was shared online first by Namokaar. It went viral and ended up receiving over 4.5 million views on YouTube, in part at least, thanks to Namokaar's reach.

But some others in the industry believe that video streaming platforms like YouTube have both helped and harmed the industry. Accessing poetry by various poets, no matter what the genre, is now easier than ever before, thanks to the internet. Is that one reason why crowds aren't flocking to these sammelans like they used to before? On the other hand, YouTube has allowed poets to cultivate mass followings and made them experience new levels of popularity. Wouldn't this, then, translate to more footfall when these poets perform? There are no easy answers.

Rahul Jain, the forty-year-old who runs Namokaar, told me that videos of nationalistic poetry, especially when it backs Modi, perform very well on YouTube. 'Most people who are listening to such nationalistic poetry are BJP-backers,' he said. 'If a person is searching for such poetry and listening to it, they have to be BJP and Modi supporters,' believed Rahul.

Rahul, rummaging through his YouTube channel's analytics data, said he found that the biggest bulk of such listeners who enjoy such nationalistic, pro-BJP and Hindutva poetry are the young, with Rajasthan being a big centre for online consumption.

Rahul told me how these poems worked very well in all the areas where the BJP and Hindutva forces were popular.

Poets told me how many organizers, when recruiting poets for a show, had started to consider their virality online as a factor before taking them in. The logic was that if poets were popular online, it would possibly help draw in the crowds.

This has, in turn, pushed poets to create content that is likely to go viral, over other types of content. In the current Indian context, hate and bigotry are easy ways to achieve virality, and that is something that young poets like Kamal realize.

Rahul said he felt Modi was like a 'master key', that could be applied anywhere for better results—poems, kavi sammelan stages, included. 'Put him on any banner or any product, and it will sell,' he said.

All this has resulted in a change in the nature of nationalistic poems written. From hailing past kings and warriors to revolutionaries and freedom fighters who drove the colonial rulers away, nationalistic poetry has now drifted towards backing the Modi government on its policies.

'Instead of poems on Tanhaji, Shivaji or Chandra Shekhar Azad, today's poems are on Ram Mandir's construction or on the Article 370 being revoked,' said Rahul.

Tentacles of an Ecosystem

In March 2021, Kamal headed to Patna for a kavi sammelan. Kamal was relieved to do this because he hadn't performed for months, thanks to the disruptions in the live entertainment industry due to Covid-19.

The night before the show, Kamal had barely slept; poet Shambhu Shikhar and he had decided to embark on a late-night drive, which allowed them only four hours of sleep. Shambhu, a popular comic poet himself, is Kamal's mentor, life coach and landlord, all rolled into one.

Patna was an old hunting ground for Kamal; he had performed there twice before. The city had become even more familiar in Shambhu's company—the comic hails from Bihar's Madhubani district, a four-hour drive from the state capital.

For poets like Kamal, who rely on their ability to strike a chord with their audience's politics, it isn't familiarity with a city that matters as much as the way the city's vote swings. For instance, his shows, he claims, have dried up in Mumbai ever since a surprise coalition between the Hindutva-leaning Shiv Sena, the Congress and the Nationalist Congress Party (NCP) materialized in October 2019 and dislodged the BJP-led government in Maharashtra. In the five years preceding that, when a BJP-led government was in power, Kamal did shows there once every few months.

One reason why Kamal's fortunes, often, diminish with the BJP's stock dipping locally is that organizers start shying away from openly promoting a brand of politics so different from that of the ruling party.

When they get Kamal on board, they know what they are getting—an unvarnished endorsement of Hindutva politics, a thinly disguised backing of the BJP and a stinging attack on its rivals.

In the Patna show, though, Kamal had nothing to worry about.

In November 2020, the BJP, in alliance with Nitish Kumar's Janata Dal (United), narrowly scraped through to a victory against a powerful opposition alliance led by the Rashtriya Janata Dal party. The victory, which seemed like a foregone conclusion before the poll campaign began, was one that came after a fight down to the wire, with a surprisingly resurgent Opposition campaign falling only ten seats short of winning power.

By March 2021, though, this margin of victory seemed to have been forgotten on Patna's streets.

Going by political banners and hoardings—of which there were plenty on the city's roads—what was remembered and consciously reinforced was the changed political dynamic within the ruling coalition—the fact that the BJP was lording over a diminished JDU. Despite contesting fewer seats than the JDU, the BJP, won seventy-four seats, while the JDU was reduced to merely forty-three seats, out of the total 243 seats that were up for grabs. The banners made it seem like it was only a minor detail that Nitish Kumar was still the chief minister.

The road from the Jayprakash Narayan Airport through the arterial Nehru Path, better known by its old name Bailey Road, and through the busy Dak Bungalow chowk all the way up to Gandhi Maidan was dotted with young BJP leaders announcing a key party executive meeting in posters swathed in saffron. The posters were everywhere—outside hospitals, under flyovers, on pavements. In comparison, green posters by the JDU, sometimes not even featuring Chief Minister Kumar, were only a handful. Not surprisingly, seventeen months after this visit to Patna, the BJP-JDU alliance collapsed. Kumar, instead, tied up with the RJD and continued to occupy the chief minister's chair.

Comfortably ensconced in saffron, Patna promises to be a friendly outing for Kamal.

Dressed in a mustard sweatshirt paired with olive casual trousers, Kamal looks like a fresh graduate when he lands in Patna on a Sunday morning in early March 2021.

~

The show was slated to start at 6 p.m., but Kamal had things to do before that. First up was an audience with Acharya Shri Sudarshan ji Maharaj, an eighty-four-year-old spiritual guru who runs a string of educational institutions across Bihar and Jharkhand.

This meeting, organized by Shambhu, sees Kamal, as well as the other poets performing that evening, head to the Maharaj's school-cum-ashram in the Jaganpura area of Patna, a twenty-minute ride from the hotel.

At the centre of the sprawling ashram is a raised pedestal on which rests a life-size statue of the Maharaj, on a throne that is bigger than him. On walking into the ashram, the Maharaj's presence remains a visible one—he smiles at visitors in various poses through posters hanging from pillars along the walk. The photos are accompanied by life lessons like:

Sleep with Smile,
Getup with Smile (sic)

Aap ki Ankhon Mein Twinkle Hona Chahiye,
Wrinkle Nahin.

There should be a twinkle in your eye,
Not wrinkles around it.

Maharaj meets us in a large gazebo with golden arches and green pillars situated in the ashram's compound. A wooden, backless settee has been repurposed to serve as the Maharaj's throne, with red satin pillows placed as his armrests. The spiritual leader walks in ten minutes after we get there, dressed in a monochromatic saffron—a bright saffron kurta along with a dhoti in the same shade, an open saffron jacket with golden embroidery and a saffron stole, all this combined with a pair of crocs.

Shambhu, who has coordinated this meeting, introduces each poet. When he reaches Kamal, the Maharaj grunts in acknowledgement. '*Yeh Kamal nahi; Kamaal hai*', he isn't Kamal; he is the Captivating Kamal, he says and laughs immediately.

Looking at me, he points to Kamal and says that his work has always stood out and that he listens to Kamal regularly. 'He breathes fire. It is like he has fire inside him,' the Maharaj says, looking into the distance.

The words have Kamal beaming. Of all the accompanying poets, he has been singled out for such effusive praise.

Such connections, with other spokes of the Hindutva wheel like the Maharaj, are vital to Kamal. They give him more clout, which in turn grants him greater legitimacy in these circles. This leads to more platforms for him to perform at, resulting in opportunities to broaden his base. They also give him access, a vital tool for ascension in this world where Hindutva meets politics meets poetry. Who you know decides where you reach—here, spiritual gurus carry the clout of superstars, their work intertwined closely with politics and governance. On his website, the Maharaj has photos that show him sharing the stage with various politicians, past and present, from presidents to chief ministers.

Proximity to such a person helps Kamal in yet another way. It draws people towards him, wanting a slice of that clout.

Waiting in hotel room as we return from the ashram are two members of the Hindu Mahasabha. They want an audience with him, and by extension, Shambhu, who he is sharing the room with.

The Akhil Bharatiya Hindu Mahasabha is one of the oldest socio-political organizations to have openly and exclusively championed the cause of Hindu nationalism in the country. Formed after a split from the Indian National Congress in 1909, the Mahasabha, in its early days, saw the participation of the likes of Lala Lajpat Rai and Pandit Madan Mohan Malaviya, but soon took a turn towards the hard right, guided by the influences of personalities like Vinayak Damodar Savarkar as well as K.B. Hegdewar and Syama Prasad Mukherjee.

In their book *The Murderer, the Monarch and the Fakir*, Appu Esthose Suresh and Priyanka Kotamraju demonstrate, by piecing together historical evidence, that the Hindu Mahasabha was at the 'epicentre' of the plan to assassinate Mahatma Gandhi.[1] Savarkar, who was an accused in the murder but was subsequently let off due to the lack of evidence, had served as the president of the Mahasabha, while Gandhi's assassin, Nathuram Godse, had been a member of the organization.

But the Hindu Mahasabha's tentacles are also entangled in something more current. Hegdewar, who was an active member of the Mahasabha, and Mukherjee,[2] who became the president of the Mahasabha in 1944,[3] also laid the foundation of the current political dominance by the BJP. While Hegdewar went on to become one of the founders of the RSS, Mukherjee founded the Bharatiya Jana Sangh, the political predecessor of the BJP.

Despite the lineage, the Hindu Mahasabha, today, carries none of that clout. Relegated to a fringe player, its hard-line Hindutva has now been co-opted by elements inside the Sangh Parivar, from the Vishwa Hindu Parishad to the Bajrang Dal, as well as smaller elements outside it, like the Hindu Yuva Vahini in Uttar Pradesh and the Sri Ram Sena in Karnataka.

Periodically, though, the Mahasabha leaps into the news with its acts. In January 2019, Mahasabha members, led by the party's general secretary Puja Shakun Pandey, *recreated* the assassination of Mahatma Gandhi.[4] In videos of the event, Pandey is smiling at the camera, approvingly, while holding an air pistol.[5] Sporting similarly wide grins with her are nearly ten others who surround her. Most are wearing saffron—Pandey is draped in a saffron saree, while the others have saffron scarves around their necks. It was an event tailor-made for outrage and, hence, publicity for an organization deprived of media exposure. Pandey held the air pistol in her hand and shot at an effigy of Gandhi. The effigy stood in a pool of 'blood'. The stunt caused anger and outrage. Two members, including Pandey, were jailed.[6] But the event successfully brought back the limelight on to the organization.

Today, two of its members are here for something similar—more visibility. Amit Sinha and Rajshree Kumari, both active members of the Mahasabha's Bihar unit are here to meet Kamal and Shambhu. Purportedly, they both want to meet the two poets and understand how they might get more visibility and political heft. But minutes

into the conversation, the purpose of their visit becomes clearer—
they don't see a future with the Mahasabha and want to hitch their
wagons to the BJP. Can Kamal and Shambhu maybe 'guide' them
on how to do that?

Kamal, later, decodes it for me—Kumari wants to fight
elections from Bihar on a BJP ticket. What will separate her from
the many other aspirants is the access that the likes of Shambhu
and Kamal could provide. Shambhu is a popular name, not just
in kavi sammelans, but also in Hindi entertainment and news
television. Shambhu has made numerous appearances on various
poetry shows on TV, the most famous being *Lapete Mein Netaji,*
Leader in a Wrap, which sees a group of Hindi comic poets take
on a politician guest on the show. Shambhu is famous for his sharp
political satire, and his work has endeared him to audiences across
the political spectrum. But Shambhu, Kamal told me, was someone
who was '*apne hi ideology ke*', someone of my own ideology. This
meant that while his satire targeted politicians across the aisles,
he had more than a soft spot for the BJP. His ideological leaning
and his body of work meant that he had a vast network of friends
within the BJP.

Sinha and Kumari seemed to know this and were hoping that
Shambhu and Kamal could pool in their networks to help a fellow
Hindutva soldier further her journey.

Kumari introduces Sinha as her senior colleague and a dedicated
leader who started off as a foot soldier in the cause of Hindutva.
Sinha latches on to the description and reminds his audience that
he has been around, even before the current period of Hindutva
sunshine. In the dark, pre-Modi days, he underlines.

'*2008 mein, jab Congress ka kaal tha, tab stithi bahut zyaada
dayniya thi,*' he says. The situation was miserable in 2008 when
the Congress was in power. The year was the near-midpoint of the
BJP's ten-year period of being away from power at the Centre. The

Congress and its allies had seemed strong and had retained power in the general elections of 2009.

Since this is the political equivalent of a corporate networking meeting, Sinha, after delivering the intriguing opening line, pauses, looks around and then dives straight into a story that burnishes his credentials. Even though the BJP had been weak in those years, Sinha says he waged a lonely battle on the ground, trying to popularize Hindutva ideals and mobilize support.

'I conducted 200–250 meetings then. Initially, there were only four to five people, which then went up to nearly 100,' Sinha says, adding that these meetings now draw 'as many as 400'.

In these meetings, Sinha would try to encourage the audience to join the Hindutva fold. 'Whoever would shy away from talking about Hindutva, we would talk to them about rashtravaad (nationalism) and tell them that rashtravaad is Hindutva,' Sinha says. '*Rashtravaad mein sab kuch aa jaata hai*' (Nationalism encompasses all these things).

This is where Kumari chimes in, looking to buff up her senior's CV further.

'Bhaiyya also pushed for more Hindutva sympathizers to be given tickets from across parties,' says Kumari, revealing Sinha's blueprint for a political discourse dominated by Hindutva ideals. 'He says they can fight from any party, JDU, even RJD, or whatever. But they should all be there to further the cause of Hindutva,' she says.

Kamal, who had fallen silent after introducing them, suddenly comes to life on hearing about this blueprint.

'*Haan, haan bilkul*. Absolutely. This is exactly what Savarkar had wanted,' Kamal says.

'*Savarkar ne kahaa tha, rajneeti ka Hindutva-karan hona chahiye*' (Savarkar had said the country's politics needs to be centred around Hindutva). 'He had never said that only one party should lay claim to it,' Kamal adds.

His barb towards the BJP's monopolization of the Hindutva agenda is quickly caught by Kumari, who goes on a diatribe against the BJP. The party, in alliance with the JDU, is doling out salaries to muezzins in the state's mosques, she says, a claim often repeated by Hindu nationalist blogs on the internet.[7]

Sinha takes over soon. He does not want to quibble over smaller policy decisions. 'This is happening because we are all fighting for the wrong thing,' Sinha says, looking around the room.

'All this talk about a Hindutva revival is "hawa", hot air,' he says, followed by a pause. 'Every day, 35,000 cows are being slaughtered across India, officially,' he says. 'But the real figure is 90,000 to 1 lakh cows, every day.' He does not quote any source for his data—in this audience, he does not need to. If Hindutva was truly on the ascent as a dominant political ideology, Sinha argues, would so many cows be allowed to be slaughtered? All this was eroding the Hindu's existence and his values.

'Hamara jo adarsh aur astitva ka manak hai, sab ko khatm kiya jaa raha hai,' Sinha says. The symbol of our identity and our existence is being finished off.

Releasing his fist and opening his hand in the air, he adds, 'Kuch bhi hamara nahi bach raha hai.' We are not able to save anything.

Sinha hopes to rouse his audience into action and activity, with his dire diagnosis of the state of Hindus.

Shambhu, the ostensible target audience for today's pitch, has so far shown scant attention and interest in the proceedings. Wearing a sleeveless white vest and white trousers, Shambhu has been lying on his bed sideways, with his eyes firmly shut, through the whole conversation, without a murmur. But Sinha's latest assertion is hyperbolic enough for him to be jolted out of his inertia. Shambhu insists that bovine slaughter is driven by economic reasons and opposition to it is merely 'political noise'.

Instead, Shambhu says that Hindu nationalists like Sinha must work on an agenda for the country once it becomes a Hindu rashtra. 'To make this country a *Hindu rashtra* is a minor thing; it will happen very easily, whenever they want. Instead of talking about all this, we must focus on a blueprint—what will we do once we are a *Hindu rashtra?*'

Sinha is stumped because he clearly didn't foresee the trajectory of this conversation.

Shambhu, now sitting up in bed, signals that he has just begun. 'Hundred years later, we will have not just a *Hindu rashtra* but an *akhand Bharat*, because people on the other side are fighting among themselves, between the Prophet's son-in-law and father-in-law,' he says, referring to the Hindu nationalist ideal of an undivided India stretching from Afghanistan in the west to Indonesia in the east and the sectarian differences between Shia and Sunni Muslims.[8]

Having regained his poise, Sinha wants to interject, but Shambhu barely gives him an opportunity to speak. When Shambhu is finally done, Sinha says he has a response he wants to offer. Shambhu, instead, has decided that he has had enough and makes an emphatic show of his disdain for the guests by lying down and shutting his eyes.

Sinha takes mild offence at this and asks Shambhu if he is listening. '*Hum aankh bandh karke sun rahe hain,*' comes Shambhu's response, my eyes are shut but I am listening.

By now, Sinha looks defeated. He knows the pitch isn't going anywhere, but he doesn't want to give up. One last time, one forceful pitch. He decides to follow his old template: one bombastic statement to garner intrigue to start off with, followed by the details.

'All the blueprints are ready, sahab,' Sinha says, addressing the eyes-shut Shambhu, but looking around the room with a grin.

He pauses for a brief moment and holds the grin. 'Our Hindu Puranas, our ancient holy texts, have already created blueprints for everything. We don't need to do anything at all,' he says, the grin now only gets wider.

He first points to the Modi government's plan to clean up the Ganga River. Those efforts, he says, are unnecessary; the answer to the dirty Ganga lies in a sixth-century text. 'The Bhagwat Puran says that in the *sharad ritu*, autumn, all rivers clean themselves. All we need to do is focus on not making them dirty,' Sinha says.

'Similarly, the Puran also says that whenever *maha yantras*, super-machines, are invented, nothing that is divya, divine, will survive. That is exactly what happened when washing machines got invented—the entire dhobi samaj has been rendered jobless. The government should have thought of these consequences before allowing washing machines,' Sinha says, referring to the community whose traditional occupation was to wash and iron clothes.

The kooky turn of events, from slamming cow slaughter to targeting washing machines, is too much for even Kamal.

He gets up, tries to speak, but Sinha isn't done. 'The only time I see a ray of hope is when I go to villages, where people don't depend on technology. *Devtaaon ke gram hote hai, asooron ke nagar, yeh bhi Upanishad mein likha hai.*' (The gods reside in villages, the demons in cities; this is written in the Upanishads).

'*Saara kuch ready hai.* It's all there in our books,' Sinha says, triumphant, his grin now wider than before, his look that of a confident debater who has clinched the argument and rendered his opponent speechless.

For a moment, Shambhu and Kamal look stumped. The room falls silent, with neither of them acknowledging the Hindutva crusader's pitch.

Shambhu opens a single eye, looks straight past Sinha and scolds Kamal, asking him to start getting ready for the show. '*Aap jaldi se shave karke aao.*' Go and get a shave quickly.

Kamal has got the message—Shambhu has lost his patience, and the conversation has to end now. He politely tries to get the two out, in the least offensive way possible.

Predictably, the meeting is a dud. It ends with no concrete promises by either Shambhu or Kamal; instead, Sinha and Kumari sheepishly say they will stay in touch.

After they leave, Kamal starts showing a sense of urgency. His show is due to start in two hours, and he has to groom himself, find a barber to shave off his stubble and get his jacket ironed. I ask him what he is planning to perform. He looks at me and says, '*Woh abhi likhna hai.*' I still need to write my material.

Thirty minutes to go before the show, Kamal takes an A4 sheet and folds it to fit in his palm, stands by the dresser and starts writing his lines. In less than fifteen minutes, he is done.

~

The venue for the evening's show is the Kalidas Rangalaya, an arts theatre located in the heart of the city, on the periphery of the historic Gandhi Maidan. The show is being hosted by a local non-governmental organization, Prayas, as the culmination of their annual week-long theatre festival.

Groups from different parts of the country participate in the festival. This time, despite the pandemic, groups from as far as Assam had travelled to Patna to present their work.

Prayas's main organizer, a short, harried man, tells me that Prayas has, traditionally, always hosted a kavi sammelan to mark the finale of the event, and Shambhu, as a local from Bihar's Madhubani district, was the perfect host for the evening.

'Shambhu ji is a massive draw here,' he tells me. 'That's why we booked his dates well in advance and told him to organize his own team for today's show,' he adds. This *team* is the band of poets that Shambhu has put together, which includes Kamal.

That evening, I get to experience Shambhu's popularity first-hand.

As soon as he enters the stage, the audience breaks into spontaneous hooting and whistling. It goes on for more than a few seconds, so Shambhu has to gesture with his hands, asking them to stop.

The auditorium is a large, bare hall with over 500 seats. Despite its prime location, it is obvious that the auditorium has seen better days. It is ramshackle, its walls cracking, even the stage's flooring—a painted concrete floor—is chipping off. The ceiling is tiled with square white tiles, with black dirt blotches visible. The seats are hard, brown plastic bucket seats.

But none of this will matter as soon as the curtains are raised, and the show starts.

Shambhu, with his one-liners and observational comedy, gets the show off to a roaring start, before introducing his team for the evening. There is Hemant Pandey, a Kanpur-based comic, poet Abhay Nirbheek from Lucknow, and Delhi's Padmini Sharma, all of whom flank Kamal sitting in the centre. While Shambhu praises them all as he introduces them, he heaps especially lavish praise on Kamal.

'His name is Kamal Agney because his poetry has the fire that can burn the enemy to ashes,' Shambhu says to the audience, with a finger pointed towards the poet. He says Kamal has done 'such important work' even though he's the youngest on the stage. He talks about Kamal's recent video series where he writes and recites poetry on 'forgotten Hindu heroes' of the past, and tells the audience that Kamal is 'filling the gaps in history'.

'You will get poems on Bhagat Singh, but not on Sukhdev and Rajguru,' Shambhu says, to illustrate how history had selectively highlighted contributions from different leaders. '*Aaj ki uplabdhi Kamal hai*,' he says, today's highlight will be Kamal, concluding the introduction to the poet to rapturous applause.

He is not wrong.

~

First up is Nirbheek, a bespectacled poet whose poetry belongs to the same genre as Kamal's—*vir ras*—poetry of gallantry and nationalism.

Nirbheek starts off with poems extolling the courage of the country's soldiers but takes an abrupt turn when he suddenly switches to slamming the '*tukde tukde gang*', a pejorative thrown at critics by the Hindu right-wing and members of Modi's BJP.

He asks for members of this *tukde tukde gang* to be thrown out of India and lashes out at the Modi government's critics and Opposition politicians who had asked for more evidence for India's 2016 military action across the Line of Control, often called the 'surgical strikes'.

His poetry soon descends into a naked, unabashed backing of the government. Referring to the Modi government's contentious move to abrogate Article 370 of the Indian Constitution and strip the erstwhile state of Jammu and Kashmir of its special status, Nirbheek hails the move, calls it a fitting tribute to the shahadat, sacrifice of Indian soldiers. Closing his act, Nirbheek trains his guns on those who had expressed worries over rising religious intolerance in India; in doing so, Nirbheek echoes the BJP's stance on the issue.

Nirbheek garners heavy applause, and Kamal, sitting centre-stage, looks pleased. The audience's appetite had been whetted.

After two other poets, it is finally Kamal's turn.

Kamal tries to warm his audience up. Dressed in a blue checked blazer, matching trousers and a white shirt, Kamal makes for a diminutive presence on stage. But from his first line, he exhibits confidence and comfort.

'Your applause to my next few lines will tell me what I should perform and what today's Bihar wants to hear,' Kamal starts.

He isn't lying. Since his content is, often, polarizing and provocative, Kamal had told me how he 'tests' his audience with such feelers. His routine consists of starting off with content that centres around nationalism without targeting it at anyone. Then, he progressively steps up the heat, pushing the limits of provocation. At each step, Kamal explained to me, he evaluates the response. Here is how the process usually flows.

Some generic poetry, first. Focus on amorphous ideas about the tiranga, flag, and *sarhad par hamare jawan*, our soldiers protecting our borders, and gauge the response. You barely ever go wrong with them, these benign, universally beloved ideas of patriotism. Then, harden your stance. Pepper Pakistan over your poetry, indulge in some subtle dog-whistling by linking Indian Muslims to Pakistan, throw some communally charged references in, without going all out with the rhetoric. Check for applause. Then, slowly, introduce your political ideology by attacking nameless enemies, from the tukde tukde gang to the award wapsi gang. Gauge the applause again. If it has been getting progressively tepid, you know that the audience isn't ripe enough, in which case, go back to some more universal themes like patriotism and references to the soldiers on the country's borders. Stick to these if the audience remains tepid. But if the applause gets louder, continue with the diatribe against all enemies, real and imagined, till you hit a crescendo, and so does the applause.

He follows the process here too. First up is a poem around the national flag. The applause is good, so Kamal comes back to the crowd. If they like his next few lines, they must show it in their applause, he tells them.

'*Yahaan rashtravaad ka parv chhidd jaana chahiye.*' This hall must turn into a festival of nationalism.

Less than two months earlier, the country's Republic Day saw near-riots break out in New Delhi. On 26 January, a protest rally by farmer groups, demonstrating against three controversial agricultural laws brought in by the Modi government, turned violent after some groups strayed from the rally's pre-decided route and clashed with the police.[9] Some farmers stormed the Red Fort, with one protester captured on video trying to hoist the Nishan Sahib, a flag representing the Sikh religion.[10]

Kamal decides to train his guns on the protesting farmers. It is a gambit. The farmers' protests have had sympathy from across different corners of the country, with many critical of the government's approach. Slamming them so early in his show can backfire, and many might tune out of his performance, or worse, boo him. Kamal knows this, but he decides to take a chance.

Ghodde bigad jaaye toh naal kheech lijiye,
Haathon se shikaariyon ke jaal kheech lijiye,
Kheecha hai jisne Lal Qile se tiranga,
Dilli waalon uski khaal kheech lijiye.

To punish an errant horse, pull his shoe out,
Pull away a hunter's trap.
The one who pulled down the Indian tricolour from the Red Fort,
O Delhi, excoriate him.

The hall breaks into rapturous applause, with many hooting through the applause. The cheering reassures Kamal: it was going to be good night. In that hall, facts didn't matter anymore. The Indian tricolour had not been supplanted by the Nishan Sahib.[11] It continued to fly where it was hoisted, while the protesters had hoisted the Nishan Sahib on a flagpole next to it.

Despite the applause, Kamal wants to go slow tonight with his political poetry. It is just the first few minutes, and he has a long set to perform.

So he holds himself back. For now, he focuses on the plight of the country's soldiers, poetry that would appeal to both sides of the political aisle.

Slowly, he veers towards one of his most popular poems, one that, like this performance, is a slow tease in revealing his political ideology. At this stage, Kamal's act is about drawing invisible lines and creating cleavages, delineating friend from foe, sifting the anti-nationals from the nationalists.

First on the radar is Mahatma Gandhi.

Rather than attack him right away through his signature work, Kamal chooses a more gradual route. As always, he reminds his audience of Chandrashekhar Azad, the slain Indian revolutionary.

He contrasts Azad with Gandhi and asks his question: What did Chandrashekhar get for his sacrifice? You could print Gandhi's photos on high-value currency notes because he is the father of the nation, Kamal argues. But could you have not put Azad's face on ten-rupee notes?

The audience cheers in agreement. The applause goes off. So, Kamal builds on it. This time, it is Nehru.

Naariyon ke jhevar ko, nar ke kalevar ko kya mila
Netaji Subhas jaise tevar ko kya mila,

Jinnah ko mila Pak, Nehru ko Hind,
Koi toh bataiye Chandrashekhar ko kya mila

The women lost their heirlooms, the men who sacrificed
themselves, what did they get in return?
The fieriness of Subhas Chandra Bose, what did he get?
Jinnah got Pakistan, and Nehru India
Someone tell me, what did Chandrashekhar get?

The audience is stunned for a few seconds, before breaking into
rapturous applause, louder than the last time. Kamal's work is
sharp and still somewhat subtle—the poem cleverly casts Jawaharlal
Nehru and Mohammed Ali Jinnah on one side, as benefactors of
the country's partition, and on the other places Azad as the one
who sacrificed his life for the country and yet, his contribution was
ignored and side-lined.

Kamal's ways are of a crafty storyteller who lures you into his trap,
bit by bit. By now, the audience, which has been roused by his patriotic
poetry about the country's soldiers, is now being asked to choose
between Azad on the one side, and Gandhi and Nehru on the other.

As the evening wears on, Kamal's performance continues to egg
his audience on pick a side.

Kamal proceeds to lash out at the 'JNU waale'. He reminds his
audiences of November 2019, when Swami Vivekananda's yet-to-
be-unveiled statue in the JNU campus in New Delhi was defaced
by slogans.[12] The miscreants had painted '*Bhagwa Jalega*', Saffron
will burn, and 'F*ck BJP' under the statue, ostensibly to protest the
statue's inauguration.

Kamal takes them on.

Yeh Vaam panth desh ka aadhar nahi,
Mandir hai Saraswati ka, bazaar nahi,

Swami Vivekanand ki murti tod de,
Unko yahan rehne ka adhikar nahi hai!

The politics of the left has no place in the country,
It is Goddess Saraswati's temple, not a market,
Those who destroy Swami Vivekananda's statue,
They have no right to stay here!

Loud clapping and whistling break out as soon as he delivers the punch line. The applause continues for a few seconds and nearly feels like it won't stop. In that moment, it is easy to believe that every single person in the room agrees wholeheartedly with him.

The applause has reassured Kamal of his hold over the audience and their ideological alignment with him. It is now time to move on, from attacking nameless, faceless groups to specific individuals.

He goes back to the abrogation of Article 370, and jokes about how its critics were left hapless and how the region's special status was 'khatm'. Over.

He reminds his audience of former Jammu and Kashmir Chief Minister Mehbooba Mufti's remarks in 2017, warning against any move to strip the region of its autonomy. 'If the special status is withdrawn, no one in Kashmir will hold the tricolour,' she had said.[13]

Kamal says Modi and Union Home Minister Amit Shah did to the special status what 'Indian batsmen Sachin Tendulkar and Virender Sehwag did to Shoaib Akhtar,' yet again drawing invisible lines around key characters, placing them in different camps. Modi and Shah are Tendulkar and Sehwag Mufti is Akhtar.

Then, he suddenly changes his tone and speaks, in a forceful, louder manner.

Desh ke tirange ko uthane waale hai karodon,
Aap khud ki arthi ko uthane wala dhoondiye.

Don't worry about the tricolour; there will be millions to hold
  it aloft
You find yourself a pallbearer.

Kamal delivers this line with animated hand gestures, ever the
energetic orator. The punch line is delivered angrily with his right
hand stretched out, his index finger pointing upwards.

The applause is even louder. I look around and see that the
hall is now much more crowded than it was before Kamal started
performing. Coincidence or otherwise, the progressively increasing
decibel levels of the applause might have played its own part in
drawing more people in. The canteen outside is now empty apart
from a few onlookers. Most youngsters, who were milling around
when the show started, are now all inside the auditorium and
listening to Kamal.

Mufti is the first politician he has targeted directly in the show so
far. If the reception is to go by, most in the audience wouldn't mind
more of this.

So Kamal takes the cue and goes after political figures one after
the other—from Farooq Abdullah to Rahul Gandhi. The audience
laps it up with a constant ringing applause. After one such political
poem, a man, seemingly in his twenties, stands up in the audience
and closes his fist, raises it to the sky and shouts, '*Bharat Mata
ki jai!*' Around him, some of the others join him in his next two
attempts.

Like a master orator, Kamal takes the cue.

In logon ne Bharat Mata ki jai bolne par bhi fatwa laga diya hai

These people have issued a fatwa even against chanting Bharat
  Mata ki jai

The audience hoots in agreement.

Banjar zameen par kabhi gulistan nahin ho sakta,
Jo Bharat Mata ki jai na bole, woh kabhi bhai nahin ho sakta.

Land that is barren, can never see the bloom of a flower,
The one who does not chant Bharat Mata ki Jai, can never be
  our brother.

The line evokes much applause and hooting. Kamal latches on to it
and, in a style reminiscent of Prime Minister Narendra Modi, asks
his audience to join in.

'*Dono haathon ki muthi bandh karke haath upar uthaye, aur mere*
saath boliye Bharat Mata ki jai!' Clench your fists, raise your hands
in the air and chant with me, *Bharat Mata ki jai*!
The audience willingly obliges three times.

With the audience on a high, Kamal makes a turn towards
Rahul Gandhi, Modi's principal rival, a critic Modi's followers love
to hate.

Kamal says he read Gandhi's comments, when the former
Congress chief said his name was 'Rahul Gandhi, not Rahul
Savarkar', after he was asked to apologize for his remark about
growing crimes against women.[14] Gandhi's statement was a dig at
Savarkar's repeated petitions to the British Empire—at least seven
of them—asking for clemency while he was incarcerated in the
Cellular Jail in the Andaman Islands.[15] Critics of Hindu nationalism
have called these petitions a sign of Savarkar's 'cowardice'.

Kamal says he agrees with Gandhi. To be Savarkar, Kamal tells
his audience, you need to be able to swim in the sea, referring to
Savarkar's attempt to escape police custody while being transported
back to India from London in a ship at the French port of Marseilles.[16]

'You can't become Savarkar sitting by the sea and getting massages done in Bangkok,' Kamal thunders, followed immediately by loud applause and whistling.

The applause continues for a few seconds. Kamal is already twenty minutes into his performance, and time is running out. The show started late and needs to be wrapped up in time. Kamal has one last act up his sleeve. He makes it clear that it's going to be his most potent work tonight.

'Main ab khatm hone tak chup nahi rahoonga. Aap khatm hone par chup mat rehna.' I won't stay silent till I finish reciting. But once I finish, you should not stay silent.

For the last one, he goes back to JNU.

Desh droh ki degree lene aaye hai JNU mein;
Fir se sankat ke badal ab chaaye hai JNU mein,
Isse kaale din kya honge Bharat ke barbadi ke,
Dilli mein naare lagte hai Kashmir ki azaadi ke,
Anjam samajhna hoga inke mansubo ko,
Bharat mein ab abhinandan hoga Afzal aur Yakubo ka.
Inka illaj karna hoga lohe ki jail salakhon mein;
Gangajal ka tezaab daalna hoga ab inki aankhon mein,
Modi ji ab bhool na jaana kiye desh ke waadon ko
Sabak sikha do ab Afzal ki inn najayaz aulaadon ko.

To earn a degree in sedition, they have come to JNU;
Dark clouds of trouble are hovering, again, over JNU,
What a black day it is for India,
When slogans for Kashmir's freedom ring in Delhi,
Their goals, their deadly intents, we must understand,
They want us to hail Afzals and Yakubs.
They must now be cured behind iron bars;
The acid of Gangajal must now be poured into their eyes,

Modiji, don't you forget the promises you made to the
  country,
Teach them a lesson for life, these illicit children of Afzal
  [Guru].

The audience claps vigorously in agreement. The applause is immediate and constant. Many in the back start hooting, some voices call for an encore. The applause is broken by faint sloganeering of *Bharat Mata ki jai*.

Kamal folds his hands and bows. The audience is roused, the clapping seems incessant, and the sloganeering is powerful.

Shambhu walks on to the stage then and says *Bharat Mata ki jai*, again. The audience repeats, this time louder than ever before in the entire evening.

Shambhu gauges the mood and adds to it. *'Bharat aaj kal mata nahi baap hai. Aur jis tarah se dadhi ugga rahe hai, shayad dada bhi ban jaaye.'* Bharat is not a mother but a father these days. And the way he is growing his beard, he might just be a grandfather soon.

Kamal, in his performance, made the audience subliminally choose between Azad and Gandhi, asked them to club Jinnah and Nehru together and reviled Modi's political opponents. Shambhu's comment, drawing an equivalence between the country and the Prime Minister, caps the night.

The audience laughs and claps even harder.

'Hum Sab Bhajapai'

Weeks after that performance in Patna, India found itself in the throes of a catastrophic second wave of Covid-19 infections.

The government's indifference towards the pandemic had turned out to be fatally misplaced.[1] A devastating deluge of Covid-19 cases overwhelmed the country in the months of April and May 2021, leaving the country's hospitals and cemeteries flooded. Patients found no place to go, nor did the dead. People were falling dead on the city's streets due to the lack of everything, from hospital beds to oxygen.[2]

For Kamal, all this had meant a slew of show cancellations and the possibility of a fresh financial crisis.

Ever since the pandemic began in 2020, Kamal's income had fluctuated wildly. The money from live shows—which was the bulk of his income—had come down to naught. After the first wave of cases ebbed, live shows had slowly started taking off. The show in Patna was one of the first ones that Kamal had performed at since the pandemic. The second wave seemed devastating, and Kamal feared that shows might not resume that year at all.

Thankfully for Kamal and his ilk, the second wave of infections peaked in May and by July, cases had dipped substantially, and kavi sammelans had started taking place. I told Kamal that I was keen to attend some more sammelans with him, to see him perform.

He was getting calls to perform at some sammelans, he said. *'Lekin kuch mazza nahi lag raha.'* It didn't sound any fun, he would say, to justify why those calls weren't materializing into performances. This, I later deciphered, meant that either the money offered was paltry or the show was too local for him to be associated with.

It seemed perplexing, because Kamal needed the money. His expenses were piling up. He had wanted to buy a new motorcycle for home so that his father did not have to depend on his brothers to be driven around. Kamal had his own expenses—from rent to the living costs that came with staying in a posh locality in Greater Noida, even if he shared it with two others.

Yet, for Kamal, saying no was important.

Kamal grew up in Gosaiganj, a small town with a population of less than 10,000 on the outskirts of Lucknow, a forty-minute drive from the heart of the city of nawabs.

It was there that he had witnessed his life's first-ever poetry recital, a *kavya goshti*. The goshti was mostly a meeting of local poets, where they would recite their own material and discuss each other's work. Kamal's father, Ashok Varma, a connoisseur of poetry, knew all the local poets closely and attended these goshtis religiously. Slowly, Kamal started tagging along. In these goshtis, one of the poets who immediately stood out for Kamal was a local schoolteacher poet named Rameshwar Prasad Dwivedi Pralayankar.

Pralayankar is a nationalist poet, and much like Kamal, his poems deal with social and political matters. Back then, he would perform at locally organized kavya goshtis and Kamal, still in school, would attend these programmes and be blown away by Pralayankar's talent, his commitment to the Hindu cause as well as his mastery over the Hindi language.

But as Kamal grew to emulate his guru, one thing struck him as odd about Pralayankar—for all his talent, Pralayankar had won barely any recognition outside of the state.

'He has never been very career-minded about his poetry. Maybe because of his full-time job as a teacher, he never wanted to push his boundaries,' Kamal told me. As a result, he would not be able to perform at bigger events that involved travelling. Be it Lucknow or Delhi, Pralayankar would end up saying no to many prestigious events because he could not afford to be gone from work for days.

As a way to make up for this, Pralayankar would accept all invitations he got around Gosaiganj, travelling across districts, even to smaller, local kavi sammelans, without regard for money or fame.

'Woh toh kahin bhi nikal jaate the, apne scooter par.' He would readily set off on his scooter for any kind of event.

Kamal used to be uncomfortable watching his guru do this. For him, readily going to smaller events, without any prestige or money meant that people took your talent and skills for granted. It also meant that you would get comfortable with whatever came your way, without having the hunger for more—bigger stages, more crowds, more money.

For Kamal, that was unacceptable.

That is where he had to make his break with his guru. Kamal was ambitious and had staked it all in the world of poetry. Money and fame were important. Each time he would get offered local gigs, with little prospect of decent money or exposure, Kamal would think of his first guru and inevitably refuse it.

It was in October 2021, around the nine-day festival of Navratri—at the end of which Lord Ram slays Ravana and marks the end of the war in the Ramayana—that things finally started to pick up for Kamal.

One of the first shows that he got was a kavi sammelan in Rasoolabad, a small town in Kanpur district, slightly over ninety minutes away from Kanpur city. The organizers of the event were the local committee that primarily organized the Ramlila, a dramatic re-enactment of the Ramcharitamanas over the nine days festival. The sammelan was meant to be the big showstopper and was slated to happen a day after Dussehra, on 16 October 2021.

Kamal said he would be free to perform 'whatever he wanted' at this event, which meant that there was no one to tame his political poetry.

Accompanying him to the sammelan was a mouth-watering prospect for me. Not just because of the event itself but the broader political context around it.

The political temperature across the country, but especially in UP, was soaring. The state was going to go to polls in four months, elections that would decide the fate of its Hindu nationalist chief minister and Hindutva icon, Adityanath. The elections would also be seen as a referendum on Modi's governance since the party had dominated UP's politics since 2014 when he came to power. The state sent eighty of the country's 543 MPs to the Parliament. It was important for Modi to continue retaining a solid grip on it. But things had seemed to be slipping away.

The protest by farmers, against the three agrarian laws enacted by the Modi government, had been heating up. Just days before, three cars, containing BJP leaders and workers, including Ashish Mishra, the son of the Union Minister of State for Home Ajay Mishra Teni, ran over a group of protesting farmers in UP's Lakhimpur Kheri district.[3] Eight people, including four farmers, one journalist, two BJP workers in the cars and Mishra's driver, were killed.[4]

The killings had caused outrage across the nation. Protests broke out, with farmer groups and Opposition parties demanding that Mishra be arrested and his father Teni be sacked from his post to enable a fair investigation.[5,6] Opposition parties made a beeline for Lakhimpur Kheri, but they were stopped from entering the district. The Congress leader Priyanka Gandhi Vadra was arrested, Samajwadi Party Chief Akhilesh Yadav was put under house arrest, while other Opposition figures were not allowed to leave the Lucknow airport.[7,8] Five days later, Mishra was finally arrested.[9]

The incident had shaken the nation, with viral videos showing the car ramming into the protesting farmers being played on loop on social media and across news channels. The BJP tried hard to deflect blame.

A crisis like this could hurt the BJP's chances, and I had little doubt that the party would do all it takes to wrest the narrative in its favour. In this, Kamal and his ilk—poets and influencers—would be crucial to plant an alternative narrative.

I decided to pack my bags and head to Kanpur.

~

Even as my flight begins its descent into Kanpur, a male pilot with an enthusiastic voice tells us excitedly that we are at least ten minutes before our scheduled arrival time.

But within minutes, his enthusiasm wanes, and passengers get an introduction to the Kanpur Airport experience. Even as he taxis on the runway, the pilot tells us that the flight won't be able to pull into the terminal anytime soon. The reason? Kanpur Airport can only handle one aircraft at a time.

Stuck on the runway in Kanpur feels like being in the middle of a vast, unending expanse of a village field. Tall wild crops, untrimmed shrubs lording over the infrequent security personnel posted here, surround the aircraft on both sides.

There is no habitation around the airport as far as the eye can see, presumably because this airport was primarily designed to be an air force station. The Indian Air Force's historical records show that this airstrip was started by India's British colonial rulers during the Second World War.[10] Even as it was fighting off the Nazi Germany-led Axis powers, Britain was also preparing for hostilities with Japan in the Far East, which was a constantly expanding imperial power.

As a colony, India offered the perfect location for it to then balance the war theatre in the west and a prospective one in the east. Kanpur, in northern India and just 400 km away from Delhi, was chosen as the place to establish a 'Maintenance Unit' for the Royal Air Force, where fighter bomber aircraft like the Liberator, Lancaster, Hurricane, Tempest and Dakota were serviced and armed during the war-time operations.[11] After India's independence, the airstrip was taken over by the Indian Air Force, and the facility continues to be a defence installation along with limited operations of civilian flights. At a distance, I can see military aircraft parked outside a wide hangar, designed to be carefully out of sight for civilians like me.

After nearly twenty-five minutes of being stuck on the runway, the aircraft finally pulls over, and we walk into a white tent that serves as the arrival section of the airport. Inside the tent, a dusty red carpet makes for the flooring, while white canvas makes for its walls. The airport doesn't have a conveyor belt. Instead, there is a hole in one of the walls from where two men rush out to drag bags from carts carrying our luggage. Towing the carts from the aircraft to the arrival section is a tractor.

The men pull and carry the bags inside the tent, after which passengers are expected to identify their bags. Cacophony ensues.

Passengers start screaming out to the men to draw their attention as bags are unloaded in rapid succession. At one point, the men give up and start leaving the bags on the sides. Their rightful claimants then start rushing in to pick the bags up.

My bag is one of the last ones to arrive. I thought this was the end of my Kanpur Airport experience, but it clearly wasn't.

The airport had only twenty-odd taxis waiting outside. Unlike other airports, since flights here are infrequent, it hardly makes commercial sense for taxi drivers to plonk themselves outside the airport for hours. Instead, there are taxis that can be availed on a prepaid basis. But my long wait for the bag meant that all the taxis had gone. The taxi booking centre, in a corner of the hall, is surrounded by angry fliers awaiting their long-promised taxis. Many of them are constantly checking for Ola and Uber cabs, but neither works in Kanpur. Within minutes, the handful of cabs at the airport have been taken, and I am the last flier in arrivals waiting for my taxi. The taxi arrives an hour later.

Kamal is waiting for me at the home of his friend in Kanpur. By the time I arrive, it is 4.30 p.m.

~

On arriving, I find out that the friend Kamal referred to is another nationalist poet, Shikha Singh, known for her poems extolling Hindutva. Shikha, a poet in her thirties, is a bit of a rarity.

Of the kavi sammelans I have attended, almost as if a formula no one wants to break out of, nearly every show has had only one female poet for every four to five male poets. In a show I attended, the host even forgot to introduce the solitary female poet on the panel and had to be reminded by another male poet, after which she was finally introduced to the audience.

If it is rare to find female poets in the world of Hindi kavi sammelans, it is rarer to find a female poet who writes and recites political poetry. All the female poets I had seen usually performed the *shringar ras*, the genre of romantic poetry.

But Shikha was different. Her work was very similar to Kamal's—both are unabashed followers of Hindutva and equally unabashed about their leaning towards the BJP, and both target critics of the BJP through their work.

On the internet, though, Shikha's digital footprints are much smaller than Kamal's. There are barely any videos of her work. But some of them have found many takers. In one December 2018 video, Shikha launches into a diatribe against those criticizing growing religious intolerance in the country.[12]

First up on her radar was journalist Barkha Dutt. Shikha digs up an October 2015 tweet by Dutt where she criticized Karva Chauth, a Hindu festival celebrated by married women who observe a day-long fast in prayer for their husband's health. Dutt called it an 'inherently regressive and patriarchal' festival.[13] Shikha then proceeded to highlight another tweet by Dutt around the Muslim festival of Ramzan, characterized by a month of fasting. In the tweet, Dutt had wished her followers 'Ramzan Mubarak'. While her tweet on Ramzan was posted in June 2016, eight months after the Karva Chauth tweet, Shikha says it was '*kuch hi dino ke baad*', just a few days later.

'All of you are intelligent, well-read people, and I want to ask you all this,' Shikha says in her performance. '*Ek samvidhan, ek desh, ek chand, do dharam, do tyohaar, toh ek pichda aur ek pragatisheel kaise?*' We have one constitution, one country, one moon, two religions, two festivals around them—so how come one festival is regressive and the other progressive?

Shikha then goes on to attack other critics of the BJP regime—from the All India Majlis-e-Ittehadul Muslimeen (AIMIM) Chief

Asaduddin Owaisi to 'leaders in Kerala who want to slaughter cows and distribute beef' to journalist Ravish Kumar.[14]

Kamal tells me he respects Shikha's work immensely and he believes she holds a lot of promise. But what has held her back, he says, from garnering even more fame is that she hasn't been able to take the plunge into poetry full-time like he has. She works in a lower court in Agra, while her husband and his family are in Kanpur.

I am hoping to finally be able to meet her, but at the last minute, Shikha has had to rush back to Agra. So, instead, her husband, Akash, thirty-four, is hosting Kamal and me. Akash, a teacher who is studying to join a booming education-technology (EdTech) company, was going to drive us to Rasoolabad for the show and back to Kanpur later that night.

Both Akash and Kamal share a common passion for poetry and a similar worldview.

The three of us set off for Rasoolabad in Akash's white Maruti Suzuki Alto. The topic of conversation between them revolves around the farm protests. Kamal is livid and directs his anger towards Punjab, the state whose farmers have been at the forefront of the agitation.

Kamal believes that the farm protests are a major conspiracy against the government and Hindus. This conspiracy, he said, was playing out in Punjab silently.

'Wahaan haalat bahut kharab hai,' things are very bad there, he tells Akash.

According to him, two simultaneous processes are unravelling in Punjab: Hindus in Punjab are being harassed by Sikhs, even as Sikhs themselves are being 'fooled' by external Christian influence.

'Bhayankar conversion chal raha hai wahaan Sikho ka abhi,' Sikhs are being converted en masse there; it's horrendous, he says. As a matter of buttressing this, Kamal pauses and then, with a level of authoritativeness, says Punjabis were refusing to see the signs of what was happening right before their eyes. 'Things are so bad that the world's fourth largest church is being constructed there, but no one is saying anything,' he tells Akash.

He was referring to the Church of Signs and Wonders in Jalandhar, which claims to be 'largest and fastest growing church in Punjab, India', according to its website.[15] On social media, many posts claiming that the church was a hub for converting people into Christianity have called it the fourth largest in the world.[16]

Kamal's confidence convinces Akash. Hurling such affronts at Punjab and Punjabis in general had wide political resonance.

In those months of the protests, the agitating farmers had been roundly attacked by the BJP's top echelons. The Prime Minister had led from the front, setting the tone by saying that farmers were being 'deceived' and 'misled'.[17] His colleagues had piled on—the Haryana Chief Minister M.L. Khattar had said there was a 'Khalistani presence' among the protesting farmers,[18] Union Minister Piyush Goyal had said the agitation, led predominantly by Punjabi farmers, had been infiltrated by 'Leftists' and 'Maoists',[19] while another minister, Raosaheb Danve, had said China and Pakistan were fuelling it.[20] The hostility sparked off by such comments had only worsened in the virtual world, where the BJP's social media followers had unleashed a torrent of abuse and, often, concocted conspiracies to criticize the protests.

Kamal was talking a political language that closely resembled the BJP's. The sammelan would tell me just how far he would go.

~

Minutes before we reach the venue, some of the poets want to stop by to meet a local, influential businessman in the area. The businessman invites the poets to drop into his agricultural product store, just off the highway connecting the town to Kanpur. That's where I meet the other poets. I meet Hemant Pandey and Abhay Nirbheek, two UP-based poets I had met during Kamal's Patna performance. While Pandey is a comic, Nirbheek, the poet who had performed with Kamal in Patna, performs on the *vir rasya,* poetry that extols heroism and bravery.

Sitting in the shop, Kamal re-introduces me. Nirbheek, a soft-spoken man, remembers me distinctly and is effusive in his greeting. Pandey has forgotten me, but his memory jogs back quickly, and he breaks out in a loud, enthusiastic namaste.

Kamal congratulates them and says he's very happy that they've accepted their new responsibilities.

I am intrigued, so I interrupt their conversation. I find that Pandey and Nirbheek, both, have joined the BJP. In their new roles, they would be in charge of using art and culture to effectively spread the party's word. 'Basically, we will brainstorm with the party over how art, culture and entertainment can be used better, to ensure that the party's popularity grows,' Pandey tells me, while sipping on his chai served in a stainless-steel glass.

Both have been given particular regions in UP where their energies will be focused, Kamal chimes in to say.

I am blown by the revelation—and by the significance of it. Both are popular poets; both travel extensively across the country. Pandey, especially, appears on television—often in shows where seemingly neutral poets poke fun at politicians across the spectrum. With their popularity and their reach, both could turn into critical assets for the party.

Such an arrangement also raises questions over just how independent they really are, in selecting the material they perform. One of them, privately, tells me that he knows that his comments on the BJP will now be limited and carefully vetted. But this, according to him, is a small price to pay for the benefits that such an alignment brings.

I prod the two to tell me more, but a bunch of poets stand up from their plastic chairs and announce that the show is starting soon. Both Pandey and Nirbheek rush out.

We are barely 2 km away from the venue, but loud announcements over the microphone are audible. Within minutes, we are there.

The venue, Rasoolabad's Ramleela Ground, is decked up. Here in Rasoolabad, the Navratri festivities go on for a day after Dussehra. The whole town is lit up for the festival, with the entire town and a few neighbouring villages are expected to attend.

Two streets leading up to the venue from different directions are lit with bright, twinkling lights in pink, white, gold and red, forming an unbreached wall on both sides of these roads. A folk artiste is singing devotional hymns from the stage when Kamal, Akash and I enter the lane. The festivities are spread over a massive ground, stretching as far as the eye can see. There are Ferris wheels and carousels jostling for space between the food stalls, which in turn try and carve out space from enterprising locals peddling wares—from household utensils to clothes to bedsheets.

It is nearly 9 p.m., and these stalls are full of crowds.

Kamal, though, is not interested in any of this. He, instead, goes to the Dharamgarh Baba temple, alongside the stalls. Akash and Kamal enter together, but while Akash pays his respects across the different deities in the temple, Kamal pauses before the main deity, and his prayers go on for a few minutes. He eventually emerges and wants to rush straight to the podium.

The announcements have started, and the sammelan is all set to begin.

~

The evening's sanchalak, the person who has curated the list of poets, is Ajay Anjam, a tall, burly poet-writer from Auraiya, 50 km east of Rasoolabad.

Ajay starts introducing the smattering of artistes from across the Hindi heartland. There are seven today, of which only one is woman. True to the formula, the solo female poet, Pallavi Tripathi, based out of Noida, will perform romantic poetry with a dash of humour.

Ajay, while introducing the poets, forgets to mention Tripathi. Some whispers on the stage and a scramble to the organizer ensue before he hurriedly introduces her and exhorts the audience to applaud her, partly to shield his own embarrassment. This is the second time that I have witnessed organizers forgetting to introduce the line-up's female poet.

When he introduces Kamal, Ajay weighs his words. Kamal, he says, 'is a young poet, but one who is on to important tasks.

'*Hindutva ke liye, Sanatan Dharam ke liye, apne desh ki jitni sansthayein hai, apne Ved, Upanishad pe, lagatar kaam kar ke apni kavita ke madhyam se desh tak pohochane wale, Kamal Agney ji.*' The man who is constantly working on all the institutions in the country, be it our Vedas, our Upanishads, and bringing them to us through his poetry, for Hindutva and for Hinduism, that man is Kamal Agney.

Applause breaks out by the time Ajay ends his statement. The applause isn't as much as the ones some of the other poets received, but Kamal doesn't show any emotion. He just looks at the audience and folds his hands.

That's when Pandey, the recent recruit in the BJP, takes the stage. He is going to host the show. As soon as they hear his name, the audience breaks into applause in anticipation of what he has for them tonight.

Pandey first calls Nirbheek, the bespectacled *vir rasya* poet and fellow BJP worker, on stage to kick off the sammelan.

Nirbheek, immediately, tells the audience that he is the son of a soldier, and he will reveal what the soldier's state of mind is. His first poem is on the Kashmir Valley, where he claims the Indian tricolour is burnt every day and blames the *tukde tukde gang* for that. The applause is tepid, but there are a few chants of Zindabad! from the audience.

Nirbheek extends his arms sideways, his oratory is loud, and his mannerisms resemble Modi's. He speaks haltingly but forcefully, almost in a bombastic manner.

'*Main thoda aur kattu hota hoon.*' I will now take a more hard-line stance, he warns.

His next poem is, again, targeted at 'enemies of the nation'. He offers differing definitions:

Jinn logo ko desh padoshi bhaata,
Jinn logo ko Bharat Maa se pyaar nahin,
Jinn logo ne 'Vande Mataram' kiya sweekar nahin.

Those who like our neighbouring country better,
Those who don't love our motherland,
Those who have not accepted 'Vande Mataram'.

All these, he thunders in the last line, should leave the country.

More tepid applause follows. He reiterates his status as the son of a soldier and, hence, he adds, he wants to ask some questions to those who doubt the bravery of the country's armed forces.

A poet, he says, is never a supporter of any regime or any party. 'The poet sees the truth and writes it as it is,' Nirbheek says, without disclosing that he was now officially a part of the ruling party.

These days, he says, he finds himself livid. '*Jab log Modi ka virodh karte karte, desh ka virodh kare*'. I get angry when people, in a bid to criticize Modi, start opposing the country.

Nirbheek the poet can easily merge into Nirbheek the BJP member.

In his bombastic manner, he says that Bharat has changed. Modi, he says, will obliterate Pakistan from the world's map. That India won't keep quiet.

Hum Balochistan tumse cheen ne se na darenge,
Aur ab Modi tumhare tan pe Shiv tandav karenge

Modi will stamp your chest, dance like Shiva on it,
And snatch Balochistan away without batting an eyelid.

But the audience isn't quite responsive tonight. The applause gets less tepid, and Nirbheek bows out with stray chants of Zindabad! in the audience.

His performance tonight seems like a near-repetition of his performance seven months ago, when I saw him in Patna. His poetry continues to target Pakistan, Kashmiris and invisible enemies like the *tukde tukde gang*, without any mention of the prevailing national mood, the farmers' protests or the killings.

Next up is a comic poet who calls himself, Munna Battery.

Midway through his performance, he pauses and tells his audience that he doesn't speak on politics at all because it's not his subject. But he has a complaint, he says. '*Kuch log*,' some people, he says, seem to have a problem with everything Modi does. He points to Covid-19 vaccinations in the country and reminds the audience that ninety-five crore doses had been by then administered. But people seem to have a problem with that, too.

'It's a good thing people in India are coy, or else some people would go and defecate in public, just to show Modi's *Swachh Bharat* as a failure,' he says, referring to the Prime Minister's pet campaign on cleanliness and hygiene.

He repeats his refrain, that he won't talk about politics, immediately before talking about the 2019 elections, when Modi got re-elected.

An old woman, Battery says, died, went to heaven and came back to tell her family only one thing. *'Jaante ho kya? Aayega to Modi hi.'* Do you know what she said? She said, no matter what, the winner will be Modi, he says, repeating the BJP's catchy slogan it had employed in the polls.

Battery pokes fun at Modi's critics, at Pakistan and at 'jihadis' in Kashmir, but his refrain remains the same—he doesn't talk about politics.

After Battery discharges himself entirely, Pandey, the host, takes the stage again. Before calling the next speaker, he tells the audience that he wants to narrate an encounter that some farmers in UP had with a politician. Pandey goes on to narrate a fictitious story about Rahul Gandhi meeting sugarcane farmers. In the story, Gandhi asks the farmer at what point will the crop start spouting jaggery. Pat comes the reply from the farmer: *'Jab tum pradhan mantri banoge, tab.'* The day you become the Prime Minister.

Laughter breaks out in the audience, followed by claps.

Next up is a Hindi humour poet, Sudeep Bhola.

Without taking names, he says everyone on the stage has been saying 'Modi, Modi'. He won't do that, he says.

'I am a man of balance,' he says, before quickly adding in, 'but deep down, I am what you are,' breaking into a laugh immediately, even as the audience starts clapping.

'These are light-hearted moments. *Baad mein, main bhi Kamal Agney hi hoon.'* As the show progresses, you will see I am also Kamal Agney.

Bhola begins with a satirical joke about how petrol prices, which had recently crossed Rs 110 per litre, were unaffordable and needed to be brought down.

He asks where are the BJP waalas here? Pandey, the host for the evening, picks up the microphone and says, '*Sab Bhajapai hi hai.*' Everyone here is with the BJP.

Bhola is a popular name and face. Like Pandey, Bhola regularly appears on Hindi news television channels, especially in shows that feature humour poets dishing out satirical takes on politics and current affairs.

Tonight, though, Bhola's performance is obviously slanted in its political leaning. It revolves around joking about Rahul Gandhi as well as all other major non-BJP leaders in UP. He calls Gandhi 'Pappu', the Samajwadi Party Chief Akhilesh Yadav 'Bhatija' and Bahujan Samaj Party Chief Mayawati 'Bua', all monikers that the BJP and its social media followers routinely hurl at these rival politicians. None of the BJP leaders see any similar moniker being used for them.

He admonishes Gandhi and his sister Priyanka Gandhi Vadra, without taking their names, for 'political tourism'. Their visits to the site where farmers were run over, in Lakhimpur Kheri, immediately after the incident, had turned contentious as the Yogi government had refused to allow the visits to take place.

Bhola sidesteps any mention of the incident but criticizes their visit. '*Arre bhaiyya,* if it was necessary to come here, you should have also gone to the farmers' protest when a man was beheaded there,' Bhola says, pointing to the incident of a Sikh man being killed, allegedly by a group of Nihang Sikhs for committing sacrilege at the Singhu border.[21]

Bhola goes on to recite an entire song about Gandhi ('*Pappu fail ho gaya*', Pappu flunked the test again). The audience laps it up and showers applause on Bhola.

Kamal is now up next.

Pandey, the poet-compere, rushes to the stage to offer an introduction.

'Kamal might be young, but his name is taken with a lot of respect around the country,' he says in his introduction. 'I want to welcome him with his own words:

Atki hai iss paar toh iss paar kahenge,
Kashti hai jo us paar toh us paar kahenge,
Chahe Kanhaiya Kumar ho ya badtameez Owaisi,
Gaddar ko lalkar ke gaddar kahenge.'

I will not dither ever,
To call a spade by its name.
Be it Kanhaiya Kumar or the ill-mannered Owaisi,
A traitor, for me, will always be called a traitor.

The response in the audience is not as loud as Kamal would have wanted. Maybe it's the feeble reception, but tonight he looks nervous, his start dithers a bit.

He wants to open with a loosener. So he jokes about the Taliban's takeover of Afghanistan.

'I went to a restaurant, and they had a dish named Chicken Afghani. I told them it should be renamed to Chicken Talibani, now,' he says. The joke falls flat, with barely any laughs from the audience. This isn't what they have been told to expect from him. So the audience looks on, waiting for Kamal's next move.

He starts with his staple—his poem on Chandrashekhar Azad. He starts laying out the groundwork: he talks about the currency notes having Mohandas Karamchand Gandhi's photo. 'Was Azad so inconsequential that we could not have his photo on even a ten-rupee note?' he asks.

I have witnessed this set before, in Patna and in countless other videos of his. He continues to stick to the line, taking digs at Nehru and Gandhi.

*Itihas mein dabbe hue hai itne sawaal, ab tak aai na jawaab ki
kahaniya
Sagar se jyaada hai talaab ki kahaniya; chehron se jyaada hai
naqaab ki kahaniya.
Coat pe gulaab ki kahaniya suna kar ke, desh se mita di inquilab
ki kahaniya.*

Questions buried in history, we never heard stories of their
answers,
There are more stories of the lake, than the sea; more stories
of the veils, than of faces
By endlessly telling us tales of roses on coats, we were made to
forget the tales of revolution.

Finally, Kamal finds his mojo. The audience, for the first time in
this performance, breaks out in applause. It isn't as much as Kamal
generally gets, but at this point, he will make do. There are chants
of *waah, waah!* from fellow poets on the stage.

Kamal is clearly buoyed by the response.

He then moves back to the developments in Afghanistan. Media
reports from the country in the weeks before the show have spoken
a mass exodus among Afghans, fearful of their plight under the
Taliban. He jokes about them, saying he wonders why they are not
wanting to sit on a dharna, *demonstration,* against the Taliban.

I know he is trying to set up his next set, and I can already see
where this is going. After Nehru, he is now all set to take on Gandhi
and his insistence on non-violence and Satyagraha.

*Ho sake toh dharne par baith kar bhole bhalein Talibaniyon ko
samjha ke dekh lijiye
Bharat toh ek baar azmaa chuka yeh shastra, ab ek baar aap bhi
to azmaa ke dekh lijiye*

Shayad azaadi mil jaaye aap ko turant,
Ek baar charkha chala kar dekh lijiye.[22]

If you can, convince the poor Afghani people to demonstrate
    peacefully,
India has done this before, now it's your turn to try it once.
You might win freedom immediately,
Try spinning the charkha just once.

This time many among those in the crowd erupt with loud cheers
at his punch line.

I notice a young man, not far from where I am sitting on the stage
to Kamal's left, cheering the loudest. During the introduction,
he had been introduced as a local poet, Shivam. Throughout
the show, but especially during Kamal's performance, I saw him
transform into one of the loudest cheerleaders for Kamal.

Meanwhile, Kamal decides to press on with the Afghanistan
crisis. He tells his audience, with an air of finality, that he is now
going to reveal the *kind* of people who are fleeing Afghanistan.

The audience watches on; Kamal pauses for a brief moment. He
isn't willing to give the answer up immediately. He says the audience
reaction to what he is about to say will show him the disha, direction,
for the show ahead.

'*Ho sakta hai is kavi sammelan ki sabse hot pankti padhne jaa
raha hoon main.*' What I am about to say might be the hottest lines
recited this evening.

Islaami deshon se yeh bhaage jo musalman,
Sharam ho toh aisa nizam chod dena chahiye,
Islaamiyon pe Islam ka hi atyachaar,
Ho sake toh aisa Islam chod dena chahiye.

These Muslims who flee Islamic nations,
For honour, they must walk away from their practice.
When Islam itself inflicts suffering on its followers,
Walk away from such a religion.

The last two lines draw in more applause than before. This time, there are also hoots. Someone from the audience shouts: *'Keh gaye re bhaiya!'* He said it! Pandey, on the stage, takes a cordless microphone into his hands and says, *'Himmat hai! Itne dum se kehne waale kavi.'* He has guts. A poet who speaks with power and courage.

Suddenly, Kamal switches to talking about a recent encounter between militants and defence personnel in Jammu and Kashmir. Then he moves to the Pulwama terror attack in 2019, one of the worst such attacks on Indian defence personnel, killing forty-four of them.

His performance today is far from smooth—there seems to be no organic flow among the topics he addresses. Instead, he hurriedly seems to be checking topics off a list. At one moment he speaks of Chandrashekhar Azad. Then he jokes about Article 370 being khatm, finished. Just as suddenly, he jumps to attack students of JNU. Suddenly, he's poking fun at Mehbooba Mufti, the former Jammu and Kashmir chief minister.

Midway through his performance, I note how Kamal has carefully sidestepped any mention of the farmers' protest or anything else that is newsy and topical. The closest he has come to referencing current affairs is the Afghanistan crisis. That changes soon.

'Woh ek hakla kya naam hai, Shah Rukh Khan?'

That stammerer, what's his name? Shah Rukh Khan?

On 3 October 2021, weeks before this show, Khan's son, Aryan, had been arrested by the Narcotics Control Bureau in Mumbai on charges of consumption of drugs and conspiracy under the stringent Narcotics Drugs and Psychotropic Substances Act (NDPS).[23] It had been three weeks since, but Aryan continued to be in prison, his bail applications rejected by two different local courts.

The timing of the arrest was convenient for the ruling BJP. Happening a day before the Lakhimpur Kheri incident, the arrest ensured that the media's attention was divided between the two events. The deaths of the farmers, its aftermath, as well as the protests against the violence by Opposition parties were overshadowed by the media's breathless reportage on Aryan's arrest—most television channels chose to ignore the violence and, instead, focus their energies on bringing wall-to-wall coverage of Aryan's arrest, posting reporters everywhere, from outside the Khan residence to the prison where he was held.

Aryan's arrest was a distraction that the BJP needed.

This evening, Kamal was about to re-employ this distraction.

Kamal reminds his audience of the actor's comments in 2015 when Khan had said there was 'growing intolerance' in the country.[24]

'*Woh keh raha hai humein desh mein darr lag raha hai,*' Kamal says, the sarcasm in his voice unmistakable. He says he feels scared to live in this country.

'*Tumhare ghar mein itni charas hai, phir bhi tumhe darr lag raha hai?*' You have so much cannabis in your house, and yet you feel scared?

Many poets on stage are visibly shocked at Kamal's words. One of them has a wide grin on his face but is quick to cover it with his hand. In the audience, though, most break out into loud laughter. But Kamal isn't done.

'Arre Shah Rukh Khan, agar yeh desh ki yuva peedhi jo mere saamne hai, who agar apne ghar se 500 ke note chura kar ke apni girlfriend ke saath tumhari Veer Zaara *ya* DDLJ *nahi dekhti toh tum aaj bhi Chowpatty mein Amitabh Bachchan ki car ka puncture banane ka kaam kar rahe hote.'*

'Listen, oh Shah Rukh Khan, if youngsters like those sitting here had not flicked 500 rupees from their homes to watch your movies, you would still be in [Mumbai's] Chowpatty, fixing the punctured tyres of Amitabh Bachchan's car.'

There are now loud guffaws in the audience, accompanied by claps and whistles.

'Main desh ke yuvaaon ko kehna chahta hoon. Yeh rishiyon ka desh hai, charasiyon ka desh nahi,' Kamal goes on. I want to tell the youth of India, that this is a country of rishis, not of cannabis addicts.

'Agar desh ko bachana hai toh yaad rakhna asli hero kaun hai. Yeh Shah Rukh, Salman, Saif asli jeevan mein zero hai, veer Shiva ke Senapati Tanaji asli hero hai.' If you want to save this nation, then you must remember who the real hero is. Not Shah Rukh, Salman or Saif, who are real-life zeroes, but Tanaji, the brave commander of Shivaji's army.

The audience, yet again, responds in broad agreement. Most are clapping and whistling. Kamal has carefully singled out only three Muslim actors for his diatribe today. He does not target any other Hindu actor in his performance that night. The underlying text of his diatribe isn't just real heroes versus reel heroes, but also Hindus versus Muslims.

Kamal is coming to the end of his performance, he now seems reassured that he has warmed the audience up adequately for the final act. He prepares them for what is coming next; he says what he is about to say is the *kadwa sach*, the bitter truth.

Jitna Taliban nahi hai Afghanistan mein,
Usse zyada Taliban hai apne Hindustan mein.
Hum bandar ke haathon mein talwar thama kar baithe hai
Bharat mein ek chotta Taliban bana kar baithe hai.
Bollywood mein khub sunni thi taakat badi Pathaano ki
Kintu hakikat aaj saamne aa gayi hai Afghano ki

There are more Talibanis in India,
Than they are in Afghanistan.
We have handed over a sword to monkeys,
We have allowed a mini-Taliban in our country.
Bollywood boasted about the strength of the Pathans,
But today, the world witnesses the plight of the Afghans.

He isn't done yet, but members of the audience have taken to their feet, applaud and hooting for Kamal. Some, including fellow poets, rush to the stage and garland Kamal with a string of marigold flowers. Kamal folds his hands to thank them.

Buoyed, Kamal carries on.

He tells his audience that his poem and its focus on the Afghani refugees is not to make light of their suffering or mock them. Instead, he says, their suffering is a warning for India's Hindus.

Maanavta ke naate hum ko bhi humdardi hai
Lekin yeh toh swayam tumhari apni dehshat gardi hai
Tumne apna jeevan apne haathon narak banaya hai
Humne sadiyon se duniya ko apna dard bataya hai.
Vishwaguru hai hum toh poori duniya ko samjhana hai
Lekin sabse pehle humko apna desh bachana hai.
Jaago jaago Bharat vanshiyon, tum na aaj jo jagoge,
Vayu yaan mein latak latak kar, tum bhi ek din bhagoge.

We sympathize with your pain,
But all this is a result of your self-created terror.
You have made your own life hell,
As the world leader, we must lead the world
But before anything else, we must save our country
But before anything else, we need to save our own country.
Wake up, Indians, if you don't do so today,
You, too, will cling to aircraft in order to flee this country.

Lakhimpur Kheri and the farmers' protests are forgotten. Tonight,
Afghanistan seemed closer to Rasoolabad than Lakhimpur Kheri.

A Secular Past

Growing up in Gosaiganj, a town 20 km east of Lucknow, Kamal lived a life that he can now barely reconcile with.

Kamal in his formative years was jarringly different from the Kamal now. And so were his circumstances. Back then, some of his family's closest friends were Muslims. Kamal would frequent their homes, and they would his. Far from being a Hindu nationalist and a BJP supporter, he cast his life's first-ever vote for Akhilesh Yadav and the Samajwadi Party. He was a firm believer in secularism, believing that religious hate had no place in the country.

Kamal has changed since then. Gosaiganj barely has.

Historical references[1] mark the town to be a market town, with flourishing trade. The region was ruled by one Raja Himmat Gir Goshain, who, it is said, stood up to the seven-foot-tall Nawab of Oudh, Shuja-ud-Daula, and denied him entry into the fort after Daula was vanquished by the East India Company in the famous Battle of Buxar, 1764.[2]

To date, enterprise remains the bedrock of Gosaiganj's economy. The market road is the town's spine. Livelihoods, religion and lives—all revolve around that spine: the local temple is just off that road, so are the government and private schools, and so is the police station. So busy and narrow is the road that it barely has enough space for a single car to pass by, at great inconvenience to pedestrians who suddenly find themselves with no space to even jostle. Cars pass by only after receiving angry glares from motorcyclists and pedestrians alike, possibly why they are rarely spotted here. In 2011, the Census said less than 10,000 people lived in Gosaiganj, a number you would never agree with if you stopped by the market road.

Every second shop in the market is run by a jeweller—either selling jewellery or manufacturing it. This includes Kamal's family. His uncle, his father and now his elder brother are all skilled artisans designing and manufacturing jewellery. The family owns a hole-in-the-wall workshop in the market as well as a shop a few kilometres away, outside Gosaiganj, where jewellery is designed, crafted and even repaired.

The family's living room bears traces of it—a wooden table has tiny pieces of silver and golden jewellery strewn across it. The table serves as a makeshift workshop for Kamal's father, Ashok Varma.

The family home, in a bylane off the main street, is a narrow ground plus one structure. When I visited in October 2021, much of it was being renovated—an additional floor was being added to accommodate rising ambitions and the growing family. The home next to theirs, nearly identical in shape and size, belongs to Kamal's uncle. The arrangement allows for just the right amount of intimacy and privacy; it enables the two families to live jointly but in their respective homes. The renovations at Kamal's home have reduced the operative part of the house to just the kitchen and a small bed, so we go to his uncle's home. The living room is long but narrow there, with a bed and a couch placed in a straight line, leaving barely enough walking space in the room, much like the street outside.

Finances can be a struggle for both families. The competition in the trade, locally itself, is so high that work can be sparse. In addition, the pandemic and the precarious financial health it put millions in meant that purchasing power, especially in smaller towns like Gosaiganj, took a hit.

The ongoing renovation work at home has been funded by Kamal, through his income from shows and the commercial writing he does. If not for him, Varma is certain the family would have to put off for longer the already long-pending refurbishments.

Varma, at sixty-one, also had his age to battle. Kamal worried that his father could no longer hustle the way a business like theirs required. Kamal's older brother has set up his own shop in the same town, but that is only just taking off. Kamal's income has to fill in each time the family wants to stretch its wings—desires like an additional floor, a better home, a new motorcycle, maybe hiring an assistant for his father; Kamal has to temper these ambitions and provide for them.

~

In many ways, Varma believes he was the reason why Kamal became what he is today, a fiery, rabble-rousing Hindutva kavi. In many ways, his assessment is accurate.

In his younger days, Varma had been fond of Hindi poetry. He would enjoy reading them and also attend kavi sammelans. Without realizing it, he passed on his enthusiasm to Kamal.

Varma would often find young Kamal reading Hindi poems and requesting Varma to recite some to him. He found nothing amiss about these requests. He figured that, like most children want stories to be narrated to them, Kamal had a similar preference, but for poems.

But slowly, Varma found Kamal's requests growing. 'He would ask me to recite the same poem four to five times, and I would wonder why,' says Varma. Nonetheless, Varma would accede to his requests. A couple of days later, Kamal would walk up to his father and recite the poem back to him. 'I don't know how he did it, but he would have learned the poem by rote and would recite it to me.'

This became a bit of a habit with Kamal. So Varma started taking Kamal, at ten years old, along to the kavi sammelans that he would attend.

Kamal loved his time there. By the age of twelve, Kamal was attracted to rhymes, even if he could not fully comprehend them. He wanted to keep listening to them. So, each time they went to a kavi sammelan, Kamal would drag his father to the stall, where poets would sell cassettes and CDs of their recitals. Back home, he would play them on loop, listen to the rhymes, try and understand the delivery of those rhymes and grasp the pronunciations.

That exposure started showing effect. Soon after, he started reciting poetry in his school whenever he found an occasion. He enjoyed the process immensely. His school, buoyed by his enthusiasm, would ask him to recite the 'day's thought', a proverb or a quote by an eminent personality meant to inspire the students. It would just be a line or two, but it soon became the part of the day that young Kamal awaited most eagerly.

But as he was doing that, Kamal, looking back, realized that he was also beefing up his public speaking abilities and getting over the most common of afflictions—stage fright. The confidence helped him get a head start. By class ten, Kamal had started writing his own poems.

Even as Kamal was immersing himself deeper into poetry, initiated unwittingly by his father, there was another aspect of Varma's life that Kamal was getting drawn to.

Among his closest friends in Gosaiganj, Varma counted a Muslim man and his family to be at the top of the list. The two families would frequent each other's homes, share meals, spend days together. Each would be a part of the other's joys and sorrows. So close were the two families that each time he saw them, Kamal would touch the feet of his father's friend.

Somewhere along the way, friendships got intertwined with business. Varma had rented out a shop his family owned to his Muslim friend, seeing as the friend needed help establishing himself. They were like family to each other, and families don't need written agreements to dictate terms, they reasoned. So neither side insisted on doing the paperwork for that transaction. It was, anyway, going to be a temporary arrangement till his friend managed to get his finances in order to buy his own shop.

But a few months into the arrangement, Varma says the two had a fall out after his friend refused to vacate the shop. The dispute grew, became bitter and even ugly. The two friends would publicly quarrel. Kamal witnessed one such altercation between them. His father, who had trusted his friend blindly, without feeling the need for any safeguards in the transaction, was being ridiculed; his trust had been broken. Kamal had had enough.

He picked up a sariya, an iron rod, and headed straight in the direction of the man his father had once trusted with his life. But before he could act upon his instinct, Varma held his hand and yanked him back. Aghast at his son's indiscretion, Varma slapped Kamal publicly. 'I told him he should not dare touch my friend,' Varma recalls now.

The incident remains etched in Kamal's memory even now, more than a decade later. Initially, the incident registered as a bitter, angry fall out, a betrayal of personal trust by a friend. But as he grew and as time passed, Kamal started looking at the incident differently. Over time, as his exposure towards Hindu nationalist poets and literature grew, he started believing what had happened to him was not an exception but, instead, was symptomatic of a larger phenomenon— of how conniving Muslims were conspiring to cheat gullible Hindus after winning their trust.

Another event, taking place almost concurrently, only solidified this suspicion in Kamal's mind.

He was in his early teens when he started hearing of Muslim families immigrating to an area outside his town in large numbers. Local Hindu right-wing units started protesting the migration and fanned fears that Gosaiganj would soon see an 'Islamic takeover' if the migration was not halted.

In a place like Gosaiganj, it's often difficult to segregate the personal and the political. The community can be so tightly knit, often, that political leanings are rather irrelevant.

Among the many that the family shared deep ties with were part-time Hindu right-wing leaders who would often convince Varma to send his young children to the RSS shakha that held sessions every Sunday near the town's temple. Varma conceded to the request only because he believed that attending those sessions would bring moral discipline and physical fitness in his children.

Arvind Gupta, a local BJP leader who was earlier with the Akhil Bharatiya Vidyarthi Parishad (ABVP), the student wing of the RSS, was a part of the agitation against the Muslim immigrants. Gupta said one of their strategies during the agitation was to hold meetings with local Hindu traders and business owners like Varma and mobilize support on the issue. Their children attending the RSS Shakha only made such an approach easier for Gupta and his workers.

Gupta, along with other Hindutva activists, mobilized locals and tried approaching government authorities to press their case. Nothing much came of it, but the mobilization helped the groups widen their base.

The feared Islamic 'takeover' never happened, but Kamal continues to hold on to the agitation in his heart. He didn't realize it then, but now he does—experiences like those simply illustrated his fears were real. Just like Gosaiganj, India was facing the prospect of an 'Islamic takeover', he thought.

~

Even while these events swirled around Kamal, he was making slow inroads into his passion: poetry.

Among the kavya goshti events that Varma would take Kamal along to, one was attended by a poet named Rameshwar Prasad Dwivedi 'Pralayankar', who Kamal ultimately embraced as his guru. His work focused on upholding the *Sanatan Dharam,* reiterating the values and ethics that Hindu epics prescribed and was conservative in his outlook. In 2010, when the Supreme Court had legally recognized live-in relationships, Pralayankar, furious, had written a verse asking if the Supreme Court was going to legalize adultery next.

Initially, Kamal was spellbound by his use of classical Hindi, the flow in which he would recite his poems. But the more he saw Pralayankar in performance, the more drawn he was to what the poet was saying. Pralayankar constantly referenced Hindu religious literature, from the Puranas and Vedas to mythological characters and gods. Pralayankar also took strident Hindu nationalist positions in his poetry.

Slowly, the events in his Gosaiganj life—from the betrayal of his father's Muslim friend to the Hindu right-wing group's agitation over a supposed Islamic takeover, combined with his attraction towards Pralayankar—drew Kamal deeper and deeper towards Hindutva thought. In Hindutva, he saw an explanation for what had happened to his father at the hands of a man he had trusted completely and what could have happened to Gosaiganj if Hindus had not hit the streets in opposition.

~

Connecting personal trauma to politics and getting radicalized into a far-right ideology as a result of the trauma, is a process that isn't unique to Kamal.

A study conducted among former white supremacists in the US in 2020 explained how commonplace this was.[3] The study, found that adverse events during childhood altered the participants' social and psychological development and made them susceptible towards extremism.

> Our findings highlight the potential for participants to rely on extremist participation as a way to rectify distress associated with individual trauma.
>
> As a result, these individuals may become especially vulnerable to white supremacist recruitment tactics which sometimes target youth who are frustrated and looking for solutions to their problems, seeking intimate relationships outside of their families, and/or typically lack maturity and are unable to fully comprehend the ramifications of a group's radical ideology.

While the study focused on extremism in the US, especially white extremism, its findings provide an understanding beyond American shores.

Even though his ideological moorings were slowly forming, Kamal's leanings when it came to electoral politics remained fluid. While by then he had been introduced to Pralayankar's poetry, Hindu nationalist literature, as well as the activities of the RSS, when it came to casting his first-ever vote in 2012, Kamal's choice wasn't as obvious.

The Bahujan Samaj Party (BSP)'s government, led by then Chief Minister Mayawati, had finished its five-year reign, and it was being challenged by the young yet inexperienced face of Akhilesh Yadav, who was leading the Samajwadi Party (SP). His father and party founder, the ageing Mulayam Singh Yadav, had relinquished the reins of the party's campaign in the hands of his son. Akhilesh with his master's degree in environmental engineering from Australia promised a break from politics-as-usual. He promised 'positive politics',[4] fresh industrial investments in the state and free laptops and tablets to students passing classes ten and twelve, respectively.[5]

Mayawati did not appeal to Kamal much. For him, her tenure had been marked by the unrelenting power cuts that Gosaiganj had experienced; even the media was full of reports of statues that the chief minister was constructing worth thousands of crores.[6]

It didn't matter to Kamal that Akhilesh and his Samajwadi Party counted Muslims and Yadavs to be their core voters. Nor did Yadav senior's avowed secular stance matter to him. Kamal voted for Akhilesh and was jubilant when his leader won.

But that jubilance didn't last long.

In the five years that Akhilesh's term in office lasted, a lot changed. Narendra Modi became the Prime Minister, with the BJP sweeping UP in the 2014 Lok Sabha polls by winning seventy-one of the eighty parliamentary constituencies in the state. Hindu nationalism was no longer alive only in the kavi sammelan events that Kamal attended.

At a personal level, by the time the 2017 elections for the state assembly came, Kamal had firmly found his ideological anchor in Hindutva. He had started stridently performing Hindutva poetry across the country, and his credentials as a Hindutva foot soldier were bringing him fame and riches.

Now, he could see Akhilesh's faults rather clearly. Akhilesh and his party had the sole intention of appeasing the Muslim community, Kamal reasoned with his new-found clarity of thought. Among the Hindus, only the Yadavs got powerful; the rest were neglected. His allure for Akhilesh, as a foreign-educated young leader, had crumbled when Akhilesh allowed Muslims 'to go on a rampage and kill innocent Hindus, all because they didn't allow the Muslims to molest Hindu women,' according to Kamal.

He was referring to the Muzaffarnagar riots of 2013, which had engulfed the westernmost part of UP, the districts of Muzaffarnagar and Shamli, where Hindu Jats and Muslims clashed sporadically over days, leading to at least sixty people losing their lives and over 40,000 their homes.[7] There were differing accounts of what had sparked off the riots—many, like Kamal, had claimed that the riots were instigated after a Muslim man had misbehaved with a Hindu woman.[8] When her brothers protested, a fight broke out and ended up as full-blown sectarian violence. Others had claimed that a motorcycle accident between the Muslim man and the two Hindu men had taken a sectarian turn and ended in riots.[9]

Even a government-appointed inquiry commission had not been able to verify just what triggered the riots.[10] But the commission's report, as well as several others, had flagged the role of BJP leaders in fanning the flames and using out-of-context videos from Pakistan to falsely depict the 'brutal' killings of Hindu men in the riots.[11] The report also charged BJP leaders with making hate speeches in an already-polarized environment, thereby actively stoking hate and violence.

But none of these factor in Kamal's recollection of the event. For him, the riots were another confirmation of his fears and a reaffirmation of his prejudices.

At a personal level, Kamal had his own reasons to feel dejected with Akhilesh's tenure. Over the five years, there had been multiple instances where Kamal and his family feared for their safety. His father had been waylaid by robbers on the highway connecting Gosaiganj to Lucknow, when he was coming back from a shop the family had newly purchased to set up a new jewellery shop, not more than 10 km away from the family home. Thankfully, Varma had escaped the situation without any injuries, but the thought of an encore was so terrifying that the family abandoned plans for the new store, in order to avoid travelling. Two of his uncles had been robbed—once by a trusted employee who decamped with gold and silver deposits and another time by robbers at gunpoint along a highway nearby.

The BJP, if voted to power, had promised to change all that with a crackdown on crime.[12] Adding to the appeal was the BJP's electoral promise to construct a grand Ram Mandir.

In Kamal's head, the die was cast, long before the campaign would even start. Akhilesh had to be defeated.

~

By then, his Hindutva poetry had started getting noticed. He was performing regularly in kavi sammelans across the state, while some of his poetry had even achieved virality online.

When elections came, he started getting approached by local leaders of the BJP to back the party. Kamal was open to the idea of campaigning for the party. So he jumped at the opportunity to address public meetings in support of a BJP MLA aspirant in Lucknow, just three months before the polls.

In the next ten days, Kamal went on a whirlwind tour of the constituency, addressing meetings in every nook and cranny of the city. Days would start by 9 a.m. and end in the wee hours of the morning, addressing meetings in the candidate's support. These weren't major political rallies. 'The crowds would range from 200 to 20,000 people. No matter how small the size, I had to perform,' Kamal says.

For the poet, campaigning was a new experience: here, he couldn't come up and just recite his poems as he had done all this while. He had to be much more explicit in his political stances and had to fill in the gaps between his poems with electoral rhetoric. It didn't prove to be a very difficult task for Kamal. He just had to stay true to his beliefs.

He would lambast critics of the Modi government and mock the liberals.

The country had seen frequent disturbances—a spate of mostly Muslim victims had been lynched by vicious mobs, often by Hindu right-wing activists in the name of cow protection.[13] One of the first such attacks took place in Uttar Pradesh, when a Hindu mob lynched a fifty-two-year-old Muslim villager named Mohammed Akhlaq on the suspicion that he had slaughtered a cow.[14,15]

The killing had triggered outrage across the nation. Upset at the silence of the Modi government and its inability to rein in some of its leaders who backed and justified[16] the lynching, eminent intellectuals and artistes returned government-bestowed honours and awards in protest. All this forced even Modi to react[17] and call the incident 'sad and undesirable'.

Kamal mentioned the incident in his speeches but mockingly punned on the victim's name. '*1 Akhlaq mara, toh usko mile 45 lakh,*' 1 Akhlaq died, and he got 45 lakh, Kamal would say, referring to the financial aid the government gave his family. He would slam the 'award wapsi gang', a disparaging reference to those who were returning their awards in protest.

But he would be careful not to say this in all his public meetings. Each night, Kamal would be handed over a chart that spelled out his schedule for the following day. Accompanying the chart would be detailed instructions: where the meetings were, the time, the prospective audience size, as well as demographic tidbits like their castes or subcastes, their class or livelihoods. With these details would come a crucial piece of instruction. 'The candidate and his team would tell me where I needed to use *acchi bhasha,* decent language, and where I could go hard (sic),' Kamal says.

Going hard was code for delivering speeches he was known for: controversial, polemical and communally polarizing.

He would also be given specific instructions if the candidate or his team felt they needed some religious polarization in certain areas, Kamal said.

Kamal would be happy in these moments. 'That's where I could be myself and say what I believed in,' he says. 'At other places, where they would ask me to go soft, I would have to dilute my ideology.'

After his month-long stint, Kamal had addressed over 200 public meetings. His effort paid off. The candidate won by over 20,000 votes, the BJP came to power with an overwhelmingly large mandate, winning 312 of the total 402 seats, and Akhilesh was denied a second term.

~

This effort, to fight Akhilesh's re-election bid and back the BJP, paid off handsomely for Kamal. The BJP's sweeping victory in the polls and the surprise elevation of Yogi Adityanath as the state's chief minister was music to Kamal's ears.

Kamal's brief but impactful dalliance with the BJP, as well as his growing fame, had put him in touch with various leaders of the RSS and its affiliated outfits. Among them was also the Hindu Yuva Vahini, a right-wing group of Hindu nationalists founded by Yogi Adityanath.

Kamal had interacted with a few of its leaders in the run-up to the polls. Those leaders had shown an appreciation for Kamal's ideological bent and his poetry. Now, with Adityanath being sworn in as the CM, Kamal felt he had made it.

Since those UP polls of 2017, Kamal has now grown in the role of a propagandist.

After Lucknow, he campaigned for leaders in other parts of UP as well as in Madhya Pradesh's Chhatarpur district. With each incoming assignment, Kamal has made deeper inroads into the invisible yet ruthlessly effective ecosystem that keeps the BJP and the Hindu right-wing ticking. All this has only added to his popularity and given him a bigger role in these ecosystems.

From Lucknow to Chhatarpur, the party's requirements for him remained similar. By now, Kamal was getting a firmer sense of his role: he wasn't just a poet spouting Hindutva before the bigwigs take the stage. He was also supposed to test the waters with the crowd, perk them up and ensure they are pepped up to hear the main speakers. Political rallies are often long-drawn-out events, lasting anywhere from three to five hours. For organizers of these rallies, the challenge is not holding such a rally but retaining the audience's attention once they have gathered. Making this a daunting task is the fact that senior political leaders, especially during elections, have packed schedules, hopping from one public meeting to another and, hence, can be very spectacularly unpunctual.

Hence, organizers must be able to retain the audience till senior leaders arrive, lest the leaders find a sparsely filled venue. This is when the likes of Kamal serve a dual purpose: they entertain as well as propagate the ideology and help in retaining the audience's interest.

Kamal had a cricket analogy ready, to understand just what he was supposed to do—he was a batsman opening the innings for his team. His role was to give the team a solid start, 'Like the opener who comes and makes forty to fifty runs quickly so that the remaining batsmen don't feel as much pressure,' Kamal says. While the more senior political leaders would need to be calculative and cautious about the words they use, Kamal can afford to be unfiltered, unbridled and politically incorrect. This combination, often, works to the candidate's advantage. *'Meri baton se logon ko pata chal jaata hai ki candidate ki yeh ideology hai.'* My speech tells the voters that the candidate is also of the same ideology as me, Kamal says.

Both these campaigns gave him a chance to witness, upclose, the BJP's election machinery and come in close proximity with some of its biggest leaders. Kamal says some of the rallies that he participated in had leaders like Rajnath Singh, Uma Bharti, and Manoj Sinha.

In the 2022 UP polls, with Adityanath seeking re-election, Kamal was roped in again, but not for any public campaigning like the previous time. Instead, Kamal started work on content that would reach a far wider audience than a rally would—through their mobile phones.

Kamal was ready—this was going to be the most important election of his life so far, and he wanted to give it all he had.

Death and Discontent

Apna toh kisi ghair se bhi bair nahi hai,
Kintu Ram ke virodhiyon ki khair nahi hai.
Ram janmabhoomi ka yeh case chod dijiye,
Anyatha yeh Ram ji ka desh chod dijiye.

I bear enmity towards none,
But won't spare those who oppose Ram.
Withdraw your claims on the birthplace of Ram,
Or else, leave this country of Ram.

In the months leading up to the 2022 UP elections, Kamal had been aggressively defending the Yogi government's record.

Like I saw in his October 2021 show in Rasoolabad, Kamal had shown no intent to be on the defensive when it came to the controversies that plagued, both, the Modi government as well as the Yogi government.

158

Kamal's performances in the last few months had targeted Hindi film actors, refugees fleeing Afghanistan and Pandit Jawaharlal Nehru. He had carefully sidestepped any mention of the thorny challenges that the BJP faced—from the protests by farmers across India against the Modi government's proposed farm laws or the mishandling of the devastating Covid-19 wave in UP just months ago, when corpses floated on the Ganga, and tens of thousands faced crippling shortages of everything, from oxygen cylinders to hospital beds.

The BJP's victory in his home state was always important for Kamal. But this time, his personal stakes were higher: like most others in the Hindutva ecosystem, Yogi was a personal favourite for Kamal. Yogi was the closest to any politician Kamal identified with; for him, Yogi was a Hindutva crusader who had refused to let power 'sober' him into diluting his hard-line Hindu nationalist ideology.

Even before Yogi became the state's chief minister, Kamal had been in close proximity with leaders of the Hindu Yuva Vahini, a far-right militant Hindutva organization that Yogi had founded and nurtured carefully till he became the chief minister in 2017.[1] The Vahini was found to be involved in communal polarization across UP since 2002 and has been linked with a string of violent riots as well as assaults and lynchings of Muslims.[2,3,4]

When Yogi was selected for the CM's post in 2017, Kamal started believing that his proximity with those leaders would keep him in good stead. He continued to harbour this hope and hence, decided that he would do all he could to ensure his Hindutva hero sailed through.

The internet was going to be a key frontier in the political battle to win UP: as always, the BJP, with its powerful social media machinery, was leveraging it to wrest the elections. The party claimed to have over 1.7 million workers across the state, all armed with smartphones and tasked with sharing digital content with voters around them.[5] The BJP was running multiple campaigns simultaneously in a bid to ensure that it was able to attract diverse sets of voters who might have different priorities and needs—from Hindutva to better control over crime.[6]

Kamal's work became crucial in this regard. In the run-up to the polls, Kamal started appearing in slickly produced videos, a series titled 'Kamal ka Kamaal', the wonders of Kamal. The videos were better produced than anything else Kamal had been a part of until then. It featured a dapper-looking Kamal, his hair neatly gelled, wearing crisp kurtas and jackets, looking a few shades fairer and a few inches fitter.

His connections among the Hindutva ecosystem ensured that the videos would be uploaded by various pages on social media platforms periodically and would see Kamal take potshots at the BJP's rivals, lampooning them. For Kamal, this was off brand. He was no longer engaged in thundering oratory, lashing out angrily at enemies of Hindutva, nor were there any livid diatribes to be delivered against enemies, past or present.

Instead, Kamal's writing abilities had been channelized into humour—in these videos, Kamal would appear, with a laughter track playing in the backdrop, and crack jokes, take digs and smilingly play with puns to target the BJP's rivals. The videos had sound effects, music, even audience clapping. Akhilesh Yadav was Tippu, Rahul Gandhi was Pappu, and Mayawati was Behenji.

The show was packaged cleverly: it took down all of the BJP's principal rivals without explicitly ever admitting just who, really, was behind the video's making. It also, cleverly, did so without praising the BJP overtly, so as to avoid suspicion among audiences of any inherent, outward bias. For the discerning viewer, the bias would come to fore with the convenient selection of its subjects and the focused targeting of the party's rivals.

Kamal told me that he wasn't aware if the BJP ever used his videos as campaign material. But what he does admit to is how a network of pro-BJP pages and groups on Facebook circulated these videos among their followers. That, he said, meant that the message was delivered to the intended recipient.

By the end of 2021, his work had started to get noticed, and Kamal found himself closer than ever before to fame and to becoming a part of the charmed inner circle of the BJP's electoral machinery.

~

Till just a few months before the polls, the BJP were runaway favourites to win the state elections. It had seemed like a foregone conclusion that Yogi was likely to make a comeback. But challenges were mounting against it. As elections came closer, it didn't seem like it was going to be such an easy ride for him, after all. Statistical odds were stacked against Yogi Adityanath: the state, in the past forty years, had not re-elected any of its incumbents. Given that the BJP had won an overwhelming majority in the 2017 polls, it seemed to have an edge. But the last three governments formed in the state were all governments formed by single parties obtaining full majorities. And none of them got re-elected.

On the ground, Opposition parties were trying hard to deliver a blow to Yogi's chances of a re-election by stitching up coalitions among themselves. The Samajwadi Party had tied up with the Rashtriya Lok Dal, a party known for its footing within the farming Jat community in western UP. The alliance could dent the BJP's grip in the region and take away the Jat votes, without which the party would be teetering.[7] Yadav had also stitched alliances with a string of smaller parties, also known to be crucial players in smaller geographical and caste-based pockets in the state.[8]

But none of this worried Kamal as much as what he saw was happening within the BJP.

In Kamal's Hindutva ecosystem, Yogi's elevation, from a leader of a ragtag far-right Hindu organization to the chief minister of India's largest state and his rising popularity whilst in power, was awe-inspiring. For many, Kamal included, the high of seeing him in power as a cheerleader of hard-line Hindutva had induced a throbbing desire in them—to see him elevated to the biggest seat of power, as the country's Prime Minister. Even a cursory search on Facebook for the number of 'Yogi for PM' groups will tell you how popular this sentiment is, among sympathizers of the BJP and supporters of the Hindutva cause.

But as his popularity has grown, so have whispers that not everyone within the party is as enthused about Yogi's rise. The rumours grew stronger in 2021, after the second wave of Covid-19 in the country, which was especially devastating for UP. The curious decision of the BJP's top brass to send one of Modi's closest aides for over two decades, bureaucrat A.K. Sharma, to UP as a member of the legislative council added to the speculation.[9] Was Modi looking to rein Yogi in? Was this done so that the BJP leadership could keep Yogi in check? The questions swirled, bereft of any answers.

With the elections drawing closer, the whispers had only grown stronger. Within the Hindutva ecosystem, many like Kamal had started believing that the BJP top brass was looking to sabotage the UP campaign fought with Yogi at the helm. There was nothing on paper to confirm the theory—the Prime Minister had started making frequent visits to the state in the months leading up to the polls, so had senior BJP leaders. But Kamal told me many felt the party top brass were trying to ensure that candidates perceived to be close to Yogi lose and, as a result, ensure that Yogi does not remain as dominant a figure on the state's and, increasingly, the nation's political map. If the party performed poorly and managed to only scrape through to form the government, it could even be an excuse to show Yogi the door. Or at least so went the grapevine among worried Hindu nationalists, according to Kamal.

It was early February 2022; the first of a seven-phase voting cycle was all set to kick off on 10 February when he got the call. The call, Kamal told me, was from a senior leader of the Vishwa Hindu Parishad (VHP). He needed Kamal's urgent help.

The first two phases, scheduled for 10 and 14 February, were going to be the most crucial and, potentially, where the BJP was the most vulnerable. In those two phases, polls were going to be held in constituencies across western UP. This region, known for its large swathes of sugarcane cultivation and its wealthy Jat farmers, had lent popular support to the nationwide farmers' protests against the Modi government's farm laws. Some of the protest movement's top leaders, including its spokesperson Rakesh Tikait from the Bharatiya Kisan Union (BKU), hailed from this region. After over a year of protests, in December 2021, the Modi government, just two months before the UP polls, had withdrawn the three contentious laws.[10]

But for many in western UP, the anger against the Modi government had remained.

Tikait and the BKU's active role in the protests had mobilized the influential farming community of Jats in UP. The Jats were angry and had threatened to inflict heavy costs on the BJP for its stubborn opposition to the farmers' demands and for mistreating the protesting farmers.

Kamal, the VHP leader told him, had to help negate this anger. Kamal agreed with the leader's concerns about western UP. He would love to help Yogi overcome this obstacle. The question on his mind was how.

The Opposition parties had tapped into Jat anger and had tried to revive a social kinship between Jats and the local Muslims, a kinship that had existed for decades in the region. Jats and Muslims were locked in a cycle of co-dependency, economically and, often, socially too. Through my travels there, I found how the two communities lived in harmonious dependence—Muslims working for wealthy Jat farmers, or wealthy Muslim dairy farmers supplying milk to Hindu traders, who in turn make a living by distributing it.

However, that compact had been broken by the 2013 Hindu–Muslim riots in the region, concentrated around parts of Muzaffarnagar and Shamli districts. The riots primarily saw Jats and Muslims clashing.[11,12] The social cohesion between the two communities had come undone.

Not everyone was complaining though. Since then, the BJP had been sweeping polls in the region.[13]

But in 2022, things had started to change. Disgruntled Jats were turning away from the BJP, and after years of reconciliation efforts, the Jat–Muslim compact was slowly starting to crystallize again. This could spell bad news for the BJP.

On the call with Kamal, the VHP leader laid out the plan— he wanted Kamal to write poetry on three characters who featured in local legends. Kamal told me the three characters were 'Hindu heroes' who had fought against the invasion by the Turkic conqueror Timur in the region in the late fourteenth century. Kamal was told to present the three characters—Gokul Jat, Jograj Gurjar and Rampyari Gurjari—in a way that would remind listeners of how they had sacrificed their lives against the invading 'Muslim' army. Muslims. The three Gurjar and Jat heroes had sacrificed their lives so that Hindus could live and prosper, the VHP leader summed up the message; what better way to honour their sacrifices than to back a government that honours them and continues to fight the wars those heroes had fought. This was a good time to remind the Jats of this; this is what the VHP wanted Kamal to convey to them through his work, the leader told him.

At a time when Muslims and Jats were finally coming together to bury the misgivings of the past, histories, real and imagined, had to be deployed to remind them of their enmity.

The VHP leader told Kamal of the urgency—they needed him to write three pieces of poetry, one each for the three characters, and record those videos narrating his poetry, all within the next couple of days. Even for Kamal, accustomed to writing poetry in minutes, this seemed like a stretch. He wanted to give this his best, and it didn't make sense for him to rush through such a big opportunity and compromise on the quality of his work. He wanted his work to stand out, to be as hard-hitting as it could, so that Hindu voters of western UP voted for their future on the basis of a past that he was going to help them imagine.

And so Kamal politely suggested that instead of three, he would focus on just one personality—a man named Jograj Gurjar.

Across Hindu right-wing websites, portals and blogs run by Hindutva sympathizers, Gurjar is described as 'ferocious' and 'mahabali', powerful, a man of epic proportions at 7 feet and 9 inches tall and with his armour and weapons 'of such heavy weight that people of today cannot even lift' (sic).[14]

In these legends, Gurjar, the 'Supreme Commander General' of his army, was one of the few to challenge the powerful armies of Timur while he crisscrossed across northern India, plundering and capturing territories. In these retellings, Gurjar attacked Timur's army when it was all set to 'attack and destroy' Haridwar. But despite suffering 'forty-five wounds' on his body, Gurjar fought valiantly and 'decimated, defeated' Timur's armies.

Kamal's job was to retell this story, dipped in Hindutva.

~

Except, this was a rather distorted version of the events. Timur spent less than a year in India, away from his seat of power in Samarkand in present-day Uzbekistan, for his 'visitation' to India. At the end of his journey, he tried to convince his lieutenants that the reason for the trip was to wage a war against 'infidels' of Hindustan.[15] However, the principal enemies he took on and defeated during his invasion were, in fact, Muslims—including the ruler of the Delhi Sultanate, Sultan Nasiruddin Mahmud Shah.[16] The truth was, Timur's invasion had been fiercely opposed by both Muslims as well as Hindus. Due to their opposition, both Hindus and Muslims had been massacred. En route to Delhi, when Timur laid siege to Bhatner fort, locals of all communities stood up to him, with Muslims, like the local Rajputs, even 'consigning their children and women to fire', before they entered the battle against Timur's army, one which they knew they were going to certainly not return alive from.[17]

There is uncertainty around the very existence of characters like Jograj Gurjar, Gokul Jat and Rampyari Gurjari. Even a book on Timur's invasion by K.S. Lal, a historian who was accused of being sympathetic to the Hindu right-wing's causes, which otherwise goes into detailed descriptions of Timur's battle in Haridwar and other battles he fought in that year, does not mention any of the three names.

On the internet, a search for these names only yields results from obscure websites, Hindutva-leaning blog posts or websites like Postcard News, a known pro-BJP website regularly found to disseminate disinformation.[18,19] In a piece for *The Times of India*, Yugesh Kaushal, a PhD scholar from Ontario's York University, said the 'concocted tales' of these characters had been 'created out of thin-air' and had found 'ardent' support in the right-wing ecosystem.[20]

But none of this mattered to Kamal, nor his new-found VHP handler. Instead, they had to carefully sift through facts and stitch together a narrative that would suit the party's interests.

Kamal got to work. In a few hours, his poetry was ready, and the next day, he had shot a video for it too.

In the video, Kamal sports a saffron kurta and a peach Nehru jacket atop. His hair neatly combed, his eyebrows are locked in a slight grimace. Behind him play illustrations—of a ruthless-looking man in an Amish beard, holding a sword possibly intended to be Timur; of temple-like structures behind, broken down by a group of people with massive hammers and of a feisty, powerful man, his shoulders broad and moustache twirled, ostensibly meant to be Gurjar.

Taimurlang ki aandhi Hindu deep bujhane waali thi
Pyaasi talwarein Dilli se aagey jaane waali thi
Haridwar ke mandir tode jaane ki taiyaari thi
Lekin unpar veer Hinduon ki senayein bhaari thi
Saare sainik desh dharam pe ladh jaane ke laayak they,
Jograj Singh Gurjar unke adbhut sena nayak they.

The storm of Timurlane's brutality was all set to extinguish Hindus,
His bloodthirsty sword was all set to go beyond Delhi.
The temples of Haridwar were all set to be broken down,
But the brave army of Hindus refused to cowed down.
Their country, their religion, each soldier would give it their all
The army whose commander was Jograj Singh Gurjar.

The poem goes on to extol Gurjar's bravery, his valiant and successful attempt at halting Timur's progress, despite the pain and suffering he had to undergo, calling him the 'real son of Mother Ganges'.

Kamal ended the poem with an appeal:

Isiliye veer Gurjaro jago,
Yahaan ekdum sahi muhurat hai,

Is desh dharam ko aaj tumhari,
Phir se badi zarurat hai.

That is why, brave Gurjars awake
The day is right for you to forsake.
For your country, your faith to remain,
We need you direly to strive again.

The video, released across social media pages sympathetic to the BJP's cause just two days before the second phase of the election, left no one in doubt about just what it wanted Gurjars to do.

Although Kamal had sent the video off, he was not sure of just how effective it was going to be. The elections were just days away—how was his VHP handler and the ecosystem going to get the video out in time? He knew that the BJP's famed IT Cell would push the video into the country's digital bloodstreams, from WhatsApp to social media platforms like Facebook, Instagram, ShareChat, Twitter, among others. Yet, how much would they really be able to achieve in a day? Kamal remained sceptical.

On 13 February, just a day before the polls, Kamal got his answer.

A stream of messages and screenshots came flooding on his WhatsApp: his video had been shared by the renowned actor Kangana Ranaut on her personal Facebook page.[21] With it, she penned an appeal:

Listen to the story of the brave, powerful Jograj Singh Gurjar who defeated the cruel invader Timurlane. I appeal to all voters, to honour and respect the sacrifices of our brave ancestors. On polling date, make sure you vote for the security of our nation.

With 7.7 million followers, Kangana's post and the appeal had given Kamal's video a boost like very few could.

On 10 March, when the results were out, Kamal had multiple reasons to cheer. Not only had Yogi won a resounding mandate to continue in his chair, but Kamal had reasons to believe he had contributed to the victory: in the second phase, which was after his video released, the BJP had emerged a clear winner, bagging thirty-two out of the total fifty-five seats.[22]

For Kamal, 2022, had been a year that started on a high and seemed to be ending that way too. With Covid-19 receding from public memory, live events were back, and so were kavi sammelans. After a poor two-year period when work had remained patchy, Kamal was finally getting frequent invitations again to perform. Throughout the year, he travelled constantly—his WhatsApp status messages offered a window to his travels, thanks into his regular stream of selfies inside aircraft.

He also consistently penned new work in line with Hindutva's constantly evolving, broadening agenda. When a local court in UP allowed a plea seeking the removal of the Shahi Idgah Masjid in Mathura,[23] Kamal wrote a poem insisting that Mathura would be the next place to be 'liberated' after Ayodhya and Kashi, a not-so-subtle indicator of what fate Hindu nationalists wished the mosque to suffer.

His work also continued to not just toe the Hindutva line but actively defend the BJP and Modi from controversies it could find itself in—be it when Opposition parties and historians criticized the Modi government for 'distorting' the form of the State Emblem of the country[24] in the Ashoka Pillar atop the new Parliament building or when Rahul Gandhi's Bharat Jodo Yatra started gathering momentum.

Kamal had poems for all those occasions.

Kamal also had poems and couplets to reiterate his hard-line Hindutva stance. Often, he would concoct anecdotes to make his point. In nearly every show of his in 2022 that I caught, Kamal would recite the same anecdote. It was about lemons.

A few days ago, Kamal would tell his audience, he had bought a lemon. It was very ripe and green, so he wrapped it in a cloth. 'Five days later, when I opened it, it was bhagwa, saffron.'[25] Kamal would pause after that line, possibly in anticipation that the audience would realize what was coming. Most times, they did not.

'This told me that those who are green today will have to turn saffron in time,' he would say, emphasizing the *have to* with a tone so menacing it felt like a warning.

Yet, there was something that gnawed at him all through the year. For years, he had been loyally contributing to building the Hindutva narrative and popularizing it through his work. He had often added to larger conversations that were already taking place within the country and within the Hindutva ecosystem. But sometimes he had also been instrumental in sparking off new debates and narratives, like when he wrote his viral poetry justifying Gandhi's assassination in 2016.[26]

Yet, Kamal had started feeling that none of that had really mattered. He had hoped for some recognition from the BJP, a mark of gratitude towards his services for the cause and for the party. His hopes were heightened, especially after Yogi was re-elected as the chief minister in March 2022, another cause he had contributed heavily to.

Maybe, Kamal thought, in his second term, Yogi would reward those like him, who had tirelessly campaigned and pushed for him to win the state's polls. But months into Yogi's second term, Kamal didn't see anything like that coming his way.

Yet, he went along, doing what he knew best: pushing the Hindutva cause, stoking hate against those he considered its enemies and demonizing critics of the Modi government.

Financially, things had started to look up—in addition to the constant stream of shows, Kamal was also being approached for writing assignments, from scripts for short documentaries to ghost-writing books and songs. Kamal's lifestyle was seeing changes as well; he had the latest iPhone model and was looking to buy a car for himself.

But at the fag end of an otherwise successful year, Kamal's life changed completely. On the night of 11 December 2022, he got a call from home.

His sixty-one-year-old father had collapsed while sitting and chatting with the neighbours in the tiny lane outside their house in Gosaiganj. He had been rushed to the hospital, but he was unconscious. Kamal was in his Greater Noida home then. Within minutes, he got into the Maruti Alto belonging to his mentor and landlord, Shambhu Shikhar, and he was on the road, driving to Gosaiganj. Eight hours later, Kamal was home. The doctors said his father had suffered a brain haemorrhage and was now in a deep coma. They would do everything they could, he was assured.

Four days later, Kamal's father, Ashok Varma, was dead.

~

Varma was a rotund, jolly man with a cheerful disposition. Kamal had grown up with his father as the fulcrum of his world.

His father had been the one to initiate him into poetry. Varma had noticed Kamal's love for poetry and had taken him to kavi sammelans, where Kamal watched, first-hand, poets present their work.

All these memories had come flooding back to Kamal in the days after Varma's death.

Within the family, Varma was the one who understood Kamal the best. Varma had told me how he had wanted Kamal to 'tone down' his rhetoric, especially when it came to his Islamophobic poetry. He had conveyed this to Kamal, repeatedly. But he knew he had been fighting a lost cause.

'*Ya to aag ugal dega ya toh chup rahega, isiliye Kamal Agney naam rakha iska.*' Either Kamal will breathe fire, or he will keep mum; that's why he is called Kamal Agney, his father had told me.

When Kamal would lock himself in a room the entire day, refusing to eat meals or entertain family and friends because he was writing, Varma would cover for him, asking the family to let Kamal be.

Kamal had now lost his cover.

The emotional trauma of losing his father soon brought a wave of financial precariousness for Kamal. The expenses from his father's treatment and the funeral arrangements had been sudden and unexpected. For the next few months, Kamal turned down work offered to him, unable to bring himself to perform, his grief lodging itself inside him, not allowing him to shake it off.

Adding to his own was his mother's grief. Kamal told me his mother had found it very difficult to deal with the suddenness of his father's death. Her world had revolved around him for three decades. In his absence, her world felt empty and was falling apart. Suddenly, from being away from home for months, Kamal had to make regular visits to his family, be it at festivals or occasions where he knew his mother would feel vulnerable, all over again, like his parents' wedding anniversary in February.

The emotional turmoil took a toll on his finances. When I met him in early February 2023, Kamal told me his bank account had just a few thousands left. He had just performed in Rajasthan the previous night, but his car broke down on his return journey to Noida and repairing it cost him nearly Rs 10,000.

Yet Kamal wasn't very bothered by this seemingly precarious existence. He insisted that he had faith in his own abilities and his craft. It was a coping mechanism he had perfected over the last few years, realizing that being a poet without a fixed source of income could mean months of such insecurity.

Initially, this insecurity was largely about his own ability. Each time he didn't get shows he thought he deserved, he would wonder if it had something to do with his talent or the lack of it. But now, after the death of his father, he was no longer insecure about his craft. His worries were about the financial instability that such periods of lack of work brought.

In those months of grief and the all-powerful sense of volatility it brought to all aspects of his life, a grieving, hurting Kamal suddenly chanced upon a new target for his ire: the BJP.

~

For decades now, state patronage has been one of the most important sources of backing for kavi sammelans, enabling them, as well as the poets, to flourish.

One of the most prestigious sammelans in the country, the Rashtriya Kavi Sammelan—colloquially known as the Lal Qila Kavi Sammelan, named after the Red Fort in Delhi, where it is held annually—is backed by the Delhi government's Hindi Academy. Similarly, at the regional and local levels, state and district administrations routinely organize such sammelans, often to mark occasions like when the UP government marked former Prime Minister Atal Bihari Vajpayee's birth anniversary in 2022[27] or when the Modi government organized such sammelans as part of the 75th year celebrations of India's independence.[28]

Access to these events is often tightly controlled, either by bureaucrats or artistes who occupy positions within the ruling administration, as part of their cultural wings and language-based academies. For poets like Kamal, there were only two sure-shot ways to ensure they get invited to these shows: either break into these circuits and become a preferred poet for the government in power, or become so big that it would be difficult to ignore them.

Kamal was neither. What hurt him was not the lack of such popularity but that the government, *his* government, one that he had worked hard to bring to power, had still not taken him into its charmed circles. The mild disgruntlement he had felt in the months following Yogi's victory had now only snowballed in the days after his father's death, in the days when he could have done with more money in his bank account.

What incensed him further was when he saw that the UP government's machinery was still promoting artistes who, unlike him, did not really belong to the Hindutva fold. At the very least, he thought, maybe poets like him could be prioritized into being given positions inside government-controlled cultural organizations.

'Instead, those in government want to be secular. They think we will invite one Muslim poet for the sammelan and no one will call us communal anymore,' he told me when we met in February 2023.

In his annoyance and anger, Kamal recalled the times that he had campaigned for the party's candidates in various seats. So often, the candidates would tell him to 'go hard', code for him to step up the Hindutva rhetoric, stoke anti-Muslim sentiments.

A couple of times he had refused to toe the line, in defiance. They requested him, saying he should speak up for Hindutva. 'I shot back at them. I asked them, "Won't you ever speak of Hindutva? Where is this Hindutva when you invite Muslim poets to kavi sammelans?" They didn't say a word.'

In his vision, fogged by the grief and anger, Kamal had started seeing such contradictions more clearly. He equated his involvement with the Hindu right-wing ecosystem to a game of chess.

He was a pawn in the larger game, a pawn with a specific role and purpose. He was okay with that. He was going to take on a pawn on the other side, within that limited capacity. But for him, what was most important was the clarity of purpose—this was an existential war, and his side had to win if they wanted to survive. He could not tolerate any compromises on that understanding. Inviting and rewarding Muslim artistes, while ignoring your own was a blatant compromise in his world.

~

Yet, as the months rolled in, Kamal started to make peace with the unfairness of being a foot soldier.

In mid-2023, Kamal had finished reading a Hindi translation of Paulo Coelho's *The Alchemist*. He started identifying with the travails of the young shepherd Santiago, and his long, arduous journey to look for buried treasure. For Kamal, what appealed most was the self-discovery the journey forces Santiago to make and the fact that, often, realizing the treasures that one carries within you takes time and patience.

He had, slowly, started taking up more work. One of the first invitations he got was to 'host' a protest, organized by Sudarshan News, a Hindutva propaganda-dishing outlet disguised as a news channel. The channel's founder, Suresh Chavhanke, had been in the crosshairs of the Supreme Court of India for delivering a hate speech in 2021, when he administered an 'oath' to Hindu nationalists to 'fight, die, kill' in order to make India a 'Hindu rashtra'.[29,30]

The Court had come down heavily on the Delhi police for not taking any action against Chavhanke. Upset by this, Chavhanke's channel had organized a 'protest' against the Court's remarks.[31] I wanted to catch Kamal in action, so I decided to join in.

The protest, comprising a few hundred people in Delhi's Jantar Mantar on a balmy Sunday morning in February 2023, featured the Hindutva galaxy of hard-line, rabid nationalists, seated on the stage and ranked by their ability to deliver outrageous hate-filled speeches.

Kamal reached late, so he didn't anchor the protest as planned. Instead, he performed his poetry and delivered a speech in favour of Chavhanke. While most speakers that morning offered words of solidarity to Chavhanke in their brief speeches, some attacked the court, while others prescribed violence against Muslims as the pathway to delivering a Hindu rashtra.

Kamal decided to go one-up on all of them. Instead of a straight-forward speech Kamal asked his audience to join as he administered them an oath to make India a Hindu nation, one very similar to what Chavhanke had delivered in 2021. The act makes him stand out; Kamal shines on the stage briefly, before making a hasty exit.

A few weeks later, Kamal is invited to perform at Bageshwar Dham, a popular site of pilgrimage for Hindus in Madhya Pradesh's Chattarpur district.

The temple had been in the news after its head priest, Dhirendra Shastri, adopted a pronounced pro-Hindutva stance. He had led the 'ghar wapsi' or the religious conversion of Christian tribals into Hinduism; he had also publicly backed Yogi's actions against Muslims in demolishing their homes and had asked Hindus to 'wake up' and 'get the houses of stone-pelters razed by bulldozers'.[32,33,34]

Apart from his Hindutva rhetoric, Shastri had gained fame as a fortune-teller who would, ostensibly, be able to tell people's backstories within minutes of coming face-to-face with them. In his now-perfected modus operandi, devotees who would be seeing him, apparently for the first time ever, would be ushered on the stage. They would have a few seconds to disclose their problem, after which Shashtri would write their backstories on a page and then read it without any help from the devotees themselves.

All this had made Shastri the darling of Hindutva votaries across the country; his videos would routinely go viral on social media and pro-government television channels would offer their viewers breathless coverage of Shashtri's antics. For Kamal to be invited to perform in front of him was a big deal in Kamal's world. He was excited at the prospect and everything that it could lead to, in the future. Kamal knew his performance had to stand out; that this was a big chance to shine before a Hindutva rockstar.

Kamal, during his visit, decided to use Shastri's own famed technique on him—Kamal would tell what was on Shastri's mind, he announced on stage. 'Guruji wants India to be declared a Hindu rashtra. Guruji will bring more people back into the Hindu fold through *ghar wapsi* programmes; Guruji wants to protect Hindu girls from love jihad,' Kamal reads out, each prediction getting more cheer from the audience than before. The fourth prediction, he said, was that Guruji had 'appropriate arrangements' to set the enemies of Hindus right. 'And lastly, Guruji wants to buy a bulldozer for his own protection,' Kamal concludes.

Shastri jumps in his seat with a loud laugh and throws his hands in the air. Kamal's speech was a massive hit.

His visit to Bageshwar Dham symbolized a confluence of Hindutva forces helping each other grow—in his performance, Kamal, as a Hindutva poet, had reiterated Shastri's greatness. In exchange, Shastri, the ecosystem's biggest newsmaker in the past few months, had validated Kamal's credentials.

It was a win-win.

Having bagged these wins, Kamal slowly started making up for the lost time when he didn't work. His shows started again, so did his assignments. His enthusiasm grew again. He shook off his disillusionment and decided that he would continue working towards the Hindutva cause, but not just as a foot soldier who delivered sharp, Hindutva-laced rhetoric wherever he was invited. He wanted more.

He had started talking to people in the BJP, the RSS and those he knew in other Hindu right-wing organizations. He wanted to play a substantial role in the party's 2024 campaign, but not for Modi. He wanted to be a part of Yogi's campaign, devise innovative narratives and ways to deliver those narratives. Those had been his strengths anyway, he told himself.

By March 2023, he had started inking a blueprint for the next phase of his journey. Kamal Agney the poet would now also dabble in being a political adviser. And he planned to start that off by meeting with his Hindutva hero, Yogi Adityanath.

PART 3

Fighting a Cultural War: Sandeep Deo

An Introduction to Sandeep Deo

Sometime around the end of 2019, on a lazy Sunday evening, I got a call from a London-based aunt. She and her husband, my uncle, wanted to chat with me, a rather unusual occurrence.

I believed it to be an impromptu, albeit surprising, outpouring of affection, a delusion I harboured till about a couple of minutes into the call. Their purpose, I soon realized, was somewhat extraordinary.

My uncle, a second-generation immigrant to the UK from Uganda, wanted to donate funds to an Indian journalist who, he said, 'exposes the truth', someone who 'tells it like it really is' and is 'fearless'. This journalist, he added, doesn't just indulge in rhetoric but is always well-researched in what he says.

I was surprised. My uncle was a firm supporter of the BJP and a firmer supporter of the Hindu right-wing. He stopped being a fan of anti-establishment journalism, ever since the BJP became the establishment. His loyalties lay firmly with the Hindu right-wing, and his family members had been part of the Hindu Swayamsevak

Sangh, widely known to be the RSS', overseas wing; none of them had expressed any love for journalists or journalism.

Which was why my ears stood up when he said that. I wanted to know more.

He told me he dedicatedly followed this journalist's work and felt that he needed all the support he could get. His journalism was crucial, and hence, my uncle was ready to do his bit—a few pounds, running into thousands of Indian rupees, would barely matter to him. But before he transferred the money, he wanted to know my thoughts about this journalist.

That is how I stumbled upon Sandeep Deo.

Forty-six-year-old Sandeep is numerous things.

He is a former journalist-turned-author and now also a YouTuber who openly identifies as a Hindu nationalist; he is an ardent supporter of the Hindutva cause, of the BJP, and yet will convincingly insist that he is an objective journalist who spares none.

But more significantly, Sandeep also likens himself to a warrior on the frontlines of what he believes is a cultural war that Hindus are fighting against enemies as disparate as the mainstream media to the West to Islam to Netflix. Hindus, he says, are under attack from all these quarters, and they don't even realize it. Sandeep counts them all as enemies and stokes the fires of fear, anger and hatred against them.

To fight this all-pervasive war, Sandeep has opened multiple war fronts.

The most visible of those fronts is his popular YouTube channel, the grandly named 'India Speaks Daily'. Sandeep is also the editor-in-chief of a news website by the same name as his channel, a website that never strays too far away from Hindutva thought. Through his channel and website, Sandeep constantly espouses the Hindutva cause, promotes it and articulates a Hindu nationalist viewpoint on everyday matters. In doing so, he backs the BJP up most days and launches strident attacks on its rivals, often by spinning a web of facts and half facts.

But that's not what sets him apart. In doing so, Sandeep is just one of the many Hindu nationalist YouTubers who are attracting millions of eyeballs, and dollars, by popularizing their political ideology. He has a greater ambition, which, if fulfilled, could help Hindutva expand into newer, more insidious frontiers.

Sandeep is the founder of a publishing house called Kapot, which specializes in bringing out books that promote hard-line Hindu nationalism. Kapot aims to propagate Hindutva through the written word, by channelling the ideology into books across various genres, from spirituality and religion to politics and history. Its books revisit history, offering a fresh spin on historical events or justifying historical wrongs in ways that suit Hindu nationalists.

The range of books Kapot publishes and distributes is vast: from books that specialize in 'unmasking the realities' of 'Abrahamic religions', a category on its website—titles like *Love Jihad or Predatory Dawah? Shocking Ground Stories of Conversion*—to books on history like *Heroic Hindu Resistance to Muslim Invaders* and *Kaun Kehta Hai Akbar Mahaan Tha?* Kapot also sells numerous books that justify the killing of Mahatma Gandhi by Nathuram Godse,[1] as well as books that recast Congress leaders who fought for the country's independence in poor light, from Nehru[2] to Gandhi.[3,4]

Sandeep's own experience as an author drives much of this curation. He has authored six books in Hindi—including *Hamare Shri Guruji,* a biography of the Hindu nationalist ideologue and former RSS chief, M.S. Golwalkar, who wanted Hindus to take a leaf out of the Nazi playbook in dealing with the country's minorities.[5] Sandeep's first book, written in 2012, *Sajish Ki Kahani Tathyo Ki Zubani,* decries the Gujarat riots of 2002 that killed nearly 1200 people, mostly Muslims, as a conspiracy against Modi.[6] He has also

authored biographies of UP Chief Minister Yogi Adityanath and
Baba Ramdev, the yoga teacher-turned-entrepreneur known for his
proximity to the Hindu right-wing.

Kapot has been growing in popularity—it sells over 2,200 titles,
and in 2022, it sold over 25,000 books, according to Sandeep's
office.

As Sandeep sees it, launching a publishing arm has multifold
strategic benefits. To him, books offer a chance to rewrite history
the way he likes it, to grant legitimacy to some of the deepest fears
and biases that Hindu nationalists hold and to propagate it to many
more. Sandeep, in line with the Hindu Mahasabha and the RSS,
also stresses on character-building as a key step in becoming a true
Hindutva warrior. For him, books are a way to bring about a moral
Hindu consciousness.

As a result, Kapot's collection ranges from the unabashedly
political to the deeply religious, always taking care to emphasize
Hindutva ideals, either way. But even as he expands his publishing,
Sandeep also wants to puncture the oligopolist online book
distribution networks that he believes pose a threat to the growth
of Hindutva.

According to Sandeep, the West, through its many private
corporations, controls the country's e-commerce networks and
thereby has the power to shape the distribution of books in India.
He is not far off. Amazon.in and Flipkart, the retail giants that
have dominated India's e-commerce landscape, are backed by
US-based multinational companies Amazon.com and Walmart,
respectively.

For him, this means that these handful of Western corporations
are dictating what Indians must and must not read. In its war against
Hindus and Hindutva, the West, through these corporations, are
going to come gunning for books that champion the Hindutva
cause.

Hence, Sandeep isn't content just publishing these books—he has publicly announced an audacious boycott of both these e-commerce websites. He refuses to use these two e-commerce websites to sell books that Kapot publishes and distributes.

Instead, he has created his own e-commerce website to bypass these, what he calls, 'anti-Hindu' e-commerce websites.

On this website, also called Kapot, Sandeep has listed all his over 2,200 titles that he is distributing and publishing across India and also across the globe. But steadily, Sandeep and his brother, Amardeep, are expanding the website to become a Hindu, 'swadeshi', homegrown e-commerce website, where they will sell only domestically manufactured objects—right from books to common household items.

There's already a glimpse of what that would look like: by Diwali of 2022, the website had started selling what it called 'Swadeshi Lights', fairy lights made in India, as well as poojan samagri, essentials for Hindu prayer rituals. The Deo brothers are conscious that the website has to be in sync with Sandeep's persona as a Hindutva warrior. This integration of ideology with commerce has led them to expand in 2023 to selling home temples and religious paraphernalia.

But Sandeep is conscious about the limitations of this war, and of fighting against his enemies in the digital world alone. His own life, his childhood growing up in rural Darbhanga, Bihar, has taught him that social media, though important, will not reach the deepest corners of the country he wishes to reach and rouse with Hindutva thought.

And so Sandeep's next step is to take this cultural war offline, to smaller cities and towns. Sandeep intends to open bookstores-cum-libraries across 1,000 Indian towns and cities, where these books can be bought as well as read in-store so that those who can't afford to buy them can still be enlisted in his war.

But the most significant of his plans, Sandeep's Brahmastra, is to open centres that will teach Hindu boys shaastra, religious scriptures, as well as shastra, the use of weapons. For him, both deep knowledge of religion, as well as the capability to physically fight 'enemies', are equally critical in this cultural war. The funds that he collects from those like my uncle, he insists, will go towards these centres.

It is clear that Sandeep's propositions are immensely popular and strike a chord: he enjoys nearly 430,000 followers across social media platforms, many of whom fund his ventures. Sandeep's effort to position himself as a part warrior, part spiritual guide to Hindus, might have something to do with this. When he isn't warning them about this impending cultural war, Sandeep, well-versed with Hindu religious literature, narrates stories from Hindu scriptures and mythologies, imbibed with modern lessons for his followers. This combination—of being a hard-nosed 'journalist' with sharp takes on politics in the day and a spiritual guiding light by night—endears him to many.

A mark of his popularity lies in the many unsolicited calls and messages he is flooded with, where harried Hindu followers reveal their moral dilemmas and life troubles, asking him for guidance. Like the thirty-year-old who kept calling Sandeep while he was in the middle of recording a YouTube livestream, while I sat next to him, in his office in west Delhi's Uttam Nagar. The man was inspired by Sandeep's words and his spiritual prowess and was turning to him as a desperate cry for help: at thirty, he said, he didn't know what he wanted to do.

The confusion was killing him, and only Sandeep could help him out.

～

In the early twentieth century, Hindu nationalism started getting 'organized' into outfits that championed the Hindu cause exclusively. In 1915, the Akhil Bharatiya Hindu Mahasabha emerged. The Mahasabha mentioned earlier in the book, was an umbrella group consisting of provincial-level smaller sabhas, assemblies of Hindus, and its agenda was 'distinctly anti-Muslim'.[7] A decade later, the RSS was founded in September 1925 in Nagpur. Both these groups held the objective of furthering Hindu predominance and consciousness in order to solidify a Hindu identity in line with their ideologies.[8]

The Mahasabha, especially under the leadership of Vinayak Savarkar, focused on singling out Muslims and Christians as the biggest threats that Hindus faced.[9] The Mahasabha insisted that the way to tackle these 'threats' was for Hindus to unite by rising above their internal disunity and divisions caused by castes and subcastes. In addition, the Mahasabha proposed the militarization of Hindus by training them in self-defence as well as the use of weapons.[10]

The RSS agreed. Golwalkar, who also served as the RSS's second sarsanghchalak, chief leader, and one of its most important ideologues, said that Hindus 'were in a state of war' and would have to fight to win their freedom.[11]

The war and the fight for freedom weren't just from the country's colonial masters. For Golwalkar, the war was a 'triangular' one: between the Hindus, the British and the Muslims.[12]

Nearly a century after some of the earliest Hindutva ideologues made these pronouncements, Sandeep is shaking the dust off them and repackaging those beliefs—of a cultural war, of an existential threat to Hindus and of the need to fight back—to newer generations of Hindus who might have never heard about the Mahasabha, otherwise.

Much of what Sandeep says is rooted in early Hindu nationalist movements, but with a new twist. His war is one that Hindutva figures believe they have been fighting for centuries. Except, for

Sandeep, this is a war that he fights, where he is the master strategist, he is the warmonger and is also the charioteer, leading Hindus into the war.

Helping him mobilize soldiers and resources for this war is the internet.

India's YouTube streams are filled with influencers like Sandeep, who are aligned with the Hindu right-wing and provide everything, from polemical, communally charged rhetoric to 'analysis' and perspective. The style is uniformly common too—live videos from makeshift studios set up in their homes and offices, mostly alone, sometimes with other 'expert' guests—offering their takes on current affairs events.

Such influencers perform useful roles for the BJP—on any given issue, they become valuable voices for the party to shape public thought and discourse covertly in ways that it wants, without directly getting involved in it. These influencers, often, lay the ground for the Modi government's actions by creating consensus on critical issues. As a result, when the government finally takes decisions on those issues, a substantial section of the party's base is already likely to have been convinced of its need, thereby allowing the party to drown out any criticism of its actions. This played out to perfection when the Modi government decided to abrogate Article 370 of the Indian Constitution, stripping Jammu and Kashmir of its autonomy. While most others were stunned at the hurried manner in which the decision was taken without consulting many of the stakeholders, the BJP's supporters backed it firmly—having been constantly fed the rhetoric that scrapping the region's special powers would help local Kashmiri Hindus 'fight back'.[13]

These influencers also, often, peddle narratives that might be too controversial for the party itself to officially peddle.

For instance, in October 2022, a minister in the ruling Aam Aadmi Party of the Delhi government, Rajendra Pal Gautam, courted criticism from the BJP when he attended an event where 10,000 people converted to Buddhism after they were administered vows that Dr B.R. Ambedkar, the Dalit reformer and architect of India's written constitution, administered to his followers wanting to embrace Buddhism.

The BJP leaders latched on to the event, circulated its videos and referred to it and Gautam as being 'anti-Hindu'.[14] Media reports called the criticism a 'calibrated campaign'.[15] Sandeep took the issue up in a video and went further, calling the AAP a party that is an agent of 'Christianity'.[16] He lashed out at Gautam and at followers of Ambedkar, saying they were malechchh, a casteist slur often used to target those born into lower castes.[17] Sandeep said 'these neo-Buddhists' were no better than Christians, and were 'indirectly' agents of those 'Abrahamic' people.

Sandeep's rhetoric targeting neo-Buddhists as well as Dalits is a rhetoric that the BJP could never employ since it had been actively trying to win over Dalit communities.[18] But Sandeep can do that, and his doing so can help the BJP—his rhetoric helps consolidate the BJP's Hindu voters by painting its main rival in Delhi, the Aam Aadmi Party, as being anti-Hindu.

In times when Hindutva is the dominant, mainstream political ideology, taking such strident stances also makes commercial sense for Sandeep. According to Social Blade, a US-based website that tracks social media analytics, Sandeep's YouTube channel, India Speaks Daily, on the back of its followers and reach, possibly earns as much as $30,000 or nearly Rs 2,500,000 a year.[19]

It's not surprising then that more and more YouTube influencers are doing what Sandeep does: promote Hindutva causes online.

A study published in July 2021 by First Draft, a global non-profit working to track disinformation on social media, had found how Islamophobic content from India flourished on YouTube and, in fact, pushed viewers down rabbit holes of anti-Muslim content on the platform.[20] The study had found how content that centred around demonizing Muslims and blaming them for the spread of Covid-19 in India flourished on YouTube.

Similarly, in June 2022, a report by the New York University Stern Center for Business and Human Rights said that the 'most troubling abuse of YouTube in India', which at 450 million users is the platform's biggest market, was the 'targeting of Muslims by backers of ruling BJP and other right-leaning Hindu nationalist groups'.[21] Like Sandeep.

Through his videos, he ends up benefiting the BJP in different ways—on rare days when the party is facing criticism, Sandeep will spin the events in a way that the criticism is forgotten: facts are conveniently chosen, and events are selectively highlighted.

In June 2020, Indian and Chinese soldiers posted along the Line of Actual Control (LAC) saw a fierce clash break out between them in Ladakh's Galwan Valley. The clash saw twenty Indian soldiers killed and many others injured. However, the Chinese side refused to reveal the casualties on its side, leading to much intrigue and speculation about the real extent of damage suffered by China in the clashes. The clashes had been the worst-ever peacetime attack on Indian soldiers in decades, and the Modi government had faced flak from several military experts as well as Opposition parties over its lack of transparency in dealing with Chinese aggression. Many within the establishment were keen to portray India as the 'winner' after the violent clash. A minister in the Modi government, former Army Chief General V.K. Singh (retd) said more than forty Chinese soldiers had been killed in the clash.[22] The Northern Army Commander, Lieutenant General Y.K. Joshi, said that at least forty-five Chinese soldiers had been killed.[23]

On pro-government news channels and social media handles, various unverified claims were bandied about, speculating on the casualties on the Chinese side.[24, 25] Claims of Chinese casualties by Indian officials ranged from forty to hundred.[26]

In some cases, news anchors even cited viral WhatsApp messages as their source to insist that the Chinese had suffered heavily at the hands of Indian soldiers.[27] Much of this was an effort to prop up a counter to the criticism the government was facing, and to help reiterate the muscular nationalism that the Modi government had cultivated for itself. Fact-checkers were having a field day in the interim, debunking many of these claims.[28]

Eight months on, in February 2021, the Chinese side finally admitted that four soldiers had been killed. From the claims of 100 casualties, four seemed an underwhelming number. But not for Deo.

In a live video on his YouTube channel, Sandeep uses the Chinese admission of deaths—even if it is a fraction of the casualties claimed by Indians—to claim a victory over the Chinese. But while he does this, he uses the Chinese admission to hit out at critics of the government as well as fact-checkers who had flagged unverified claims of Chinese casualties earlier.

His performance begins with lavish claims—about Chinese propaganda being run from 'a massive building in China', and how China has cultivated agents everywhere, across the globe, as well as in India.[29] While he does that, on the screen, alongside his face crops up a 2008 photo of former Congress Chief Rahul Gandhi, in a handshake with Chinese President Xi Jinping. Gandhi, he says, is 'Chinese agent number 1, who is the umbrella agent … and keeps talking in favour of China.'

He does not offer much proof. He refers to a statement Gandhi made, criticizing the fact that Indian soldiers had been unarmed, as per media reports of the incident.[30] Incredulously, Sandeep says that China admitting to the four deaths was proof that 'their necks were broken', and that Gandhi was wrong, refusing to remind his viewers that the Indian side lost twenty soldiers. Chinese admissions had exposed Gandhi and had shown that he was lying, and his propaganda had failed he insists. With his claims, Sandeep manages to divert his followers' attention from the underwhelming Chinese admission and the inaccurate Indian claims. Instead, he takes their attention towards a familiar old enemy in Gandhi.

As his video rolls on, his audiences lap it up. The comments section is buzzing—one man named Chandrabhan Pandey, writing in all caps, is furious. 'WHAT STOPS US FROM HANGING THESE TRAITORS?' he asks. Another asks for a ban on Alt News, a fact-checking agency that Sandeep targets. Alt News had earlier called out the unverified claims of dozens of Chinese casualties to be misinformation. One more user asks that the BBC be banned from India. Many ask for Gandhi to be jailed; some call him a traitor, others call him worse names. During the thirty-seven-minute-long video, over 150 people have commented on it, and it has got over 35,000 views in minutes.

Sandeep's deed is done.

~

Sandeep's speeches on his YouTube channel often come across as masterfully crafted performances that evoke a range of emotions, from fear to anger to hate and relief. His speeches typically begin with him invoking fear and anger against an enemy—it could be anyone, from a rival politician to the Muslim community, to the West, to the media. Slowly, he builds his case up and simultaneously builds up his audience's anger. Sandeep's build-up makes them feel like they are wronged, or that they have been betrayed, or they are in danger, depending on the occasion.

The fear and the anger hit a crescendo—in the live comments, people start suggesting drastic solutions to the issue and claim helplessness. If they are looking to Sandeep for his sympathy, they are wrong. He chides them, nearly mocks them for being content with venting their ire in the comments section. What are you doing to fight this enemy, he would ask. The answer was implicit in the question: nothing.

But I am doing something, he would then say. He would list out his work: the publishing house, the books that it brings out, the training centres he wants to open, the e-commerce website. But what are you doing, he would ask again. Is it enough to just keep listening to these videos? Sandeep will tell them that he is trying to protect Hindus and build a Hindu ecosystem. Single-handedly.

Sandeep tries to inject guilt into an audience that is angry and scared. He lets those emotions fester through the talk. Then, just before he ends, Sandeep offers them a solution—fund me, he will say. Support me with money. 'The food for your body is not free, is it? Then how can food for thought be free?' he once asked in one of his many carefully crafted pieces.

By the end of the video, the audience, livid, scared and overwhelmed by the task of fighting the enemy, gets an easy solution from Sandeep—they don't have to go fight the war themselves.

All they have to do is to back Sandeep. He is their warrior. He will fight for them.

A Glimpse, a Warning and an Enemy: The Grip That Deo Enjoys

It's just days before India's Independence Day in 2021. On a warm Sunday morning, Sandeep, along with members of his staff, was headed to Delhi's protest site, Jantar Mantar.

Jantar Mantar is an eighteenth-century site in the heart of Delhi that was originally designed to be an astronomical observatory but now serves as an iconic site for protesters of all hues.

That morning Jantar Mantar was all set to see a public rally titled Bharat Jodo (Unite India) movement, where protesters were gathering to demand the scrapping of colonial-era laws of India's legal systems. Hidden by the anti-colonial fervour of the demand was an insidious link to the Hindu right-wing: through the protests, led by BJP leader Ashwini Upadhyay, the movement demanded the ushering of a uniform civil code by scrapping religion-specific personal laws, an old demand in the Hindu right, especially aimed at Muslim personal laws.

Dressed in his favourite mustard honey shirt and a beige cloth mask, which kept falling off his chin, Sandeep headed to the rally. But he soon realizes that the police had changed the location of the rally at the very last minute and have blocked off the roads for vehicular traffic. Sandeep had no option but to walk for nearly 2 km, a fact that he will then repeatedly mention in his live video that night as proof of both his commitment to the Hindutva cause and the government's strong-arm tactics in quelling the protest.

Hours after the rally, he was back on air, hosting a live interview with Ashwini, the main organizer of the protest.

Ashwini, a little-known BJP leader and a Supreme Court advocate from Delhi, is a regular on Sandeep's YouTube channel. For years, Ashwini's claim to fame was that he was a 'founder-member' of the Aam Aadmi Party who was unceremoniously shown the door by the party for 'anti-party activities' after he criticized party supremo Arvind Kejriwal. Six months later, he joined the BJP.

While he might not be courted by prime-time television channels for their nightly debates, Ashwini has been a regular on Sandeep's live shows. The relationship is a symbiotic one. For Ashwini, it's a platform to showcase his work, which is primarily to file Public Interest Litigations (PIL) on issues closely connected to the Hindutva cause. For Sandeep, who constantly refers to Ashwini as his 'old friend', it's a chance to burnish his credentials further by showcasing his proximity to the BJP, albeit on the 'right' causes.

In the Hindu right-wing circles, Ashwini enjoys a semi-charmed reputation—while he might not be famous, many believe his petitions prod and push the government to take up the Hindutva agenda. One digital news outlet introduced Ashwini as 'the man whose PILs force the government into making laws'.[1]

Sandeep, introducing Ashwini, recounts how the lawyer had
filed petitions urging the SC to scrap Article 370 and Triple Talaq,
much before the Modi government moved to do so.

That night, though, the circumstances are very different. The
Jantar Mantar protests made headlines, albeit for the wrong reasons.
Ashwini had called for the agitation to press the government to
accept his demands. A few thousand protesters turned up, but the
agenda was no longer the stated one—the meeting featured members
of militant Hindu right-wing organizations who raised cries of a
genocide against Muslims.[2] One clip showed a group of men, likely to
be in their twenties and thirties, in frenzied sloganeering, threatening
to kill Muslims while invoking the name of Ram.[3] Another clip
showed the same members asking other Hindus to boycott Muslims
economically.[4] Ashwini, too, gave a speech comparing the mass
exodus of Kashmiri Hindus from Jammu and Kashmir in the early
1990s to the situation in West Bengal, a trope employed by many
other leaders of the BJP in criticizing the violence in the Trinamool
Congress-run state.

Ashwini had spent the last few months spearheading a demand
to repeal 222 'black colonial-era laws', including the Indian Penal
Code of 1860, which is the bedrock of the country's criminal
justice system. Instead, Ashwini had demanded those laws be re-
drafted to reflect contemporary realities. His demands were not
politics-agnostic. Among the new laws, he had also demanded five
in harmony with the Hindu right-wing's politics—from a new
law to control the population growth to a uniform civil code for
all religious faiths, both of which are key demands of the Sangh
Parivar. Ashwini had also demanded a uniform educational code,
a thinly veiled attack on centres of Islamic learning such as the
Madrasas.

On that day, all the people who had backed his politics all along
were roused into action at Jantar Mantar.

The hate speeches and hate slogans went viral on social media, sparking outrage among users. As the gathering started dominating the headlines, the pressure on the Modi government, which controls the Delhi police, grew. Just two weeks before the event, the visiting US Secretary of State Antony Blinken had given Modi enough indications that the US was watching the country's flailing human rights situation.

Amidst mounting pressure, Ashwini appeared on Sandeep's show that evening—one of the few shows that he was seen on.

~

First, Sandeep appears on the screen, looking anguished.[5] He has a bone to pick with Ashwini, but not about the hate-filled slogans. 'Why wasn't the protest organized any better? People had come with clothes, thinking they will occupy the site for three to four days at least, but the protest wrapped up in half a day,' he asks Ashwini.

On his part, Ashwini apologizes and blames the Delhi police for shifting the location of the protest at the very last minute and for blocking roads in order to dissuade protesters from reaching the site. Sandeep chimes in, repeating how he had to walk for kilometres at end.

Ashwini talks about a 'conspiracy' to scuttle his agitation; Deo agrees. Both are circumspect, but the target slowly becomes clear— the Modi government and its Delhi Police. As the conversation rolls on, Sandeep is angrier than Ashwini. 'I don't want to take names, but governments only point to problems of Hindus and spread negativity just before elections to win votes. They don't solve anything,' he says, adding that even the revolutionary Chandrashekhar Azad was betrayed by his own people.

Emboldened, Ashwini takes one more thinly veiled dig at the Modi government. 'People have realized that they have been made fools, by constantly reminding them of what Mughal emperors did,' he says. 'They want a permanent solution now,' Ashwini adds with a straight face.

Sandeep jumps in. 'I have been working at providing a solution,' he says, listing out his priorities. 'Through an app, through publication and through e-commerce. We need to give Hindus a solution, or else nothing will change.'

This 'solution' in their world can mean very different things—for Sandeep, it means fighting, what he calls a 'cultural war', with tools like more books, videos, Vedic education, while for Ashwini, it means laws to control the population or demanding a law against 'deceitful conversions' or making yoga compulsory in schools for children between the ages of six to fourteen.

But the subtext, either way, is clear—the Hindu identity needs to be reinforced and reiterated, the 'enemy' needs to be called out, through publications or law.

For now, there are other battles to be fought, including one against their own. The pressure to act against Ashwini and the sloganeers is growing; that night, the Delhi Police, under Home Minister Amit Shah, announce an FIR and probe against Ashwini and six others.

By the end of the fifty-minute conversation, the pressure shows, and Ashwini is in tears.

Sandeep tells Ashwini not to be disheartened. After all, he adds, Ashwini's morning meeting had 'injected the people with some hope'. Neither of them discusses the hate slogans, nor is there any condemnation. Instead, Sandeep hails all those who participated in the meeting, calling them '*shuddh, sanatani, 24 karat Hindu(s)*'.

It was a tricky predicament for Sandeep.

Had that march and the subsequent police heat on Sandeep occurred in a state ruled by an Opposition party, he would have had the playbook ready. He could have blamed the police for being biased and 'anti-Hindu'.

But in this case, the authorities acting against Ashwini were firmly in control of Union Home Minister Amit Shah. Blaming their actions would mean pointing a finger towards Shah, a demigod in the Hindu nationalist pantheon.

So, what does he do? The next day, Sandeep is back again on his YouTube channel, alleging that the leftists and liberal media organizations had unleashed a 'conspiracy' against the march to characterize it as a march against the 'M community'.[6] He claims to have 'point-by-point proof' that it was a *badi saazish*, big conspiracy, to defame the march. He zooms in on a discussion hosted by journalist Barkha Dutt and targets each participant in the debate, alleges that all of them are critics of the BJP and, hence, deserve to be discredited.

This reasoning is consistent throughout the livestream. He then moves to target another journalist, Vinod Kapri, who had shared clips showing incendiary slogans being chanted at Jantar Mantar. Sandeep has nothing to say about the slogans but takes offence at Kapri sharing them, saying that Kapri provoked outrage with his tweets and that was a sign of 'conspiracy' designed to break Hindu unity.

These attempts are unsuccessful. The next day, Ashwini is summoned to the police station and is detained through the day till the wee hours of the morning before being arrested.

For Sandeep, the arrest feels like a personal blow. His patience with the Modi government now wearing thin, he realizes that he can't continue to blame the media for the arrest while sheltering the BJP government.

That evening, when he comes online, the gloves are off.[7]

Dressed in a navy blue collared T-shirt, Sandeep appears dishevelled. His t-shirt has creases, and he has stubble, for which he even apologizes. '*Bhaag daud ho rahi hai, isiliye aap ke beech aa nahi saka. Shave karne ka samay nahi mila.*' I have been running around and haven't had the chance to come before you all any earlier. I haven't even had the time to shave.

Talking about the arrest, Sandeep says Ashwini 'was treated like a terrorist, like a criminal' by being detained till 3 a.m.

The evening's talk is a demonstration of the influence that people like Sandeep, small players in the large sea of the Hindu right ecosystem, carry and wield at will.

Sandeep's criticism of the Delhi Police's treatment of Ashwini is the first indication of the surprising turn his rhetoric is going to take that evening. He lists out Ashwini's past PILs, on scrapping Article 370, on Triple Talaq. 'He filed the PIL much before the government took those decisions. The credit for the decisions went to Modi and Shah, but the work was his,' Sandeep says. And yet, Sandeep argues, the leadership had all but abandoned Ashwini when he raised issues close to the Sangh Parivar. He carefully criticizes the leadership, without going overboard.

The live chat window, beside his YouTube video, is a window into the minds of his viewers. On days like these, it offers a silent demonstration of Sandeep's grip over them. Within minutes, the chat window, hosting tens of thousands of viewers, echoes his anger and criticism of the BJP's top leadership. One viewer says he doesn't trust 'MoSha' anymore. Another, under the pseudonym 'Hindu Traveller', is blunt. '*Modi toh dhongi nikla.*' Modi turned out to be a fraud. This sentiment of betrayal is consistent. 'Another viewer says, '*BJP dhokebaaz nikla.*' The BJP is a deceiver.

Such vindication only fuels Sandeep's rhetoric. He says that if Ashwini had been arrested by a Congress-led government, Hindus would have been on the streets. 'But today, I am not able to say anything. There is an attempt to limit Hindutva to one party, one man and one organization,' he says, with thousands watching.

'*Vikalp-heenta ki paristithi nirman ki gayi hai,*' he concludes. You are being made to feel that you have no alternatives.

A user in the chat section sends a response. '*Mullah Modi,*' he writes.[8]

Sandeep has achieved what he set out to do; the anger against the government is growing.

This show of 'independence', where Sandeep criticizes the BJP on occasion, is important for his credentials as a nationalist, Hindutva warrior-journalist. Such critique by him shows his followers that he fears none, nor will he be ready to take favours from anyone. Such occasional criticism allows him to burnish his credentials as the BJP's conscience-keeper; for his audiences, it's a message that he will stick to the *truth* no matter how inconvenient it is for the powers that be, even if they belong to his own party.

Hours after Sandeep's video was broadcast, Ashwini is granted bail by a local court.

~

Sandeep's power over his audience does not come from his strident political views alone. For his followers, Sandeep is a political pundit but also a spiritual guide. He is a frank, fearless journalist as well as a morally righteous family man. He is a Hindutva warrior in the truest sense—a man who straddles moral, spiritual duties and responsibilities with equal ease.

With an eye on his long-term plans, Sandeep has sought to position himself as all this through the multiple avatars he has.

His day avatar sees Sandeep offer his sharply worded opinions on political happenings, often slaying both friend and foe. But come night-time, Sandeep takes on a different form as the spiritual mentor, discussing and offering wisdom from Hindu mythology and religious texts. He even appears on a different channel, 'Journey With Sandeep Deo', where each night he discusses one episode from the Hindu mythologies, mostly the Ramayana and Mahabharata, and underlines the lessons that those episodes hold for the modern life. Sometimes he dips into history, at other times into religion.

Late one night, Sandeep talks about Prahlad, the son of the demon king Hiranyakashyapu, who grew up not to follow his demon father's path but Vishnu's. It was a miracle—how could the son of a demon's, demon, not become like him. Sandeep believed this was because the Guru Narad had given a mantra to Prahlad's mother, Kayadhu, when she was pregnant with him. This was the first time the concept of psychology was employed to transform the sanskar, the social behaviour of a foetus, and transform him from a demon to a disciple, Sandeep tells his audience. This tale was proof that expectant mothers could shape the child's sanskar. But this had been forgotten in the modern era, Sandeep lamented.

'Aaj kal yeh naya fashion chal gaya hai … surrogacy mother.' There's a new trend in town, that of a surrogate mother. He said it was fine for those women who had trouble conceiving children. 'Lekin fashion mein, kahi hamaari body kharab ho jaayegi … Priyanka Chopra, Shah Rukh Khan ki wife, alag alag heroine jo aap dekh rakhein hai, yeh log toh garbh mein bachon ko rakhna bhi nahi chahti.' But, this trend, that pregnancy will affect the way we look … be it Priyanka Chopra or Shah Rukh Khan's wife, all these different heroines that you see, they don't even want to keep children in their wombs.

Sandeep said this degeneration threatened to overturn what Prahlad's mother had managed—a transformation from demon to human. 'Yeh toh aur bhi danav ki pravruti inn sab mein aati jaa rahi hai.' This will only increase demonic tendencies in society.

Sandeep doesn't stop at imparting wisdom. He also fields questions from troubled followers who share their woes, moral conundrums and frustrations. One night in May 2022, Sandeep delivers an angry, stinging monologue on what he sees as the absolute refusal of Hindus to back other Hindus like him when they stand for their religion's cause.

He reminds his viewers of how Vishnu, the Hindu God of creation and protection, killed Hiranyakashyapu, the father of Prahlad, because the King was becoming a threat to his son's devotion. In the modern context, he equates Prahlad to Yati Narsinghanand Saraswati, the head of a Hindu temple in Dasna, who had only in January 2022, four months before this video, been arrested for his speech in a religious convention after he called for violence against Muslims so that India could be 'Islam-free'.[9]

Sandeep has just returned from a meeting with Saraswati and is livid at how the latter had been treated. Hindus, Sandeep thundered, were refusing to back one of their own. His monologue attacked the BJP government in Uttarakhand, whose police force arrested Saraswati. But he also doesn't spare the Modi government. He is angry that Saraswati was not being allowed to hold a mass-conversion event, where Muslims would be brought into the Hindu fold, *ghar wapsi*, a return to home in the parlance of the Hindu right-wing ecosystem which believes all Muslims to be forcefully converted Hindus of the past.

'*Yeh woh sarkaar hai, jo UAE ka Badshah agar guzzar jaaye, uske liye Bharat ke jhande jhuka deti hai, yeh sarkaar soch rahi thi ki yeh ho gaya toh unki badnaami hogi.*' This is that government which, when the UAE's king dies, lowers the Indian flag. This government feared a bad name if such an event were to be held.

His words rattle his listeners. One asks, how will Hindus win this war? Another says he wants to send money to Saraswati. Yet another says the time is ripe for a bank that caters only to Hindus. Sandeep agrees to all of this. He reveals that he is working on a proposal, where Hindu victims will get financial help. He doesn't reveal much more; he doesn't need to. The screen flashes the next question from another worried follower. He moves on, so do his followers.

~

For many of his followers, these worries become existential, and Sandeep is forced to alternate between the roles of a political rabble-rouser and a spiritual guide.

In the same month, Sandeep holds a 'Q&A' session where he takes questions from his viewers. One viewer writes in, overwhelmed with his worries for the Hindu community:

> *Rashtra ki aur lautna hi hai, M ki pushtakein padhni zaroori ho gayi hai … chain nahin aa raha hai, padhai mein mann nahi lagta. Kaise bachein yeh sochta rehta hun.*

We must start paying more attention towards our nation. It has become critical to read about M (Muslims) … I just can't be at ease, I keep worrying about how we will survive.

Sandeep can relate to such fears.

In March 2021, on a hot summer day in his office-cum-newsroom-cum-studio in Uttam Nagar, such thoughts had occupied his mind, too. I had been visiting him for a few days already; these were some of our first in-person interactions, delayed thanks to the Covid-19 outbreak.

Late in the afternoon, after he had finished recording his live video for the day, we stepped out for lunch. A minute's walk away was a restaurant named Himalaya Sagar, where Sandeep clearly seemed a regular. The manager's eyes lit up when he saw Sandeep and came to our table enthusiastically. Sandeep shared his enthusiasm. He asked the manager the day's specials. The manager spat out a quickfire list of items. Nothing seemed to impress Sandeep. He looked around, distracted. Weighing his options, Sandeep warily placed his order and then, finally, asked the manager what had been on his mind for all these minutes since we had walked in. '*Kitchen mein sab apne hi log hai na? Woh log toh nahi na?*' You've employed only our people in your kitchen, right? None of *those* guys, right?

The manager broke into a reassuring smile and told Sandeep that the kitchen only had *our* people. '*Yeh log thukte hai khaane mein.*' These guys spit in our food, Sandeep offered as an explanation, looking at me and his brother Amardeep, who had joined us for lunch.

Such worries remain ingrained in Sandeep even though he tries to fight them publicly.

But in a live video session nearly a year later, Sandeep, donning the counsellor's robes, had to rise above his own worries.

As soon as a worried Hindu follower expressed his anxieties, Sandeep immediately shook his head in disapproval. 'Why are you thinking of yourself as Vishnu?' he admonishes the worrier. Sandeep refers to mythology to convince him. 'Don't be disheartened at all. Did Krishna ever get disheartened when Arjun was not able to understand his instructions?' Sandeep says.

'This battle', Sandeep says, without offering many details, 'will last a thousand years. What are we going to do in just forty to fifty years anyway?'

Such counselling comes naturally and frequently to Sandeep. After the first lockdown was imposed across the country in March 2020, Sandeep said he started getting calls and messages from many of his followers, many of them couples.

'Wives called me and told me their husbands were at home the whole day and fighting with them,' Sandeep says. Most others would have dismissed the complaints. Sandeep did, too, initially.

'I thought to myself, I haven't opened a counselling centre.'

But he wasn't at ease knowing he was ignoring those pleas for help. So Sandeep's night-time avatar took over, and he decided to narrate *bodh kathayein*, short stories that generally carry moral values. Each night, Sandeep, locked in his Uttam Nagar home, would arrive online and narrate these tales. He did not need books to refer to; Sandeep had read so many such stories growing up that narrating those came easy.

For Sandeep, it was a simple and effective way to ensure an end to domestic squabbles. 'In those days of the lockdown, people had trouble sleeping, they would be confused and anxious.' But after he started narrating these stories, those troubles abated, he says. 'They told me they were now getting sound sleep, after listening to my stories.'

Sandeep realizes that it is this popularity, on subjects far beyond the everyday politics, that makes him stand out in a sea of YouTube influencers and Hindutva warriors. They, he argues, are not fighting for the cause like he is. Most are *bike hue,* sold out. Some sold out to fame, some others to a political party, some more to money.

'Most of them come online and deliver hard political analyses in the night. Why? Because that's when NRIs wake up, and the NRI viewership is very high during nights.' But Sandeep says he doesn't do that. 'Because I realized that delivering such news and analyses to my viewers in India at night was disturbing them, was not letting them sleep well.' Despite the obvious financial losses to him, Sandeep says he won't do such shows in the night because of the impact it has on his followers.

In March 2021, Sandeep says the opposite on one of his shows. During one of his sessions, he explains to his audience that he keeps 'expose-related shows' for the night because that's when his NRI audience can also join in.

Yet, such contradictions aside, his audience laps up his many avatars. Two years ago, when Sandeep was in his office, a well-dressed young man walked in. He was despondent, he told Sandeep. He was thirty, and he didn't know what to do with his life. 'He told me, "I see your videos, and I realize that I have wasted my life,"' Sandeep says.

Sandeep's passion for the subjects he talks about, the panache with which he does his work and the way he influences opinions—the young man had wanted it all but had none of it. So he found Sandeep's office address online and decided to walk in, confident that the man he had admired so deeply would have an answer.

'I told him to stop saying you have wasted your life,' Sandeep said, before pointing to the Kentucky Fried Chicken (KFC), the popular American eatery chain. 'The owner founded the brand when he was sixty.'

But that wasn't enough, Sandeep realized. He didn't know much about this man, but it didn't really matter. 'I told him, if you are depressed, it means you are looking at others more and not within yourself. You have spent thirty years judging others, but not yourself.'

Sandeep banished him after advising him to look within. He never heard back from the man. Such unannounced visits are common at Sandeep's office, he says. 'I have got many to quit their jobs,' says Sandeep, laughing.

But the most common and the most frequent of these visits and requests for interventions comes from parents and their children.

'Sometimes, parents drag their children here, and sometimes, it's the other way round.' Both have complaints against each other and can't seem to reach a point of resolution. Sandeep believes this is a crisis of moral clarity. 'Parents are confused and, hence, children are confused. It is like being on a boat but not knowing where to go.'

Sandeep is clear about where the problem lies. 'It is not the youth that have a problem. The problem is at the root of the tree, not in the fruit.'

In his diagnosis, the problem emanates from the source of all that is morally wrong in contemporary Bharat: the West's all-pervasive influence. Parents follow Western ideals and send their children to talent hunts. Parents want Western education, and this disconnects them from their roots. The litany of complaints against the West's influence on Bharat reaches the country's roads. There is no love left within the family, Sandeep pronounces to me one evening and nothing illustrates this better than a common sight on the roads— children seated in child seats in car backseats. 'If there was love within the family, the parents would have never sent the child to sit behind in the child seat,' Sandeep says.

That singular act, according to Sandeep, forms an indelible mark on the child's psyche. 'The child is seeing all this, and as soon as he grows up, he will dump the parents in the same back seat and get his girl to sit next to him when he drives.' It's such analyses and prescriptions that his followers flock to Sandeep to hear.

'Somewhere, they see I am of a spiritual bent, and that clicks with people.'

~

This eclectic combination—of being a political analyst, an 'investigative journalist' as well as being a spiritual and a moral guide—has shaped and defined Sandeep's objectives.

Sandeep is poised for a larger battle—against what he believes is a slow, purposeful but invisible erosion of everything that Bharat stands for.

In Sandeep's mind, this war is being fought against Hindus, most of whom, like the men who push their parents to the backseats after getting married, are so blinded by the West that they don't even understand what they are being fed. They are victims of the war that they don't even know they are fighting. The ones fighting the war for them are awakened Hindus like Sandeep.

When hapless young men, parents, their children in tow come to him seeking answers to their moral conundrums, this cultural war gets reinforced in Sandeep's head. This war is taking over minds and relationships, changing homes and families, separating parents from children. That is why, Sandeep wants to act urgently against the enemies that face Sanatan Dharam, the everlasting, eternal religion that Hinduism is.

When he started fighting this war, his mind often went back to what Adi Shankaracharya, the eighth-century Hindu philosopher and theologian, had said.

In August 2019, Sandeep opened up for the first time about as a similar war that Adi Shankaracharya had fought. Hinduism was being threatened by the advent of the Vajrayana or Tantric Buddhism, which embraced the use of five essential elements:[10] madya (wine), mamsa (meat), matsya (fish), mudra (parched grain) and maithuna (sexual intercourse).

Adi Shankaracharya had identified these five elements, known as 'panchamakara', as subversive and a threat to Hinduism.

'Yeh jo panchamakara tha, usne Sanatan ko itna nasht kar diya tha, itna dushit kar diya tha, ki isse Sanatan samaj ko bachane ke liye, bahar nikaalne ke liye, bahut saara kaam karna pada,' Sandeep says, in his 2019 video. These panchamakara, they had destroyed and polluted the Hindu religion so much that Adi Shankaracharya had to toil hard to save the religion and to extricate it from this.

Shankaracharya, he says, wrote and interpreted new scriptures and finally founded the Advaita Vedanta school of Hinduism. This managed to breathe a new life into Sanatan Dharma and fight off the threats. Now was the time to face a similar war and extricate Hinduism again. Just that, this time, the enemies had changed. Without saying as much, Sandeep goes on to do what the Shankaracharya had done over 1,200 years ago. He says he is all set to coin a new term, a new phrase for the enemies that Sanatani Hindus need to fight, a new set of panchamakara.

The wheel of the Sanatan rath, the chariot, is stuck in the daldal, the muddy slush, of these panchamakara. He was also going to make a slight change in the word. The 'makara' in the original phrase meant elements. Instead, Sandeep calls them the 'Panchmakkar', replacing makar with makkar, a Hindi term hurled as an insult, loosely translating to frauds and tricksters.

'Par is baar, na Adi Shankarachayara aayenge, na Gorakh Nath ji aayenge. Yeh kaam humein hi karna hoga.' But this time, neither will Adi Shankaracharya come to save us, nor will Gorakh Nath ji. We will have to fight this war ourselves.

With that, Sandeep anoints himself the charioteer of this new cultural war.

Sandeep Deo: The War against the Panchmakkar

Growing up in Darbhanga, Bihar, Sandeep turned to tales at every chance he got. During meals, before an afternoon nap, at bedtime, whenever Sandeep and his younger brother, Amardeep, could, they would pester their grandparents to tell them tales.

Their grandparents told them stories from Hindu mythology, of the morally upright nature of Ram, his obedience as a son, of Lakshman's devotion as a brother, of an ideal family, of Krishna's wise counsel to Arjuna, of various Hindu kings and their epic battles.

These stories would help them escape the tough life that living in rural Bihar of the 1980s entailed. Ravaging floods were common in their village, so were power cuts. Once, the village power transformer broke down. Sandeep remembers how it took nearly a decade to fix, till which time the families had to survive on inverters. The pitiable state of roads limited their mobility—travelling 20 km would take over two hours.

Stories would help ease those struggles. Through repeated retellings, Sandeep imbibed those stories within his psyche. They remained with him long after the storytelling sessions. Some aspects felt more relevant than others. Like the way Goswami Tulsidas, the Hindu saint and poet, who wrote the Ramcharitamanas, an epic Sanskrit poem hailing the virtues of Ram, didn't just stop at writing it. For Sandeep, Tulsidas' greatness didn't rest at him writing the epic poem that eulogized Ram's character and conduct. What, instead, caught his eye were Tulsidas' efforts after he finished writing the poem: Tulsidas enacted the 'Ramacharitamanas' into a dramatized version in order for the poem to reach the masses. The enactment is what we know today as Ramlila. Sandeep never forgets this sequence of events.

'It was only through the Ramlila that the Ramcharitmanas reached every home, isn't it?' says Sandeep.

Or the way Lord Krishna refused to stay neutral when war broke out between the Yadav cousins, the Pandavas and the Kauravas in the Mahabharata. Instead of reiterating his neutrality in a war between his cousins, Krishna decided to join the Pandavas and back them to the hilt, thereby ultimately tilting the scales in their favour.

For Sandeep, all these stories have lessons that he employs in his life even now.

Tulsidas' efforts to popularize his epic ensured that the tales of Ram reached even those who had not or could not read the 'Ramcharitamanas'. This taught Sandeep the importance of doing all that it takes to reach as many people as you can if you are fighting for a just, rightful cause.

It told him that one must not rest on their laurels like Tulsidas refused to even after writing an epic like the Ramcharitmanas. Sandeep constantly repeats this, reiterating how it isn't enough to appear on videos or write articles for the Hindutva cause. Like Tulsidas, Sandeep wants to reach out and do more.

In the same way, Lord Krishna's open support for the Pandavas in the Mahabharata was an example for Sandeep of the importance of picking a side. Journalists claiming independence and neutrality was hogwash. After all, since journalists also cast their votes, can they really claim to be independent and neutral in their political leanings? For Sandeep, instead of them holding on to this fig leaf of neutrality, it would serve better if journalists came out and stated their true ideology.

He leads by example. '*Main saaf kehta hoon*,' I say this clearly, he says. 'I am a BJP supporter, but I keep criticizing the party. I criticize them a lot, even Prime Minister Modi.'

Somewhere, while imbibing lessons from the mythological stories he listened to in his childhood, Sandeep has made these stories come alive. These stories are no longer in books of history or mythology. They are alive and are unfolding in the present.

Except, in these re-told, re-lived stories, he is the protagonist; he is the central character who is fighting the righteous war. He is Tulsidas, trying to do all he can to reach out to people, awaken them. He is Krishna, the charioteer who is clearly picking a side in the polarized political environment of today. He is also Krishna, the philosopher and moral guide who counsels his followers like Arjuna was counselled. He is Ram, of irreproachable moral conduct—he constantly talks about how he refuses to accept advertising money from BJP governments at the Centre and states to maintain his credibility. When he asks his followers to subscribe to his products, Sandeep, in his mind, isn't asking for subscriptions, but for a *guru dakshina,* a fee usually paid to one's teacher, for the knowledge gained. 'I am giving them my thoughts, my resources and my knowledge. And knowledge should never be free,' Sandeep believes.

It's in this imagined universe of his that Sandeep is also Adi Shankaracharya, who identified and fought against the panchamakara, the five threats that Hinduism had faced. Centuries after Shankaracharya, Sandeep would dust the term off, and make it his raison d'être.

∼

Soon after he graduated with a BA in sociology from the Banaras Hindu University in 1997, Sandeep had his targets neatly defined. The country's NGO sector had always seemed suspicious to him. Fed by foreign funds, Sandeep felt the sector's interests were always at cross-purposes with the nation's. He wanted to understand this rot in the sector better. The BA wasn't fetching him any jobs, anyway, so he decided to enrol in a two-year post-graduate diploma in human rights from the Indian Institute of Human Rights in New Delhi.

Straight out of the course, Sandeep decided to jump into journalism as a way of fixing all that he saw was wrong in society.

He started off on the editing desk at *Veer Arjun*, a Hindi daily newspaper published from New Delhi best known as the newspaper where former Prime Minister Atal Bihari Vajpayee had worked in 1951 as its city editor.[1] Within a year, he switched to *Dainik Jagran*, the country's most popular newspaper, with a readership of over 65 million.[2] Between 2003 and 2012, Sandeep jumped from *Dainik Jagran* to *Nai Dunia*, another Hindi news daily, then back to *Jagran*.

While reporting from Delhi for both these newspapers, Sandeep covered 'A to Z beats', from tracking governance to crimes to politics, railways and even courts. A decade-long experience was enough to show Sandeep the greys in which the media operated.

Sandeep had debunked a piece of news that a Hindi news channel had aired about a 'driverless' black hatchback seen on Delhi's streets.

Kaun Chala Raha Hai Car? Who is driving the car?[3] The news report, using suspenseful music and dramatic beats, speculated whether there was a 'Mr India', the popular Hindi film character who could make himself invisible at will or whether it was *koi shakti*, some mysterious power, driving the car. Sandeep said he spoke to local cops who told him it was merely a case of a man wanting to play a prank by driving the car, sitting behind the driver's seat, using his stretched legs. The news channel's editor, livid at this debunking, called Sandeep's editor, asking him to be fired. Sandeep survived but was shaken.

Later, when he investigated alleged impropriety involving the Congress's Gandhi family, his editors sat on the piece and didn't let it get published. Sandeep says he leaked the story to another news agency, which promptly published it. His editors were livid. 'They told me I would now have to answer to Ahmed Patel,' Sandeep says, referring to the close confidante and political secretary of Congress Chief Sonia Gandhi.

No such meeting ever took place, but the Congress, Sandeep concluded, was corrupt and suppressed free media. His dislike for the party grew intense in the time he spent in newsrooms. The Congress's ten-year dominance in New Delhi coincided with Sandeep's reporting years. Sandeep says he saw political reporters constantly toeing the Congress line, refusing to ask the party tough questions.

In Sandeep's world, the contrast between the ruling Congress then and the ruling BJP now was stark. The way he sees it, the country's media is now vindictive and punishing with Modi, the way it never was with the Congress.

'Have you seen the way the media abuses Modi? No other Prime Minister has been abused by the media like he has been.'

Facts don't bear Sandeep's beliefs. Since 2014, India has slipped from 140[4] to 150,[5] its lowest-ever in the World Press Freedom Index, brought out by Reporters Without Borders. In a statement issued in 2022,[6] the organization, along with nine others, called upon Indian authorities to 'stop targeting journalists and online critics for their work'. In 2021, the index listed[7] India under countries considered 'bad' and one of the most dangerous for journalists. Modi, ever since he came to power in 2014, has yet to hold a press conference on Indian soil.

Dismayed by what he saw, Sandeep quit journalism in 2012 to come out with a book, *Sajish Ki Kahani, Tathyo Ki Zubani.* The book uncovered the *conspiracies* against then Gujarat Chief Minister Modi around his role in the Gujarat communal riots of 2002. Official data[8] showed that the riots had left at least 254 Hindus and over three times the number of Muslims dead, but Sandeep said allegations around Modi's collusion or his dereliction of duty were imaginary and, instead, concocted by the Congress. The book got Sandeep attention among the Hindu nationalist community.

Soon after, he joined the BJP as a member of a committee appointed to draft the party's manifesto for the upcoming Delhi assembly polls in 2013. The post didn't offer much limelight, neither did it offer much of a role for Sandeep. But at least it was his way into the party he was ideologically in tune with. Sandeep took it. Within months, though, he was disillusioned, yet again.

He found himself stifled. Too little democracy, too many restrictions. Too much of expression but very little criticism. 'One is pulling the other down. *Poora kheechad tha,*' Sandeep says, calling it a muddy slush he didn't want to be dirtied by. He quit the post and the party soon after.

Sandeep spent the next few years in the wilderness. He opened six different ventures and shut each of them down. He changed offices as many times. Each time, he got funding from private investors, but each time, the venture collapsed. *Logo change karo, content tone down karo, aisa mat likho, waisa mat likho*, Sandeep recalls. Change the logo, tone the content down, don't write this, don't say that. He says his independence was being threatened by those private investors. Nothing was working.

In those dark moments of dejection, Sandeep started seeing a pattern.

Each failure, every moment of rejection, made Sandeep see more clearly the decay in society. Each time he didn't succeed, he had some more insight into just what ailed the country.

Despair had no place in his life. Sandeep had now figured out who the enemy was. Like Shankaracharya, Sandeep realised that the enemy he was confronted with, the Panchmakkar, was a hydra-headed monster. Like Shankaracharya, Sandeep was going to fight it head-on.

~

In a video delivered to his YouTube audiences in 2019, Sandeep listed the enemies out. *Pen down karlo,* he says before he starts.[9] Pen them down. Sandeep was going to bring out his own version of the five enemies that Hindus faced.

The first was 'masiha-waad', missionaries. Through his two-year diploma in human rights, Sandeep had firmly understood how the NGO circuit worked and had concluded that NGOs and missionaries who were carrying out mass conversions as well as human rights activists, all deserved to be bucketed under this umbrella term. These NGOs did this by attracting the poor with the promise of rations, and hence, they deserve to be clubbed as an enemy, like Shankaracharya had classified mudra (grain) to be.

Sandeep's exposure to journalists within media organizations had convinced him that most of them were waampanthis, leftists, and those intoxicated by the promise that leftist thought held. Adi

Shankaracharya's fight against madya (wine) was to be replaced by Sandeep's fight against 'Marx-waad', Marxism, whose influence was as strong as an intoxication could offer.

The third threat to the nation came from anti-nationals, those who threatened to break the country into *tukde tukde*, pieces. Adi Shankaracharya had to fight against matsya (fish), but fighting these anti-nationals reminded Sandeep of the threat of matsya. After all, big fish ate the smaller fish, and that's what these anti-nationals, Urban Naxals and Maoists wanted to do: control Indian regions like Kerala and West Bengal, before slowly taking over the country.

All the attempts that Sandeep had made to create inroads into various sectors, be it media or entrepreneurship, had been thwarted by elites everywhere—the rich who had captured the top and were dictating terms to him. Those who spoke in English, thought in English and looked down upon those who couldn't were the fourth threat that the nation faced, and Sandeep called it the threat of 'Macaulay-waad', named after the colonial administrator Thomas Macaulay, despised by Indian nationalists for *westernizing* Indian education.

Adi Shankaracharya had listed maithuna, sexual intercourse, as the final threat that Hinduism had faced.[10] In today's India, Muslims were using the lure of this maithuna to target Hindu girls, draw them into Islam, produce babies and ultimately, surpass Hindus in number, Sandeep told his audiences.[11] Maithuna had been weaponized; Sandeep had no option but to list it out as the final threat facing Bharat—'Mohammad-waad', manifested by those of *kattar Islamic soch*, Islamic extremists, jihadis.

These enemies, the Panchmakkar, were going to define Sandeep's life, hereon, and give it purpose. The video hinted at his determination. Its title read: *Adi Shankaracharya destroyed the ancient Panchmakara. Who will finish off the modern Panchmakkar?*

By the end of the video, Sandeep didn't need to answer the question.

∼

Sandeep is always aware of his enemies and is alert at every opportunity in this fight. On a warm afternoon in May 2018, he marched into Delhi's Constitution Club of India. The venue was hosting famed television editor Rajat Sharma, owner of India TV, one of the country's most popular news channels.

Sharma's reputation as a high-profile television anchor-turned-media-company-owner had commonalities with Sandeep's—someone seen to be a sympathizer of the BJP and perceived to be close to the party. If anyone thought this commonality was enough to unite the two, Sandeep proved them wrong soon enough.

Dressed in a fuchsia-coloured shirt with his sleeves rolled up, Sandeep raised his hand as soon as Sharma finished delivering a speech.

Just four months ago, an eight-year-old Muslim girl had been abducted, raped and murdered near Kathua town in Jammu and Kashmir. She had been starved for days and then thrashed with a stone repeatedly, after which her corpse was thrown into the forest, from where it had been discovered. As soon it came to light, the rape infuriated the country and shortly thereafter, polarized it—the Muslim girl had been taken[12] to a local Hindu temple where she was sedated and then, allegedly raped repeatedly by a group of men that included the temple's priest and his son.[13] Hindu nationalist groups had demanded the release of the accused, saying the Hindu men had been framed. BJP leaders, including its ministers in the Jammu and Kashmir government, had backed those protests and participated in them.[14,15]

Sandeep had consistently called the police investigations into the crime as being biased against the Hindus. It was a conspiracy by the state's Chief Minister Mehbooba Mufti, who was in power with the BJP, and it was her way of destroying Hindu culture, he had said. The BJP ministers who had attended the rallies in favour of the accused had not backed the accused but, in fact, had only demanded a probe by the CBI, said Sandeep, even though there was evidence to the contrary. The outrage over the rape had been created by dangai (rioter) media and by Delhi's NGOs, both part of the Panchmakkar group of enemies, Sandeep said in his shows.

This was his chance to finally confront one such biased channel's owner.

Standing up, the microphone in the left hand, his right hand wildly gesticulating in the air, Sandeep wanted to ask Sharma a question, '*kyunki bahut bade sampadak hai aap*', because you are a big editor.[16]

'Why has the mainstream media forgotten ground reporting?' Sandeep asks, reminding his audience that he has been a reporter for fifteen years, so he knows what he is saying. Sandeep's problem was that reporters from channels like Sharma's were trusting the police investigations into the case. 'Why are you creating propaganda on the basis of the police chargesheet?' he thunders. The room suddenly breaks into applause, so spontaneous that Sandeep seems taken aback. He stops, wanting to soak the applause in.

For Sandeep, the applause was validating because attacking the media and pointing out its flaws were crucial parts of the ideological war that he was fighting. The media was one among the Panchmakkar, and it had to be fought, after all. But such spectacles had other uses, too.

In his world, Sandeep is a fearless, frank and forthright journalist, who doesn't mince words and cares two hoots about those in power or authority. He is not a journalist reverential of authority. He, instead, is a journalist who questions all, spares none. Taking on Sharma, a hugely popular journalist and one who frequently rubs shoulders with the highest echelons of the BJP, is a signal that for Sandeep, there are no holy cows.

Yet another way such confrontations help Sandeep is to reiterate his insider-outsider relationship with the media. He wants to emphasize his status as a journalist, but constantly differentiate himself from the likes of Sharma.

When he introduced himself, Sandeep said he had been a journalist with a fifteen-year-long career. He may not have spelt it out it but putting himself forth was Sandeep's way of saying that he was a *real* journalist, unlike the *mainstream media,* represented by the likes of Sharma. Such differentiation was not just necessary but also an existential requirement for the likes of Sandeep as well as the vast influencer army that has been propped by the BJP.

In their book, *The Art of Conjuring Alternate Realities*, Shivam Shankar Singh and Anand Venkatanarayanan,[17] break down Donald Trump's presidential campaign of 2016 and highlight a concerted effort to attack traditional media outlets in the US that could have been critical of Trump. Such attacks helped reduce the legitimacy of these media outlets and took the sting out of their investigations against Trump.

In India, a similar process has been underway since 2014, when Modi came to power. Traditional media has come under strident attack by those in power, led by Modi himself, who coined the term 'News Traders'.[18] His colleague and Union Minister General V.K. Singh (retd) coined 'Presstitutes', a term that is now routinely hurled by Modi supporters at any media critical of the government.[19] Such rhetoric at the top has been matched by insidious propaganda on social media and within messaging applications like WhatsApp. Disinformation flows freely, often with a note of caution for those sceptical of the post's content: *Bikau media yeh sach aapko nahi dikhayegi.* Sold-out media won't reveal this truth.

All this has helped delegitimize any criticism that might come from traditional media sources towards the government.[20] With the credibility of these media outlets invalidated, the field is left wide open for those like Sandeep, who present themselves as the *real media,* showing what the mainstream media hides, displaying what *real journalism* looks like.

When Sandeep confronted Sharma on that warm May afternoon, for Sandeep and his followers, it was a clash that had been set up a long time ago. In doing so, Sandeep presented the problem and, in effect, presented himself as the solution. Sharma tried to respond to Deo's questions, but the audience, so charged after his question, kept interrupting and heckling him through his response. In that hall, the audience had picked whose side it was going to be on already.[21]

~

The media, though, was just one of the problems Sandeep was tackling.

By early 2021, television shows and movies on over-the-top (OTT) platforms like Netflix and Amazon Prime were being consumed in growing numbers. Theatres were shut due to the Covid-19 pandemic, even television shows were stuttering to be produced. As a result, audiences, frustrated with the pandemic and hungry for entertainment, had flocked to OTT platforms.

Sandeep was disturbed and anxious—who knew what the Western platforms were peddling in the name of entertainment? He had to know for himself before one of the panchmakkars strengthened its grip. After all, entertainment is a potent way in which biases can be fed and thoughts altered in a gullible population. This new anxiety had increased the work that Sandeep had to put in. Apart from scanning the mainstream media for its biases, Sandeep was now forced to look into the content that these platforms were churning out.

Each night, Sandeep would finish his day's work and then switch on a movie or a web show.

What he watched over a few months astonished him. All content had a similar pattern, a similar narrative that played out within their storylines—all of them were attacking cultural values inherent to Indian society. There was nudity, there was abuse, both novel for Indian audiences because strict government censors would not allow theatrical films to show that. But what was more damaging, according to Sandeep, was how this content was constantly showing the breakdown within Indian families—dysfunctional families, partners cheating on each other, children not obeying their parents, or worse, abusing substances.

One web series showed school-going children addicted to drugs. Another film he watched, a crime thriller named *The Girl on the Train*, featuring actor Parineeti Chopra, had Chopra playing an alcoholic divorcee who, unable to get past her own broken marriage, threatens to uproot the life of a seemingly happily married couple she is jealous of.

Sandeep saw the reiteration of the pattern. Why did they have to show that Indian families were failing? Why not, instead, show a happy home?

Sandeep already knew the answer. For long, the West, especially the UK and the US, had been trying to brainwash Indian minds and break the hold that Hinduism, its culture and values have held over Indians. 'Wherever Europe and Arabia went, they were able to destroy the culture of those places,' says Sandeep. 'But not here. For thousands of years, they have tried. But even now, we are chanting the Gayatri mantra.'

Except now, these forces had launched a renewed attack with the advent of social media and OTT platforms. This was what Sandeep had been alert about. This was why he was constantly scrutinizing every new movie, every new show that these platforms churned out.

Hinduism's foreign enemies had realized that if they had to infiltrate Bharat, they would have to break the cultural strength that

Hindus had, reasoned Sandeep. The OTT shows and films he saw were proof that the attack had begun.

'The most fundamental thing in Indian society is the family. *Pehle family, fir apni jaati, fir dharam, fir apna samaj aur phir desh.*' Family comes first, then your caste group, your religion, your society and your country, says Sandeep. 'If you break the family, the rest becomes easy to break.'

In order to break the family, the nucleus of the family had to be targeted. 'The family is bound together by the women. Hindu religion has a presence at home because of the women of the house. So, the West wants to target the women.'

This targeting, Sandeep believes, is done through movies like *The Girl on the Train*. Such movies give women ideas, paint such dysfunctional relationships to be commonplace and, often, push them to take feminist stances where there are none to be taken. Sandeep is already seeing this venom spread through society.

'Whatever you watch on OTT, it is directly entering your bedroom,' Sandeep says. 'For example, marital rape. *OTT yahaan marital rape dikhata hai, aur Supreme Court mein wahaan cases aane lagte hai.*' Here, OTT content shows marital rape, and almost immediately, we have cases filed against marital rape in the Supreme Court. Marital rape, for Sandeep, was the perfect alibi the West could provide to break Indian families up. 'When two people are inside the room, how will one ever be sure that one of them has been raped? The woman will always be believed, and that will break the family up.'

For Sandeep, all this circled back to his formulation of the Panchmakkar. This, after all, was 'Macaulay-waad' redux. 'This is exactly what Macaulay had wanted. That our Indian minds should become Western in all ways.'

More people were waking up to his concerns. Two months before, a show on Amazon Prime named *Tandav* had upset many when it showed[22] an actor dress up as Lord Shiva and mouth obscenities as part of a college play. The scene had raised hackles of those like Sandeep. Hindu nationalists filed police complaints across the country, and the show's crew and officials at Amazon Prime faced imminent arrests before the Supreme Court stepped in to provide relief.[23]

The situation needed an urgent solution before OTT got into every bedroom in the country. And that solution was a Hindu OTT platform, Sandeep had announced.

The platform would imbibe Sanatan Dharam values to its audiences; it would uphold, not break, societal and familial values among Hindus. It would also warn against the conspiracies that OTT platforms were a part of—to rob people not just of their time but their attention as well as their values. Sandeep wanted to get started on it urgently.

For that to happen, Sandeep needed to be able to raise funds in time. He had already mentioned the idea to his followers, asking them to join in and support his endeavour with funds. This was a cultural war, and the war would have to be taken to every front that the enemy was present on. OTT was one; books were another.

∼

The central belief in Sandeep's war against the Panchmakkar is that the war can't be won by fighting it on a single turf. Nor can there be a single strategy to fight it.

Sandeep believes that since Macaulay-waad saw West trying to push its values into Indian minds by eroding traditional values, Hindus could not simply be passive in response. Hindus had to do a lot more. Like reiterating the values at stake, reiterating the ideals that Sanatan Dharam stood for; reminding people of the glorious, *real* history of Bharat, and correcting the leftist history that

Congress-led governments had filled the country's school textbooks with.

This was also an area in which Sandeep had experience and insights. After his first book on the conspiracies to scuttle Modi's political career, in 2015, Sandeep signed up with Bloomsbury India, the Indian arm of the internationally renowned publishing house. At Bloomsbury, Sandeep found a vehicle for his moral and political project. He wrote biographies of yoga-guru-turned-entrepreneur Ramdev, the spiritual leader Ashutosh Maharaj, as well as philanthropist and social entrepreneur Bindeshwar Pathak, apart from the biography of UP Chief Minister Yogi Adityanath. He also wrote something that reflected his beliefs, a book that explores the growth of the communist movement globally and in India, titled *Kahani Communisto Ki*. The book presses ahead Sandeep's belief on communists infiltrating India's freedom struggle through the Indian National Congress and insists that Jawaharlal Nehru carried the communist movement forward through his 'leftist agenda and approach'.

The Bloomsbury website calls[24] the book a 'historical and sociological study of development of leftist ideology' and talks of the Communist Party of India's split after the death of 'Nehru, who was responsible for institutionalizing the communist ideology in country's policy'.[25]

The partnership between Sandeep and Bloomsbury blossomed. *Kahani Communisto Ki* was the first of a three-part series that would investigate how communism developed in the country. Bloomsbury wanted him to write more, and Sandeep was only too keen. To have a platform with one of the largest global publishers, with a presence in different global centres, from London to New York to Sydney, was a high for Sandeep, who was simultaneously facing a string of entrepreneurial failures with multiple investors backing out. The publishing deal also got him credibility—suddenly, he was no longer a journalist on a rant, but an expert author with global publishing credentials. Sandeep says the royalty from his books would cross a few lakhs a year, enough for him to sustain his family through his teething struggles as an entrepreneur.

But in 2020, the partnership faced some unexpectedly rough weather.

In August 2020, Bloomsbury announced the publication of a new book titled *Delhi Riots 2020: The Untold Story*, a book that its authors Monika Arora, Sonali Chitalkar and Prerna Malhotra had said would 'uncover the Jihadist–Naxal conspiracy' that was at play behind the communal riots in the capital city in February that year, which had left at least fifty-three people dead, many more injured and hundreds of homes and properties charred by rioters.[26] The violence had been preceded by hate speeches by BJP leaders as well as leading Hindu right-wing figures, threatening violence against Muslims.[27]

Months after the riots, the new book threatened to cause a fresh outpouring of tensions that had just about settled. For the book's launch, the authors had invited, among others, BJP leader Kapil Mishra, who had been accused of igniting the riots with his hate speech.[28] Even before it could be launched, it faced severe flak, with many accusing Bloomsbury of offering a platform for propaganda and falsehoods.[29]

Sandeep had been closely watching the controversy from the sidelines as it ballooned. The criticism around the book, leading up to the launch, was simply the left-liberal mafia at work, as Sandeep saw it. The mafia was only doing what it knew how to do—create narratives against any such attempt to bring out what was true. He wasn't too worried. It would pass.

But within days, Bloomsbury India announced that it was withdrawing the book. Facing severe flak for its decision to associate with the likes of Mishra, Bloomsbury decided to withdraw the book, citing a 'deep sense of responsibility' that it harboured towards society.[30] When he heard Bloomsbury's decision, Sandeep snapped. Bloomsbury had buckled under pressure, and the mafia had won. This was problematic for ideological reasons, because this showed the space for such books was constantly being contested by the left-liberal lobby. But it also made Sandeep insecure. If Bloomsbury could so easily disown this book, Sandeep could be next. What stopped Bloomsbury from pulling the plug on his books the next time there was such criticism?

With this realization, Sandeep realized that all the work he had done—be it 'exposing' the left ecosystem in *Kahani Communisto Ki* or unravelling the conspiracies to falsely target Narendra Modi for his role in the communal riots in Gujarat in 2002—could, one day, be pulped overnight, in a fashion as perfunctory as the one he had just witnessed. He didn't want to take a chance anymore trusting a platform that he thought could give in easily to the left ecosystem he so detested.

Two days after Bloomsbury announced their intentions, Sandeep announced his. He was withdrawing all his books from Bloomsbury. The publisher would have to stop publishing all his books immediately, and he was also withdrawing the rights to an upcoming English translation of his book on communism.

Sandeep announced the withdrawal, but not his plans: he was all set to launch a Hindutva publishing network that would soon rival Bloomsbury. Except, he would never need to withdraw books.

New Ways, Old Ways

For over a century now, Hindu nationalists have cultivated publishing as a crucial ally in their quest to popularize Hindutva ideology.

Starting as far back as in the mid-nineteenth and early twentieth century, printed literature—from journals to weeklies to newspapers and newsletters to books—emerged as a key tool to not just propagate Hindu thought but also mobilize Hindus for religio-political causes, be it calling for an end to cow slaughter or to defend the Hindu caste structure. This was a trend observed both in Hindi as well as regional language literature.

One estimate showed that over half of the Bengali-language books published between 1844 and 1852 were religious, with over a third of all the books being focused on the Hindu religion.[1] One catalogue for Tamil publications, in 1865, showed that nearly 70 per cent of all Tamil language publications were religious works and 29 per cent of all the books were focused on Hinduism.[2]

Various religious movements started seeing the advantage of reaching out to wider audiences using the print medium. For instance, a weekly in Ajmer named *Rajasthan Samachar*, started in 1889, was meant to be the mouthpiece of the Arya Samaj movement and continued to do so for over two decades before it shut down.[3] The success, albeit temporary, that the Arya Samaj movement got with a printed mouthpiece offered a shining example to similar other movements keen on broadening their support bases. Hindu nationalists were not far behind. Publications like *Sanatan Dharma Pataka* and *Dharma-Rakshak* cropped up but soon sank.[4]

In 1925, a journal named *Hindu Panch* was born with an avowed political stance—on its cover, it stated its mission statement—*Hindu sangathan* (organizing Hindus), *shuddhi sanskar* (reconversion of Christians and Muslims to Hinduism), *achhootodhhar* (eradicating caste-based untouchability), *samaj sudhar* (social reforms) *and Hindi prachar* (popularizing Hindi language).[5] The journal even spelt out its focus areas: '... restoring the dignity of Hindus, saving the Hindu name, bringing Hindu rule to India and waking up Hindus from their slumber'—a discourse eerily similar to the one commonly found among Hindu nationalists in today's times.

Among all these efforts, the most concerted one to use publishing to further Hindu nationalism and popularize it came from Gita Press, a Gorakhpur-based publishing house that specialized in publishing Hindu religious and cultural texts. From publishing the Bhagavad Gita, Ramayana, Puranas and the Upanishads to magazines as well as moral and cultural guides, Gita Press, started by two Marwari businessmen in 1923, has slowly risen to become the world's largest publisher of Hindu religious books.[6] It publishes in English as well as fourteen regional languages.

But even as it grew, it quickly developed deep ties with the leading lights among Hindu nationalists—from the Akhil Bharatiya Hindu Mahasabha, to which both its founders were connected, to later the RSS and its many affiliates. Cross-pollination of ideas was common between the two: such links lent these organizations a natural platform in the Gita Press publications, to disseminate their ideas. On the other hand, often, Gita Press publications would play a pivotal role in shaping public opinion on issues that would then be taken up by Hindu nationalists. In his book *Gita Press and the Making of Hindu India*, author Akshaya Mukul says that it was 'foot soldiers' like Gita Press that lay behind the success of Hindu nationalism.[7]

Nearly a hundred years after the Gita Press embarked on its mission, there are new foot soldiers like Sandeep to take the journey ahead.

~

Sandeep's journey in publishing began with an event entirely unconnected to his life—the pulping of the book on the Delhi riots of 2020 by Bloomsbury. Sandeep's decision to withdraw his books from Bloomsbury meant that his flourishing career as an author of four books with an international publisher had ended overnight.

Yet, Sandeep was not worried over the fate of his books. 'All the top publishers, who are now my friends, called me and told me to come to them with my books,' he said, in a video he uploaded the night he announced his withdrawal. But the struggle to get there, he told his audience, had been long and arduous.

'When I had sent out the manuscript of my first book, the one on Modi and asked these very publishers to publish it, they refused to touch it. Some said, "*Sandeep bhai, yeh kitaab aag hai, aag.*"' Sandeep, this book will singe us like a fire. Now, the tables had turned. Six books later, they all wanted a piece of him.

But he wasn't going to trust such publishers again. Sandeep wasn't ready to relent, and instead, decided that he was going to take a big leap and turn this moment into an opportunity: his own publishing house would not just print his books but, instead, create a pool of Hindutva literature by bringing together different writers. Instead of having to kowtow to big publishing houses who can censor their thoughts, allow or block book ideas on a whim and then, overnight, pulp their books after a protest, Sandeep's publishing house will allow everything that deserves to be printed. The disclaimer being that the end result has to be in favour of Sanatan Dharam and the larger Hindutva cause.

In that moment was born Kapot, Sandeep's publishing house.

Such a step was also going to help Sandeep in the larger cultural war that he was fighting—creating an avenue like this for publishing Hindutva literature meant that Hindu nationalists like him could retain firm control of the knowledge that was going to be produced. The possibilities were immense: he could now, freely, publish investigations and expose conspiracies like he had with the Gujarat riots. He could now set about writing 'real' history—the way he saw it, history had been thoroughly suppressed and, instead, Congress-backed historians had presented a version of history that exaggerated the role of the Congress in the freedom struggle while neglecting the glorious heights that Bharat, the Hindu rashtra, had reached before it had been invaded by the Mughals. So far, attempts to tell this 'real' history have always been checked by publishers. But now, no more.

He immediately started getting in touch with various people: like-minded authors who had already written books with other publishers, 'experts' like him who could churn out books on any subject, as well as journalists who thought like him. But even as he had excitedly set about announcing his plans for Kapot, it dawned on him that drawing in authors or publishing a book was not the most difficult part. Even if he did manage to do all that, without a solid distribution network, his efforts would come to nought.

In starting from scratch, the natural option for him was to lean on existing e-commerce websites like Amazon.com and Flipkart, where readers could order the book. But Sandeep flinched at the idea. These platforms, he said, were *Hindu-virodhi*, anti-Hindu. To depend on them, while nurturing a business that is supposed to reclaim Hindu values, was anathema to him.

'These businesses don't care about Hindu sentiments; they sell toilets with our gods and goddesses on it,' he said. In 2017, Amazon.com had faced a storm of outrage after its US retail website was found selling toilet seat covers and other toilet accessories with images of Hindu deities printed on them.[8] For Sandeep, it was a sign that the e-commerce giant and others like it did not respect Hindus. To lean on them and get them more business was out of the question. He knew boycotting them would mean incurring a loss: these websites count for upwards of 50 per cent of book sales in India currently, according to industry estimates.[9]

Instead, Sandeep unveiled the next part of his plan, one that would not just solve his current logistical predicament but also become a potent tool in his desire to build a Hindu ecosystem: an e-commerce website dedicated to Hindus and Hindutva.

Such a website would serve as the ideal platform for Sandeep for multiple reasons. Having his own e-commerce website, Sandeep realized, would also make it possible for him to sell books that not only appeal to his Hindutva sensitivities but which were published by other publishers. These books could give him a small source of income, but apart from that, they could also help Sandeep buy time: Kapot could take off and establish itself on the backs of a ready catalogue of Hindutva literature even as Sandeep would gradually develop and commission original books. Most importantly, having his own distribution network would mean no one would be able to censor the kind of books that Sandeep publishes or limit its reach.

Across far-right circles globally, such concerns around the censorship of books by Amazon and other online retailers are widespread. Amazon.com, in the US, has banned several books written by White nationalists as well as by Nazi sympathizers and Holocaust deniers.[10] It has also blocked contentious books around gender and mental illness, publicly drawing a line on the way these subjects are depicted.[11] Such bans have drawn furious reactions from Republican politicians as well as from the far-right, decrying Amazon.com for its censorship.[12]

Not depending on Amazon and having his own e-commerce website would help Sandeep bypass such control, altogether. What the website would also help him do was to promote and publicize little-known books that already exist and propagate the Hindutva cause but have poor reach.

Kapot, now, is doing exactly this.

Sandeep's company now sells nearly 2,200 titles across nine different categories, from Ayurveda to literature, from fiction to religious to, of course, politics and non-fiction. In 2022 alone, it had managed to sell over 25,000 books, shipped across India as well to diaspora audiences like my uncle in the UK.

Its catalogue might show a diverse variety, but Kapot's focus is clear: Of the total, 839 fall under the 'Non-Fiction' category, the largest chunk. The next biggest chunk is dedicated to the 'Religious & Spiritual Literature' category, with 730 books. Both these categories lie at the heart of what Sandeep envisions himself as: a spiritually awakened crusader, waging the righteous war against the adharmi, unholy, enemies of the Hindus.

The books he sells seek to enhance that reputation. Among the non-fiction books are categories you may not find in an average bookstore: 'True Narratives' and 'Abrahamic Religions', subjects that are, in some ways Kapot's raison d'être.

The Abrahamic Religions category consists of books devoted to Islam and Christianity, but in a way that would appeal deeply to Hindu nationalist followers.

'True Narratives' is a term that Sandeep constantly refers to in his public talks and is a term his followers are likely to be aware of. The term broadly refers to a belief in the Hindu right-wing ecosystem, about how 'real history' has been shielded and, instead, has been manipulated to reflect a history that is shaped by the 'left-wing' and 'liberal' ecosystems. Such 'manipulated' narratives are called 'Fake Narratives' in Sandeep's world, and the efforts to 'correct' them, then, become 'True Narratives'.

On his YouTube channel, Sandeep has an immensely popular ongoing series of videos called 'Games of Fake Narratives', where he claims to unearth and expose 'narrations': from how the American elite were conspiring to target the Modi government or how Indians had been secretly 'brainwashed' to celebrate Christmas—a day, as he calls it, when *plastic ke pedh par bulb lagte hai*, when bulbs are hung on plastic trees. The evidence he presents in these videos ranges from non-existent to flimsy. To justify his belief that the American elite were hatching a secret conspiracy against Modi and his government, he has as proof a letter written by three US senators to the Indian ambassador to the US in December 2020.[13] The letter, coming at the height of the protests by Indian farmers, referred to the heavy-handed efforts mounted by police authorities to quell these protests in New Delhi using water cannons, barricades and tear gas shells, and quoted the senators being 'deeply concerned' urging the Indian government to uphold the protesters' right to assemble peacefully. That letter, in Sandeep's world, becomes the sign of a deep, underlying conspiracy.

Similarly, to target Christmas festivities, he points to the Bible—the holy book does not specify Christ's birthday to be on

25 December. Neither, he says, is there any proof that Christ was, indeed, born on the day. Despite this, he lamented, Hindus were celebrating Christmas thanks to their 'herd-like mentality'. Sandeep is right, but selective. The accurate date of Christ's birth has been a matter of contention[14] for years, and Christmas festivities actually began over three centuries [15] before Christ's birth.

The video is a prototype of how Sandeep works—he makes his case by holding on to figments of truth, but selectively. He applies such logic and demands accurate historical information for denouncing Christmas celebrations, but chooses to ignore what the consequences would be of applying similar benchmarks of historical and factual accuracy to Hindu festivities and beliefs.

Such agendas are carried forward by Kapot's books under both the sections mentioned previously.

Among the books listed under the 'True Narrative' section is a book called *Bleeding India: Four Aggressors, Thousand Cuts*, a book that lists 'Islamic fundamentalism, Christian evangelicals, Urban Naxalism and media-NGO-human rights issue nexus' as the 'gravest threats' facing India, a concept similar to Sandeep's own belief of the Panchmakkar.

In the same section are books on themes that Sandeep harps on. On religion, the collection includes a book called *A Quiet Case of Ethnic Cleansing: The Murder of Bangladesh's Hindus*. In a description mentioned on the publisher Akshaya Prakashan's website,[16] the book peddles a belief that is dominant among many in the Hindu right-wing—that Hindus in Bangladesh have been ill-treated and their numbers have diminished dramatically. This builds upon the historical belief among Sandeep and others in the ecosystem that Islam is inimical to Hinduism. What many miss mentioning in this light is that, in absolute numbers, the Hindu population in Bangladesh has been on the rise since the country's liberation in 1971. However, the Hindu community has diminished in its share of the total percentage for multiple reasons—from a slower rate of 'population growth as against that of the Muslims as well as smaller family sizes and late marriages'.[17, 18]

There are a bunch of other books that deal with Islam as well as Christianity in a similar vein: ensconced in controversy, laden with biases and prejudices, the books' core stoked by hatred and fear. This finds an echo in books ranging across categories: in history, books that document a 'heroic' resistance by Hindu rulers to Muslim invaders; about the 'real history' of what happened to Hindu temples under Muslim rulers; books on love jihad, the imagined fear among Hindu nationalists about Muslim men deceitfully converting Hindu girls to Islam; and even books analysing 'Muslim separatism', which the Kapot website describes to be the 'pattern through which Islam has been breaking Hindu society and its motherland'.

In politics, there are books that challenge popular history, recast it in a new light and chip away at historical legacies inimical to the Hindutva ideology. An entire section of books is devoted to M.K. Gandhi: many titles seek to 'question' Gandhi's achievements, many others glorify and even justify the actions of his assassin, the Hindu nationalist Nathuram Godse. Featured prominently on the website is a book titled *Godse Ki Awaaz Suno*, with a fat strapline beneath: '*That court testimony which was banned by the Congress government 65 years ago. Who is responsible for India's partition?*' it asks in bold.

The cover leaves little to guess about its answer: it is a large photo of a smiling Gandhi. The book's introduction blames Gandhi for force-feeding the 'secularism brand of opium and allowing the Muslim league to carve out a separate Islamic nation in Pakistan'. The book, priced at Rs 35, is a best-seller. There are at least two other books, *Gandhi Vadh Kyun?* and *Gandhi Vadh Aur Main*, on the same theme.

Another book in the same section revolves around Gandhi's relationship with women. Titled *Mahatma Gandhi Aur Unki*

Mahila Mitr, the Kapot website praises this book for its in-depth research on the subject of the women associates that Gandhi had. It is a translation of the English book *Brahmacharya Gandhi & His Women Associates*, published in 2013. A review by journalist Gouri Chatterjee, published in the *DNA* newspaper, called the book and its insinuations around Gandhi's relationships with these women the 'trite explanations of a conventional, unimaginative mind wholly unequipped to delve into the complexities of someone as unusual as Gandhi'.[19] The review ended with a suggestion: the book 'must not be cast aside lightly; it is to be thrown away with great force'.

~

Within less than two years of it being live, the Kapot website has grown significantly. All the books that Sandeep sells go through a rigorous process that he, frequently, describes in his videos. All prospective books to be sold on Kapot first go to Sandeep for him to read them 'minutely' and check for nuances and slants.

'Even if they say that they are Hindu-waadi, pro-Hindu, books on the cover, sometimes when you read it, you realize they are actually against our ideology,' Sandeep tells his followers. He does not appreciate any such subversive tactics—to guard against such snarky mutiny, he says, he has to go through the entire book. Apart from the book, Sandeep also digs into the author's antecedents.

After all that, when he is sure that there are no red flags, Sandeep green lights the book. From that point on, his brother, Amardeep, takes over and handles everything—from placing orders with the publishing house to listing it on the website, to handling the distribution and packaging, as well as redressing customer grievances in case of botched or delayed deliveries.

Among the books listed and distributed by Kapot, only eleven have been published by Kapot. The rest, an overwhelming majority of the books that Sandeep sells, have been published by other, often smaller, publishing houses.

A big chunk of these books—286 or over 14 per cent—comes from one publishing house: Prabhat Prakashan. The New Delhi-based publishing house was started in 1958 and has since then risen to the top as a leading publisher in the country, with books in Hindi and now, increasingly, in English. Prabhat has earned its niche in publishing books on higher education as well as to aid prospective entrants to competitive government exams, from the civil services to defence services.

Officially, Prabhat does not mention its political leanings. But on its website catalogue, displaying its publications, its political section makes its leanings clear.[20] Among political books, two in every five books are on themes that would warm the cockles of a Hindu nationalist's heart.[21]

These books either promote Hindu nationalist thought— one book, capturing the RSS and the BJP's journey, is titled *A Remarkable Political Movement*—or they attack rivals and critics, like a book that tells *The Truth About Teesta Setalvad*, attacking the civil rights activist and journalist who worked extensively among victims of the 2002 Gujarat riots, earning the ire of the then Chief Minister Narendra Modi. The book is written by Anirban Ganguly, a BJP leader,[22] along with Amba Charan Vashishth, who, according to a *Times of India* report,[23] was a part of the editorial team of the BJP's mouthpiece, *Kamal Sandesh*. There is also a book titled *Fascist Tendencies in the Congress Party*, which attacks the Opposition party for what it calls 'its contempt for democratic traditions and its dalliance with dictatorship'. Most other books are glowing tributes to the RSS, to its leaders, as well as to Modi and his tenure as the country's Prime Minister. There are multiple books authored by Modi himself listed on Prabhat's website: a book named *Jyotipunj* on the RSS, profiling some of its leaders, as well as a book titled *Social Harmony* that is a collection of articles written by Modi 'which show his love for the under-privileged, his endeavour to share in their joys and sorrows, the excellence of his thoughts and processes and his sensitivity towards the society,' according to the website.

Prabhat may be the largest, but it isn't the only one. Hindi Sahitya Sadan, a publishing house based out of New Delhi, might not ring bells, but it has published over 35,000 books in its seventy-seven-year-long existence so far. Its political books catalogue can read like the timeline of a Hindu nationalist Facebook community: from *Bharat: Islami Rajya Ki Or Ek Chetavani* to *Bhartiya Musalmano Ke Hindu Purvaj Musalman Kaise Bane?* The latter's cover gives out the answer: a bearded man sitting atop an angry-looking horse stomping upon human remains, a blood-stained sword in his hand.

Sahitya Sadan has many books in a similar vein: the titles, often, give out nearly everything you need to know about the leaning the book has. Consider this: *Secularvadiyon Aur Islam Ka Asli Chehra* or *Challenges Before The Hindus* or even *Gandhi Benakaab* as well as *Hindu Jagran: Kyun Aur Kaise?*

Accompanied by such sensationalistic and bombastic rhetoric is graphic imagery and use of bright colours. A book named *Jihad ke Naam Par Duniya Ko Musalmaan Banaya Gaya* features an illustration, bloodied red in tone, of strong, angry-looking men with beards attacking people. A book titled *Two Faces of Islam* has a cover that features an illustration of a rose and a sword lying alongside each other.

~

Sandeep, though, isn't content having established Kapot as a platform to sell such books. The platform, as helpful as it is for him to popularize his brand of Hindutva and cement his image in the ecosystem, is only the first step in a long journey.

Sandeep's conviction about e-commerce giants like Amazon.com being 'anti-Hindu', has pushed him to dream about the day when a Hindu, Hindustan-bred e-commerce rival can topple Amazon.com's dominance and, in the process, also help support products that further Hindutva. For him, Kapot is a step in that direction—to establish a homebred e-commerce site that can take on other foreign giants and help the Hindu nationalist ideology grow. For him, this would be perfect revenge for selling toilet seats with Hindu gods and goddesses painted on them.

Such a plan ties into Sandeep's deep suspicion of Big Tech, too. Twice already, YouTube has shut down Sandeep's channel. He doesn't even know why. Since then, Sandeep, though dependent on the platform, has also been wary of it. He knows a third ban might come anytime, a price too big to pay for him since it would involve re-establishing himself on the platform and re-gaining his 338,000-odd followers that he had painstakingly gathered.

He has made amends to avoid the ban, not by toning down his polemic but, instead, by either avoiding certain words or finding replacements for them. For instance, Sandeep avoids using the word 'Rohingya' in his talks. Thousands of Rohingyas, attacked and displaced due to violence against them in the Rakhine state of neighbouring Myanmar, have sought refuge in India. But Hindu nationalists have consistently opposed their intake, insisting that their inflows are linked to a secret Islamic conspiracy to 'engineer demographic changes'[24] and increase the Muslim population in India to overtake the Hindu numbers.

Some Hindu right-wing groups have called them a terror threat, alleging that they were, essentially, conduits for terrorist groups who wanted to carry out attacks in India.

Sandeep concurs with both those fears. But now he no longer refers to the word 'Rohingya' and finds novel ways to refer to them. One evening in March 2021, while I sat across him, after finishing a live video on YouTube, Sandeep was checking his phone when he suddenly looked up, startled. He screamed out for his video editor, who was sitting six feet away from him, and asked him to quickly scan the video he had just recorded. 'Did I say Rohingyas anywhere? *Jaldi dekho.*' Check quickly, he asked his editor.

Sandeep was in a state of mild panic till the editor finished scrutinizing the video. Even before he was done, Sandeep was already shouting out instructions: '*Rohingya shabd ko kaat do, beep mat karna, kaat dena.*' Cut the word Rohingya out, don't beep it, cut it out completely.

Even as the editor was carefully going through the video, Sandeep looked at me and explained the panic. '*Yeh YouTube waale, yeh "Rohingya" shabd ko dhoondte rehte hai. Agar aap ne apne video mein Rohingya daal diya, toh yeh log usko ban kar dete hai.*' These YouTube guys keep searching for the word 'Rohingya'. If your video has that word in it, then YouTube bans the video. '*Mera account do bar bandh ho gaya tha, isi wajah se.*' My account has been shut down twice in the past for this very reason, Sandeep adds.

There's no evidence to suggest that YouTube, or for that matter, any of the social media platforms, would implement a blanket ban like the one Sandeep mentions—any mention of the word Rohingya and the post would be taken down. Such a policy would, in effect, mean that no one would be able to discuss one of the most critical humanitarian crises in recent times on social media. Obviously, this isn't the case: a simple search on YouTube with the word Rohingya reveals countless videos, in thousands, posted by all kinds of channels: from international and national news organizations to local and regional news organizations, from the United Nations to

NGOs, to even smaller YouTube channels in India—have all posted videos on the Rohingya refugees.

But Sandeep's own brush with regulation of content by social media platforms has convinced him that the platforms are locked in a conspiracy against both Hindus as well as Bharat.

As evidence, he points to the list of major shareholders who have invested in the social media app Twitter: among them is Saudi Prince Alwaleed bin Talal Al Saud, the founder of Kingdom Holding, a publicly listed conglomerate based out of Saudi Arabia's capital city Riyadh. The prince, according to the Bloomberg Billionaires Index,[25] owns 30.1 million shares in Twitter, as well as shares in other top global firms like Citigroup as well as Snap, the parent company of the popular messaging app Snapchat.

The prince's investment comes to less than 5 per cent of Twitter, according to MarketScreener.com, a financial news website.[26] But for Sandeep, this is evidence that Islamists are carefully controlling Twitter and using it to promote dissent against the Modi government and, effectively, throttling Hindutva thought. He makes it a point to repeat these suspicions 'with data' to his followers regularly in his videos.

Such suspicion of the Big Tech players is common across the global right-wing communities. In 2017, a group of engineers and investors came together to announce an 'Alt Tech alliance', which described itself as 'defenders of free speech, individual liberty and truth … tired of the status quo in the technology industry'.[27] Their launch statement expressed[28] sentiments similar to Sandeep's. 'Silicon Valley companies,' the statement read, 'are being propped up with billions of dollars from foreign interests. They are extraordinarily hostile to any form of conservatism, populism and nationalism among other ideologies.' To fight this hostility, the alliance said, they were launching 'Alt-tech' companies,[29] which were alternatives to the popular social media platforms and where regulation would be scant.

For instance, for Twitter, there is an Alt-tech platform called Gab that is very similar in function as well as design. There is NewTube, the right's alternative to YouTube; there is also an Alt-tech company that serves to replace Wikipedia; it's called Infogalactic, and it looks very similar to the former. There are even dating sites dedicatedly serving white nationalists since the mainstream dating platforms often discourage open displays of such ideologies.[30]

India, too, has seen some similar, albeit not as explicit, experiments. In March 2020, a Bengaluru-based company launched 'Koo', a homegrown alternative to Twitter. After generating an initial buzz, the app was mostly forgotten. It came into the news a year later when the Modi government clashed with Twitter over the government's demand to block and ban tweets and accounts of news organizations, activists and journalists that were critical of the government's handling of the farmers' protests in the country.[31] Twitter had blocked more than 500 accounts on the government's request, but that wasn't enough as the government demanded more action and threatened to jail Twitter executives in the country if that wasn't done. At the height of the war, the Modi government took to promoting[32] Koo by getting its ministers and leaders to open accounts on the app en masse.

But beyond that, India hasn't seen too many attempts at creating Alt-tech start-ups. Sandeep wants to change that.

~

For Sandeep, similar thoughts of creating homegrown, nationalist alternatives to global digital platforms led to the creation of Kapot. But even as Kapot gradually grows from a website selling books to an e-commerce website, Sandeep is already eyeing newer ventures.

His experiences with YouTube—what seemed like arbitrary bans or the fear of his videos and account being struck down—made him realize that what was urgently required was an alternative platform where he could stream his content.

He has been making slow inroads: on his website, IndiaSpeaksDaily.com, Sandeep has now started live-streaming his videos at the same time as on YouTube. In addition, Sandeep is also now on the American live streaming platform Twitch, especially popular among gamers. On Twitch, Sandeep has a temporary home for his live videos until he manages to create his own homegrown streaming alternative.

In addition, Sandeep has also created his own mobile app, which allows him unmediated access to his readers. Through such an app, he does not have to worry about arbitrary bans or shadow-bans, nor does he have to worry about beeping or cutting out words, nor use alternative words when he wants to throw slurs.

The goal, Sandeep tells me, is to become 'Atmanirbhar', self-reliant, a word brought back into circulation by Prime Minister Narendra Modi when he, during the first wave of the Covid-19 pandemic in mid-2020, announced the Atmanirbhar Bharat, Self-reliant India campaign, to reduce Indian dependence on exports. *'Atmanirbhar banna hai. Yeh foreign apps pe depend nahi hona hai,'* I want to be self-reliant; I don't want to depend on these foreign-funded apps, Sandeep says, echoing Modi.

But all these attempts are to gear up for the most ambitious of them all—to take his work offline. The first step in this is setting up a chain of libraries and bookstores across 1,000 Indian towns and cities, where his curated books will be sold. Such an idea, Sandeep says, is the real attempt to 'take our work offline'.

Sandeep says such centres, which he calls gyaan kendra (knowledge clinics), are necessary because populations in smaller towns and cities across India might not be able to access his e-commerce website as easily as others in bigger cities would. And gyaan, knowledge, can't wait.

Sandeep's decision makes sound business sense, at least in terms of sales numbers. A February 2022 report[33] by eMarketer, a New York-based market research firm that focused on digital marketing, said that e-commerce was still just 7.8 per cent of the total retail sales in India. The eMarketer report estimated that e-commerce sales in the country will double from 2021 to 2025, making India likely to be one of the fastest-growing economies on e-commerce sales in Asia-Pacific.

Sandeep has also learnt to tie this sound business proposition into his ideology. These centres will be attached to a much broader, more ambitious and polemical plan: to attach weapon and martial arts training centres for Hindus with these gyaan kendras. Sandeep calls them shaurya kendras, loosely translated as 'bravery hubs', where Hindus can enlist themselves and be trained in self-defence techniques against enemies who, at least for now, go unnamed. The self-defence, in Sandeep's vision, will range from teaching valorous Hindus martial arts skills to the use of weapons like trishuls, tridents, as well as other non-lethal weapons like lathis, sticks, and maces.

In Sandeep's imagination, the two—gyaan kendras and shaurya kendras—will function concurrently, out of the same premises. '*Shastra aur shaastra, dono ka gyaan yahaan milega,*' Sandeep says. Shastra are weapons, shaastra is knowledge from ancient Hindu scriptures. Knowledge of both these aspects will be available at these centres, Sandeep tells me.

Those emerging out of these centres will be *asli Hindu*, the real Hindus, who will be armed with knowledge and strength to take on enemies and protect their Hindu motherland.

Arming and militarizing Hindus is a concept as old as Hindutva itself. One of the earliest proponents of such Hindu militarization was Dr Balkrishna Shivram Moonje, a leader of the Akhil Bhartiya Hindu Mahasabha, and a mentor to the RSS founder, Dr K.B. Hegdewar.

In their book *The Murderer, the Monarch and the Fakir*,[34] authors, Appu Esthose Suresh and Priyanka Kotamraju, detail how Moonje proposed the mobilization and militarization of Hindus in the 1920s. The trigger for Moonje was the anti-colonial rebellion by nationalists in Kerala's Malabar region. The rebellion was led by Muslim peasants, known as Mappilas, in the region and was pitched against the British colonial administration as well as local colonial-appointed high-caste Hindus who were in authority.

Moonje, alarmed at reports of Muslim peasants killing Hindu feudal lords during the rebellion, blamed 'Hindu weakness' and 'unfit' Hindus, divided on caste lines, as the reason behind the killings of the Hindus in the uprising. Many with links to the uprising[35] have termed such an unidimensional communal spin on the uprising as inaccurate,[36] arguing that the uprising was against colonial forces and the locals backing those forces.

But the uprising spurred Moonje in 1934 to call for setting up a 'Hindu military school'. In his four-page application, explaining the rationale for such a school, Moonje laid out his reasons. Suresh and Kotamraju explained in their book:[37]

The four-page note (by Moonje) brings out the fear of an imagined enemy at the gates and his frustration at the divisiveness of the Hindu caste system, which was a deterrent against a unified defence of the motherland from potential aggressors from within and outside. At its core was the idea of a 'military regeneration of Hindus' by breaking caste barriers, establishing one such school in every province and eventually setting up an All India Military College for training the teachers employed at these industries.

Moonje's thoughts and actions were heavily inspired by Benito Mussolini, the fascist Italian dictator. On his way back from the Round Table Conference in 1931, where he represented the Hindu Mahasabha, Moonje stopped in Rome and held a meeting with Mussolini and even visited military schools, colleges and institutes of fascist indoctrination in Italy.[38]

'Signor Mussolini, they say, never forgets. We also want our boys to never forget the obligations of their own history,' Moonje wrote, in a note explaining the architecture of a military school he finally set up in Nashik, Maharashtra, named Bhonsala Military School.[39]

Such sentiments of Hindus being weak and unable to fight off invaders have also been repeated by Vinayak Damodar Savarkar in his writings.[40]

Sandeep agrees with Moonje and Savarkar's assessment and has repackaged the enemies of Hindus in his Panchmakkar framework: Christian missionaries, leftists, anti-nationals, elites and Islamists.

Both Moonje and Sandeep share similar concerns of the Hindus being unable to defend the motherland. Their solutions, too, are similar: dedicated centres to facilitate militarization of Hindus. But Sandeep has added a twist of his own into these plans by combining this militarization with indoctrination through classes that will make young Hindu men read literature that Kapot produces— revisionist history about Mughals, material that stokes anger against figures like Gandhi and Nehru as well as incites readers to harbour hate and suspicion towards Muslims and Christians.

The commercial benefits of such a venture can be immense: Sandeep says he envisions students paying a fee for these classes. The fee apart, the venture will help Sandeep broaden the reach of his books and, thereby, broaden the market for all his products, from books to his app to his live videos and his social media profiles.

This plan, to militarize young Hindus and propagate strident Hindu nationalism in them, is laden with dangers. Within the country and beyond, there are examples galore of just why such a plan can be fraught with possible harm.

In 2014, partly as a response to growing Russian aggression, a volunteer-based paramilitary militia was formed in Ukraine. Known as the 'Azov Battalion', the group grew in popularity and attracted far-right, neo-Nazi supporters to join its ranks.[41] The battalion was one of the many volunteer-driven militias that sprung up in Ukraine after the 2013–14 wave of civil unrest, demonstrations and protests known as the Revolution of Dignity against the then President Viktor Yanukovych, which ended with his ouster.

While the battalion was soon absorbed by the Ukrainian government into its National Guard, it kept attracting white supremacists and far-right ultra-nationalists to its training camps, where it had started imparting military training to participants. The camps, combined with the battalion's demonstrated affinity towards Nazism, have attracted white supremacists globally. Those radicalized at these camps are, in turn, using their training for violent and hate-filled attacks against ideological rivals. For instance, the Federal Bureau of Investigation (FBI) has found that the Azov Battalion (now regiment, after being integrated into the National Guard) had been engaged in 'training and radicalising US-based white supremacy organisations'.[42] The FBI had also found[43] links between Azov and some of the violent white supremacists responsible for the violence in Charlottesville, Virginia, United States, in August 2017, when members of a white supremacist rally[44] clashed with counter-protestors, leading to at least three deaths and numerous others sustaining injuries.

Closer home, similar experiences have shaped one such military training school: Moonje's Bhonsala Military School. The

Maharashtra Anti-Terrorism Squad, while investigating the 2008 bomb blasts in the Muslim-dominated town of Malegaon, stumbled upon evidence that some of the accused in the case had been closely linked to the Bhonsala Military School. Some accused, including the now BJP MP Pragya Singh Thakur, had allegedly held a meeting in the school's premises in Nashik to plan the Malegaon blast.[45]

In times of rising nationalism in the country's political discourse, the existence of schools like Bhonsala Military School and the kind that Sandeep proposes could further exacerbate the religious polarization that already exists in the country and even cause real-world violence.

Dhirendra K. Jha, in his book, Shadow *Armies*, warns that military training schools like Bhonsala could end up injecting religious poison into the country's defence services too. 'A number of Army men seem to drift towards Hindutva organisations after retirement. Possibly because the communalism at such places (Bhonsala) is garbed as nationalism,' Jha writes.[46] With its 'curious combination of Hindutva ideology and military training', places like Bhonsala, writes Jha, 'seem equipped to capture the imagination of such army men whose sense of patriotism can easily get mixed up with Hindu communalism.'

For Sandeep, though, such mixing of communalism and patriotism wouldn't be an accidental one, but one by design. Before the pandemic struck, he had finalized the first-ever such shaurya-cum-gyaan-kendra, above his office in Uttam Nagar in West Delhi, less than 20 km away from the Parliament. But with the sudden lockdown and the resultant disruption of business, Sandeep has had to shelve his plans.

The disruption had made Sandeep reassess his plans. He realized that having a physical centre was fraught with uncertainties, especially for someone like him, having meagre resources anyway.

Instead, he has come to believe that the centre can start in the virtual world, with online classes while he garners more funding.

Like Moonje did nine decades ago, Sandeep, too, is trying to raise funds for the centre. The plan, he says, is to ultimately have a residential centre that can allow students to stay on the campus and be trained in these skills and knowledge full-time.

Just a matter of time, he says with a smile.

A Change of Heart, a New Start

By the end of 2021, Sandeep's life was getting more and more frenetic.

The second wave of Covid-19 had dashed his plans of starting his knowledge clinics and bravery hubs to impart training in arms and martial arts as well as ancient Vedic knowledge. But the setback notwithstanding, Sandeep was focused on ensuring that the publishing arm takes off.

Earlier that year, Kapot had commissioned and published a book that neatly tied into his own work and philosophy. The book *Patrakarita Ka Kaala Adhyay*, written by his journalist friend Manish Thakur, seeks to 'expose' the corruption within Indian journalism.[1] Thakur has quit journalism and now runs the YouTube channel 'The Manish Thakur Show' with over 310,000 subscribers, which offers 'an unbiased analysis of the day-to-day headlines' and 'the truth behind misleading contents (sic) on Indian TV media', urging people to subscribe and 'join the fight against the Anti-National Agenda'.[2]

The book seems like an extension of the YouTube channel's mission statement: Kapot describes the book as an 'exposé' on the 'anti-India and anti-Indian society ploys that are crafted behind iron doors, in the name of journalism'.

It is a theme that is close to Sandeep's heart and is the subject of much of his own work, including YouTube. Sandeep prides himself on being a media expert with first-hand experience in newsrooms.

Not surprisingly, he jumped at the opportunity to publish this book. The book took off, going on to sell over 2,000 copies in a year, according to him.

~

By the end of 2021, Sandeep was increasingly being consumed by pangs of anxiety and restlessness.

Elections in UP were due in early 2022, and Chief Minister Yogi Adityanath, Sandeep's hero numero uno, was up for re-election. Contingent on UP was the Hindutva project: a loss here would severely dent the prospects of the BJP's re-election in 2024 and, as a consequence, the dream to rebuild the country with Hindu ethos. For the project to live on and for Sandeep's career to be buoyant, Yogi had to come back and come back stronger.

For Sandeep, the next few months were going to shape the future of the Hindu rashtra they all wanted to see.

Sandeep had always harboured deep appreciation for Yogi. He was everything that Modi offered and a lot more: he was not just a leader who had prioritized Hindutva, but he was also a Mahant, the chief priest of a temple representing the influential Nath community of the Gorakhnath temple in UP's Gorakhpur.[3] For Sandeep, who had never been hesitant to display his own understanding of Hindu scriptures, Yogi was the complete package.

It is a sentiment common among hard-line Hindu nationalists. In my travels across the Hindi heartland, among both Hindutva supporters as well as activists of the Sangh Parivar, Yogi finds immense popular support—much more than Modi, most times. Many fancy him as the natural heir to Modi and a more fitting one at that. Supporters tell me how Yogi, like Modi, has no family and, hence, is non-corrupt and focused on his work. But where the UP Chief Minister edges out the Prime Minister is his unabashed courting of the Hindutva vote, as against what they see as Modi's tempered approach.

They point to Modi's rhetoric of being an icon of 'inclusive' development with slogans like *Sabka Saath, Sabka Vikas, Sabka Vishwas* (Backing of all, development of all, trust of all), or him urging his party to reach out to sections of the Muslim community,[4] his own interactions with Muslim community leaders, calling them a part of his family.[5] All this, many often tell me, shows that Modi had dialled down his Hindutva credentials. With Yogi, there had been no such troubles.

His first term as the UP chief minister had only added to his allure for such backers—Yogi has been blunt about who he was going after—from shutting down animal slaughterhouses, run primarily by Muslims,[6] to enacting laws that criminalize interfaith marriage, meant to target instances of Muslim men marrying Hindu women,[7] to demolishing properties belonging to protesters critical of government policies.[8] So popular were some of his steps that other BJP governments took the cue and followed up with similar moves in their states. In July 2022, Karnataka Chief Minister Basavraj Bommai said he gave Yogi 'a hundred out of hundred' score for his governance and said that if needed, 'the Yogi model' would be employed in Karnataka, too, to deal with criminal elements.[9]

Leading up to the elections, Sandeep kept reiterating his support for Yogi through his work.

But in the weeks before the elections, something drastically changed within Sandeep. From telling me that he was a journalist who supported the BJP, Sandeep no longer wanted to be associated with the party, even as a supporter. Suddenly, he was critical of the BJP and its top leadership each time he got an opportunity.

He was very clear that he would no longer bat for the BJP. His only aim was to make Yogi win. But in Yogi's win, he started looking for ways to defeat Modi.

Modi was now his bête noire. I saw this change unfold and I could not wait to find out why.

~

Amidst all the other projects that were slated to be inaugurated on the eve of the UP polls, one held a special place for Sandeep—the opening of Kashi's Vishwanath temple complex after giving it a Rs 800-crore makeover.[10] The revamp involved 'decongesting' the lanes around the temple by demolishing hundreds of homes and shops around it and creating unhindered access from the temple to the holy Ganga river.[11]

For Sandeep, the temple carried special memories. As a student of arts at the Banaras Hindu University two decades ago, Sandeep would head to the temple each time he was troubled. 'I would line up outside the temple at 3 a.m. so that I could enter as soon as it opened,' Sandeep said. He found the temple soothing in ways he could not explain. He could feel divinity around him; his worries would dissolve in the air.

But as the revamp project started taking shape, news started filtering in that centuries-old homes were being forced to make way for the grand corridor. Along with the homes, word spread that the old temples in those narrow by-lanes where Sandeep had walked through a countless number of times were also being demolished.

These allegations reached a crescendo as the date of the inauguration of the project, 13 December 2021, inched closer.

For weeks, Sandeep had been hearing about it. 'But I don't want to say anything about this before I actually go and check it out for myself,' he would tell his audience on YouTube. Just weeks before Modi was supposed to make a grand inauguration in December 2021, Sandeep declared a visit to Kashi to verify these rumours. However, within days, he changed his mind. One night he explained to his audience that he was 'under pressure' from people; one senior BJP leader, Sandeep claimed, had even called him and told him to put off the visit.[12] Reluctantly, Sandeep had agreed.

The glitz and glamour around the corridor's inauguration were reaching a feverish high. Kashi was being decked up, over 3,000 guests were to be invited and Modi's office had billed it as a top event, insisting that Modi had taken a personal interest in the project's progress.[13]

'*Akele vyakti ki koi sunta bhi nahin.*' In any case, no one would have heard my sole discordant voice, Sandeep reasoned his silence later.

But that changed on the night of 7 December. It was late, and he was driving his metallic grey sedan back to his home on the outskirts of Delhi with his wife, Shweta, next to him. Suddenly, a stray dog dashed in from the side, jumped right in front of the car and crashed into the front.

The impact dented the car's front bumper badly, left it mangled and pushed it all the way into the engine. Although Sandeep and Shweta had no injuries, he feared the worst for the dog.

But seconds later, the dog appeared, without any visible injuries and walked away from the car. 'Smilingly', Sandeep would later describe the dog's walk.

He was astonished. The dog's miraculous escape and their own close shave with a grievous accident had left him stupefied. He was stunned that the dog, despite the ghastly accident, had managed to survive. His mind was in a haze. But slowly, as he kept going over the incident, a realization dawned upon him, cutting the haze. The accident wasn't an ordinary one; it was a message to him.

His mind harked back to his grandmother's stories. He tried to understand what the dog's presence meant in the mythological stories he had heard.

Suddenly, he remembered.

In these narrations, the dog was the vehicle of Kaal Bhairava, an avatar of Shiva. Bhairava, with his appearance of a dark-skinned god sporting a garland of skulls and snakes, is known as the God who annihilates fear, the One who helps his devotee vanquish any anxieties that hold them back from being on the path of righteousness.[14]

With that realization, he knew what had happened. It was no ordinary dog. The dog was a messenger of Bhairava Baba, he later told his viewers. Bhairava Baba had realized there were anxieties and fears that had held him back from doing what was right and hence, was sending him a signal—do your duties, unafraid of the consequences.

Sandeep took the accident to be a message: he needed to do his karma and go to Kashi.

'My nani used to say, it's okay if you can't please humans, but you should never displease the Parmatma, God,' Sandeep told his followers in a video at the end of December, when he recounted the accident and the realization that had followed.

Days after Modi inaugurated the project, Sandeep and Shweta headed to Kashi. But what they saw there left him scarred and, as he later said, 'in tears'.

Back from Kashi, Sandeep took to YouTube on 27 December and launched a stunning attack against the temple project and, by extension, on Modi.

At the start of the video, Sandeep holds a copy of the Bhagavad Gita in his hands and declares with a cinematic flourish that he won't lie. He recounts his memories of going to the temple as a student. 'I would be spellbound; I would find it hard to even utter words,' he says. 'I would cry.'

But this time, he didn't feel the same. The sense of divinity he had always felt was lacking this time.

Over the next seventy minutes, with the use of photos, Sandeep shows his audience why. He alleges that the project, built at Modi's behest, has resulted in the uprooting of 400 pracheen (ancient), temples; many of those temples had been demolished, the deities' idols discarded.

He shows photos of a path, unpaved and full of debris, as if on a construction site. That spot, he says, was where the great sage Tulsidas had constructed a temple for Lord Hanuman. The temple was now a part of the debris.

'There is no temple anymore, but I still can't dare to wear shoes, because I know the temple existed right here,' he says, pointing to his photo. In the photo, Sandeep is standing sideways, dressed in a navy blue kurta and white pants, with a tripundra on his forehead, his feet bare on the rubble underneath.[15]

'Do you not feel like crying?' he suddenly launches, his pitch soaring. 'This is the same Tulsidas who, despite Akbar, dared to write the "Ramcharitamanas". His temples have been broken today. Do you not feel like crying?'

His anger boiling, he fires another salvo, keeping in line with his political objectives. 'I found out that these demolitions were so painful that Hindu workers did not agree to carry them out. Eighty per cent of the workers who demolished those temples were *harre tidde* (green locusts),' Sandeep says, employing his slang code for Muslims.

'And they were having a great time demolishing those temples,' says Sandeep, without bothering to burden himself with the need to furnish proof for this. He knows his audience doesn't need any. 'I know this because I checked everyone's identity cards and found 80 per cent of them to be *harre tidde*.'

Sandeep occasionally blames bureaucrats for the destruction, but his target becomes clear eventually. 'This is what Aurangzeb used to do [demolish Hindu temples]. Now, my own government has done it,' Sandeep says, without naming Modi.

'Yogi knows all this, but even he can't make Modi understand.'

The incident, his brother, Amardeep, later told me, had changed Sandeep's outlook towards Modi and the BJP. Sandeep had decided that he could no longer back the party as long as it was ruled by a man who would happily preside over the demolition of ancient temples and seek to overshadow this destruction with pomp and grandeur through the inauguration.

'*Bhaiji bahut disturb ho gaye,*' Amardeep told me. Brother was very disturbed by what he saw there.

Later, Sandeep told me he had decided to start scrutinizing the Modi government's policies closely and was left disappointed. According to him, these guys were running a government in the name of Hindutva, but '*minorities ki funding toh badh gayi hai*'. Government funding for the welfare of minority groups has increased instead. Sandeep said he had read through government documents and data, and reached this heartbreaking conclusion.

This isn't borne out by facts. A report in the *Frontline* magazine had shown that while the budget for the Central Ministry of Minority Affairs had risen rapidly between 2006 and 2013, it had registered a very nominal increase after that since Modi came to power.[16] In the 2023 budget, the ministry even suffered a 38 per cent budget cut.[17]

Yet, Sandeep had made up his mind—he could no longer back Modi.

Weeks later, with just days to go before the UP elections, he recalibrated his position. He would back the BJP and Yogi. Yogi had to win so that he could go ahead and replace Modi.

From then on, he went about shoring up support for Yogi as a replacement for Modi.

He would list out his grievances with the Modi government. This government, he would say, is more interested in appeasing minorities rather than caring for the Hindus.

'*Meri hi sarkaar, chaalis yojna hare tiddon ke liye leke aati hai. Hinduon ko sirf tripund lagakar khush kar diya jaata hai, par saari yojnayein alpasankhyako ke liye hai.*' My own government brings forty different welfare schemes for those green locusts, nothing for us Hindus. Come elections, they just apply tilaks on our foreheads and appease us.

But there is a way out of such misery and doom, Sandeep reassured his listeners. Yogi Adityanath is that way out.

The Centre was drafting schemes for minorities, but not Yogi. '*Yogi aap ke liye yojnayein bana rahe hai.*' Yogi is drafting schemes for you, he says.

He lists them out. '*Love J waali*', he refers to UP's Prohibition of Unlawful Religious Conversion Act, approved in 2020 and which prohibits religious conversion by marriage, among other factors—a legislation that was meant to tackle the Hindu right-wing's fear of Muslim men luring Hindu women into Islam by marriage, calling it love jihad.

Done selling the present and the recent past, Sandeep now wants to make one final pitch for Yogi through the promise of a brighter, more saffron future. But the pitch wasn't to make the Gorakhpur temple head monk the state's chief minister. It was a pitch to envision him as the country's Prime Minister and imagine the future with him.

'*Yogi aayenge toh Article 25 aur 30 mein badlaav hoga.*' If he comes to power [in the Centre], Articles 25 and 30 will be changed, Sandeep says. Both these articles of the Indian Constitution are frequent topics of animated conversation and consternation among the Hindu right-wing. All discussions around these topics revolve around vociferous demands to scrap them, banish them from the Constitution forever. Here's why: Article 25 allows Indians the freedom to profess, practice and propagate their religious beliefs.[18] Article 30 enshrines the rights of minorities to establish and administer educational institutions and asks the state to not discriminate against such institutions.[19] For Hindu nationalists like Sandeep, both these Articles lie at the heart of why India is still not a Hindu rashtra, thanks to such 'appeasement' of minorities and offering them rights that allow them to establish and propagate their own religious identities.

Sandeep goes on. If Adityanath is brought in, a Uniform Civil Code will follow suit, which, in effect, would not allow for religion-based personal laws to continue—again, a long-standing demand by Hindu nationalists, primarily targeted at Muslim personal laws.[20]

If Adityanath comes to power, he will bring in a law to control the country's population, a move demanded by Hindu nationalists for decades, based on the imagined fear of an Islamic takeover of India in the future. If Adityanath comes to power, he will ensure that slaughtering of cows gets banned across the country.

But for all this to happen, Sandeep underlines, '*unko majority se laana hoga*'. He will have to be elected with an overwhelming majority. '*Full majority dena hoga, warna woh dab ke, RSS ka, secularism ka bayyar ho jayega.*' Give him a full majority, or else he will turn secular if the RSS manages to pressure him.

Sandeep is peddling promises of a future that is distant and uncertain. At a time when Adityanath was struggling to hold his fort together, amidst dissensions, Sandeep was promoting him not for a second chief ministerial term but for the Prime Minister's chair. Sandeep doesn't mention much about the Adityanath government's performance, nor much about what the BJP's manifesto for UP promises.

But it isn't really needed. By the time Sandeep finishes his monologues, a flurry of comments on his live video confirm the effectiveness of his sales pitch.

> *'Yogi ji satta mein rahe … tabhi Sanatan Dharam bach sakta hai.'*
> We can save our [Hindu] Sanatam Dharam (religion) only if Yogi remains in power.

> *'Yogi ji hai toh Sanatan hai. Hari Om.'*
> [Hindu] Sanatan religion will survive only if Yogi will.

> *'Modi hatao desh bachao … Yogi lao desh bachao.'*
> Get Modi out, save the nation … bring Yogi in, save the nation.

⌒

Sandeep's prayers work.

On 10 March 2022, after a gruelling seven-phase election season, the BJP, with Modi and Yogi as the face of its campaign, win convincingly by bagging 255 of the 403 assembly states. While the party has got an outright majority by itself, no one could miss the undertext: the party suffered a serious loss of face, its seat tally dropping from 302 in the previous polls, while its rival Samajwadi Party bagged 111 seats from just 47 in 2017.

Sandeep believed that this reduced majority was the handiwork of the BJP's top brass, who saw Yogi's popularity as a threat to their own ambitions. Sandeep felt the party's campaign had been sabotaged from within—deserving candidates were not given seats, senior leaders plotted defeats of their own men.

All this steadily contributed to Sandeep's loss of faith in the present BJP leadership as the deliverers of Hindutva utopia.

Throughout 2022, Sandeep's disillusionment with the BJP steadily grows. He is frequently critical of the party in his videos and his website's coverage of the party and its affairs. His 'study' of the party's policies in the interim only makes him drift wider.

He looks into India's exports of beef, and his findings add to his anger. 'They used to oppose cow slaughter, but India is now the biggest exporter of beef,' he says.

Indian government data shows that exports of 'meat and bovine animals (frozen), after being more or less stable since 2014, registered a substantial increase 2021 onwards'.[21] However, despite the increase, India was the world's fourth biggest beef exporter, not the biggest, as Sandeep alleged.[22]

Similarly, he started feeling that the Modi government, having campaigned against the Congress's *Musalmaan tushtikaran*, Muslim appeasement, had started doing the same itself, except it labelled it 'truptikaran', fulfilment, referring to a speech by Modi in July 2022, asking party workers to reach out to minorities, among others, and move from the politics of tushtikaran to truptikaran, 'from appeasement to fulfilment'.[23]

Sandeep repeats his charges several times that year through his work and public speeches. By the end of 2022, though, this criticism exacts its cost on him.

He starts experiencing a dip in his own fortunes in the online world. His videos on YouTube, which would earlier easily garner tens of thousands of views, were now barely managing a few thousand views. His 'live' videos, which would draw in viewers in hordes, now had only a couple of hundred people tuning in.

Sandeep told me he decided to tap his network of sources within the BJP to see whether this was by design 'I found out that the top leadership in, both, the BJP and the RSS were unhappy about my videos,' Sandeep said. 'That is why the BJP's IT Cell had my channel shadow-banned,' he told me, referring to an unspoken practice adopted by social media platforms where they mute the presence of an account and limit their reach, but without notifying the user.[24]

I decided to investigate if his suspicions had any credence. Checking data for his channel, India Speaks Daily, on Social Blade, an online portal offering analytics for YouTube channels, I found his reach had rather drastically reduced around the time of the UP polls after his videos criticizing the Kashi Vishwanath corridor project had released.

In February 2022, he would garner over 3.5 million views through the month. That number nosedived to around 1.5 million monthly views in March. One month later, by April, his channel could barely garner 1.2 million monthly views. Since then, throughout 2022, his channel's reach has dropped further to less than a million monthly views, last checked in August 2023.[25]

This also slowed down his channel's growth—from garnering 69,000 new followers between January 2021 and January 2022, his channel gained only 35,000 new followers in the year after that. All this also translated into the drying up of his income from YouTube.[26]

The gloves were now off. They had hurt Sandeep, and he was going to hit back.

~

He got his opportunity on 9 January 2023, in an unlikely event: an interview with the RSS chief, Dr Mohan Bhagwat.

The RSS chief was being interviewed by editors of its mouthpieces, *Panchjanya* and *Organiser*, on a wide range of subjects, including his stance on homosexuality. In response, Bhagwat, whose organization's leaders had previously called homosexuality a 'psychological problem' that had to be treated, offered a surprising about-turn.

Bhagwat said that Indian civilization had always acknowledged homosexuality, and even pointed to an episode in the Mahabharat, involving two generals of a king named Jarasandha—Hamsa and Dimbhaka. Bhagwat said the epic offered indications of a homosexual relationship between the two.[27] 'Humans already have this type (of relationship). It has existed since the dawn of time,' he said, to argue for deep links between Hindu cultural traditions and homosexuality.

Sandeep saw red at that. He was incensed at Bhagwat's response and thought of it as a ploy to increase the RSS's support base and co-opt younger generations of Indians, more likely to back the cause.

I asked Sandeep what his objection really was. 'His claim is entirely false. Nothing like that exists,' he said. After Bhagwat's interview, he consulted Hindu religious scriptures. 'I read the Sri Harivansh Puran and realized that what he said was not actually correct at all,' Sandeep said.

Sandeep didn't see this statement as a mere slip-up; he saw this as a calculated strategy by the RSS against Hindus and Hinduism, especially after the demolition of ancient Hindu temples in Kashi for a grander, new temple complex. The strategy, he said, was to take Hindus farther and farther away from Hindu ethos and traditions and, instead, transform them into prototypes of 'Abrahamic religions' in order to make them appealing to the West. This, he insisted, was a deep-rooted conspiracy by the West in cahoots with the RSS and the BJP's top leadership. Hinduism had to be altered, one step at a time, and its traditions and values had to be discarded.

He also pointed to another unlikely event as further proof of his hypothesis—the death of Prime Minister Modi's mother, Heeraben Modi, on 30 December 2022.[28]

After attending her funeral, Modi carried on with his official duties the same day by inaugurating a slew of projects through video conferences.[29] His decision was hailed by BJP leaders as a sign of his commitment and was lauded as a 'karmayogi' by his colleagues. But Sandeep didn't agree. Hindu traditions, he said, needed close family members to observe a mourning period and stay away from celebrations and happy occasions. Sandeep said close family members, especially sons, were also expected to shave their heads or, at the very least, their facial hair off.

'Par yeh toh seedhe inauguration mein chale gaye,' Sandeep said angrily. But Modi went straight to events to inaugurate new projects. Not just that, he didn't even shave his hair off. Sandeep found it offensive. 'Yeh toh naya dharam bana rahe hai.' He is creating a new religion. Sandeep is worried that young Hindus, seeing Bhagwat's arguments and Modi's practice, will seek to emulate them.

'Tomorrow, when a Hindu boy tells his parents he is a homosexual, and his parents oppose it, he will just show them Bhagwat's remarks. They will have nothing to say.' His worries for the upcoming crop of Hindus do not end there. 'Now when there's a death in the family, a son will say, I won't shave my hair because Modi ji also did not.'

Sandeep said he had to fight back. So, on 23 January 2023, exactly two weeks after Bhagwat's interview was published, Sandeep did the unthinkable—he filed a police complaint against Bhagwat.[30]

He marched into Delhi's Bindapur police station, a short walk away from his office, with a letter asking for an FIR to be filed against Bhagwat as well as the editors of *Panchjanya* and *Organisers*, who conducted and later published Bhagwat's interview.

In the letter, Sandeep said the three should be prosecuted under the Indian Penal Code's Section 295A, meant to prosecute those who indulge in 'deliberate and malicious acts, intended to outrage feelings of any class by insulting its religion or religious beliefs'.[31] The punishment under this section, if found guilty, can be a jail term that may extend up to four years or a fine or both.[32]

The Delhi Police, under the direct control of Union Home Minister Amit Shah, refused to accept his complaint. Sandeep's complaint went viral on social media, with other Hindutva supporters sharing it and backing it.[33] The complaint was reported extensively across the media. He knew the complaint wouldn't be filed by the police, so he had a back-up plan. Sandeep was going to go to a local judicial magistrate's court and ask it to exercise its powers and order the police to register his complaint under section 156 (3) of the Code of Criminal Procedure.

Sandeep had made a splash and had announced his rebellion in style.

~

While he went ahead and took the BJP and RSS head-on, Sandeep also decided to push the pedal on his own work and double down on his commitment to the cause of Hindutva.

He was now going to be even more careful in curating the list of publications that Kapot brings out. *'Bahut dilution ho raha hai.'* Our ideology is getting diluted, he told me, one sunny day in February 2023, at his office in Delhi's Uttam Nagar.

The authors that he was mentoring, so that they write books that agree with his ideological leanings, were all getting 'diluted'. They were Hindutva-wadis of convenience, Sandeep said, not authors who really got into the depth of Hindu scriptures to understand it well before writing about it.

His brother, Amardeep, who handles the e-commerce wing of Kapot, had also started having reservations about these authors. Kapot had been founded on the premise of boycotting Amazon. com, Flipkart and all other e-commerce giants who had proved themselves to be anti-Hindu and anti-India. 'But these authors, after getting their books published by us, want to sell these books through those platforms to increase their sales,' Amardeep explained. 'This is not acceptable to us. We don't care if we sell less, but we can't depend on Amazon, etc.'

So, Sandeep decided that he had to start scrutinizing the authors that Kapot would produce even more than before, investigate their knowledge of Hinduism and weed out any opportunists who were not as committed to the Hindutva cause as he was. All this would take time, he realized. Money was always an issue for Kapot—author advances, publishing costs, distribution expenses, all these would cost a lot. More scrutiny would mean that the number of books that Kapot published would also go down, as each book would take much longer to come to fruition.

Kapot's model needed an overhaul.

So, Sandeep and Amardeep decided that while they would focus on bringing out a careful selection of dharmic- and Sanatan-based books, Sandeep would republish old Hindu religious books that were possibly out of print while continuing to distribute books by other publishers that broadly speak to the same theme as his: promoting Hindutva ideology, 'exposing' the Panchamakkaar enemies, rewriting history the way it should be.

In this model, Kapot carefully fills a void—of being a one-stop shop for all those who want to buy books that further Hindu nationalism, promote an alternate history, and viciously attack Hindutva's enemies.

When it couldn't publish new books, Kapot would also facilitate publication of Hindutva books by using its networks with other publishers. In 2022, Sandeep said, he got other like-minded publishers, not as vigilant about possible ideological dilutions, to publish manuscripts that wouldn't pass muster at Kapot.

These alliances meant that the Hindutva publishing networks would continue to churn out books, and Sandeep's Kapot would only grow its umbrella wider in trying to give these books a consolidated Hindutva platform to sell.

Stepping into 2023, Sandeep realized that this was an important year to bring out books that could shape voters' mindsets and push them further towards Hindutva ideals. But while he was plotting all this, he realized that there was a bigger enemy that he needed to tackle urgently—the BJP.

Literature, social media posts, YouTube videos were not any match for the BJP's prowess in nearly all of these departments. He had tried enough and realized its limitations. He had to tackle the party in a way that would hurt.

That's how he arrived at his life's most audacious move so far: jumping into the electoral fray and taking on the BJP electorally in the 2024 general elections.

~

For Sandeep to accomplish this uphill task with any success, he knew that he couldn't be alone. But he also realized that finding an ally would be difficult. After all, if he wanted a party with an even more right-wing position than the BJP on matters of Hindutva, the options were very limited—Shiv Sena, a party that called itself the true-blood Hindutva party, was a regional party and no longer an option after it allied with the Congress, anathema to Sandeep.

The Akhil Bhartiya Hindu Mahasabha, the original Hindutva party formed in the early twentieth century, was now a pale shadow of itself, existing less in electoral politics and more in stunts and publicity exercises for oxygen.

Up in the north, though, Sandeep spotted some promising green shoots.

For a few months now, a new political force had been taking shape in the troubled state of Jammu and Kashmir, a force that shared his objectives as well as, more importantly, his new-found animosity towards the BJP.

Ikkjutt Jammu, United Jammu, a party formed in December 2021, was slowly gathering steam in the region of Jammu.[34] Its name was an oxymoron: the party's raison d'être was a division; their demand was for a separate, Hindu-majority state of Jammu to be carved out from the Muslim-majority union territory of Jammu and Kashmir.

The party's founding ideals, as well as its founder, both, had Sandeep's approval.

The organization had been formed by an advocate, Ankur Sharma, who has spearheaded allegations of a conspiracy to deliberately and silently change the demography of the Hindu-majority areas in Jammu by facilitating the 'sudden influx' of Muslims into it.[35]

Sharma sees signs of this conspiracy everywhere: In 2014, he filed a petition in the J&K High Court against a state law, the Kashmir State Lands (Vesting of Ownership to the Occupants) Act, 2001, widely known as the 'Roshni Act', asking for it to be repealed.

The Act had proposed to regularize the occupation of state-owned land by occupants till 1990, and the proceeds the government would collect on regularizing were to be pumped into building hydropower projects for the state, thus the name 'Roshni', brightness.[36]

But Sharma saw this regularizing of occupation as a way to 'trigger land jihad', as he said in an interview he gave to a Kashmiri media outlet.[37] The conspiracy, according to Sharma, was to give away land to primarily Muslim occupants in Jammu so as to bring about 'a demographic change' in Jammu, claiming that as many as 85 to 90 per cent of the occupants of such lands in Jammu were Muslims.

The campaign grew in Jammu, other right-wing groups, as well as sympathetic media outlets, joined in and stoked fears of a reprisal of the 1947 Jammu massacre, when tens of thousands of Muslims were killed by Dogra ruler Hari Singh's paramilitary force.[38,39] Sharma's petition resulted in the J&K High Court declaring the law 'unconstitutional, contrary to law and unsustainable',[40] but the court found little merit in his arguments around a demographic change. The court, displeased with communal overtones on the issue outside the court, specifically insisted that the verdict was not targeting any community.[41]

Local news reports pointed to government data that revealed how less than 3 per cent of the potential beneficiaries of the law were Muslims.[42]

Sharma also saw this conspiracy in another unlikely place, in the earlier mentioned rape and murder of the eight-year-old girl from the nomadic Muslim Bakarwal community in 2018, in Kashmir's Kathua. The rape-murder drew shock after it emerged that the seven men accused in the case allegedly repeatedly sedated and raped the girl in a temple in Rasana, Kathua.[43] Sharma decided to represent Sanji Ram, the temple's chief priest and the main accused in the girl's murder. Ram, the police investigations showed, had planned the girl's murder as a ploy to 'scare the nomads away'.[44]

In his defence, Sharma told the court that the murder had been committed by 'jihadis' as a ploy to 'change the religious demography of the area'.[45] Sharma was also associated with Hindu Ekta Manch, the Hindu Unity Forum, a Hindu nationalist body that took out a protest march in defence of the accused.[46]

The court threw his arguments out and convicted his client, sentencing him to life imprisonment.[47]

Undeterred, Sharma has continued to push his rhetoric along.

He has fashioned his party as that which 'does not care about Kashmir' and has its eyes 'only on Jammu'.[48] The BJP, he says, has let down the Hindus of Jammu because they wanted to 'appease radical Islamists in Kashmir'.[49] Sharma alleges that a 'Hindu genocide' was silently underway in Kashmir and lays the blame on the Modi government for terrorist killings of Hindus in the valley.[50]

Sharma, like Sandeep, realizes that the space for Hindutva votaries can get cramped within the BJP and its aligned organizations. What unites them both is their inherent belief that the way to grow, then, is to prove that you are one-up on the BJP; that they, not the BJP, are the true-blood protectors of Hindutva and everything Hindu.

They both realize that the only way to grow within the Hindutva space is to take stances even the BJP might be too shy to adopt and do things that even the BJP might be embarrassed to associate itself with.

Competitive Hindutva, after all, requires innovative thinking.

And collaborations, as Sandeep has realized.

In early February 2023, Sandeep travelled all the way to Jammu from Delhi and spent two days with Sharma. By then, Sharma had embarked upon his yatra, the 'IkkJutt Jammu Party's Yatra for Separate Jammu State', through which he visited numerous towns and regions across Jammu, mobilizing support for his party.

Sandeep's meeting with Sharma left him impressed. Sharma, he says, '*Bolte bahut badhiya hai*', is a great orator, he told me, and shares and shares the same concerns as him: Hindus have been left powerless by the BJP, and it is time that *real* Hindu voices resonate within the Parliament.

That's when the two inked a partnership. Ikkjutt Jammu was not going to be restricted to Jammu any longer. With Sandeep on board, the party wanted to create a national presence and send "asli", real, Hindus to Parliament.

The agenda for the party was clear, Sandeep told me, even if the manifesto wasn't ready until then:

> Eliminate any extra rights or affirmative actions for religious minorities, scrap the Minority Affairs Ministry, scrap the Minorities Commission, bring in the uniform civil code, 'equal rights' for Hindus; curbing Article 25, which offers equal rights to all citizens to practice their religion and scrap Article 30, that allows minorities to establish educational institutions; a strict control on infiltration so there is no 'demographic change' that these 'infiltrators' can effect on Hindus; and a complete, unflinching ban on slaughter of all bovine animals.

Sandeep said that the fight to get into Parliament wasn't going to be easy, and that they were not delusional. 'We will expand only to a few Hindutva-waadi states, where we will focus on just a handful of seats—seats where we can find strong contenders,' he said. On the radar are the states of Madhya Pradesh, Gujarat, Rajasthan, Himachal Pradesh, Uttarakhand and a couple of seats even in southern Karnataka. Sandeep said the target was to look at a total of around twenty-odd seats.

'We are very clear that we will only go and fight where there is a majority of Hindu voters. We don't care about being secular; we don't want to appeal to non-Hindus.'

It is an uphill task, but Sandeep said that Sharma and he are ready for the struggle. At the end of the struggle, though, Sandeep doesn't see any rewards for himself. He won't fight the elections, nor will he take up any positions in power.

This decision, like most others of his, was driven by his Nani's tales. 'Every Ram needs a Vasishtha. Every Chandragupta Maurya needs a Chanakya,' he smiled.

Afterword

I write this with just months to go before the 2024 general elections.

Over the course of the four years that I have now known them, a lot has changed in the lives of Kavi, Kamal and Sandeep Deo. Their personal and professional upheavals have all been documented in the book.

Yet, for all three of them, the 2024 polls are crucial. All three have a point to make; all three are desperate to contribute.

For Kavi, her separation from her husband and the breakdown of her ties with her father brought about big changes in her life. In April 2023, Kavi moved back in with her biological family in Alwar. Slowly, adjusting to this change, she started producing songs again. Except most of them were devotional, dedicated to various Hindu gods and sometimes historical Hindu figures like Maharana Pratap.

Kavi confessed that this move, away from Hindutva, was deliberate. 'My Facebook ID keeps getting blocked, or Meta stops the monetization of my page when people report my posts,' she admitted. Even on her YouTube page, some of her songs, including one that pushes for a law to control population growth as a response to an imagined Islamic demographic takeover, have been mass reported. This has caused her earnings to suffer.

But slowly, she has told me, she is getting her mojo back. She is in the process of finalizing a song on Modi, she said. The lyrics told me a lot about which way Kavi was going to drift, come 2024. *'Phir se Kamal Khilana Hai, Ghar ghar bhagwa lehrana hai / '24 mein tumko Ram kasam, Modi ko laana hai.'* The lotus has to bloom again, Saffron must fly atop each home / In '24, swear by Ram, that you will bring back Modi again.

Kamal, on the other hand, has been making deeper inroads into the BJP and the Hindu right-wing ecosystem. By August 2023, he was already working on the re-election campaign for one chief minister in a BJP-ruled state. In that same month, on 11 August, while the Modi government's ministers and Members of Parliament participated in a 'Tiranga Yatra' in New Delhi,[1] Kamal was invited to perform at a kavi sammelan organized as a part of the Yatra. Kamal was now performing more regularly, travelling across the country again. Things had started to look up and he was insistent that he would have a meatier role to play in the 2024 polls, especially for Yogi.

Sandeep's efforts to take on the BJP have only gained strength. His party, Ikkjutt Jammu, had been rechristened 'Ekam Sanatan Bharat Dal', and by August, the party had expanded enough to appoint party chiefs across twenty-one states.

He was also adding the finishing touches to a 'training module', a bunch of online courses that seek to imbibe a 'Sanatan Hindu' perspective on politics and political philosophy. His party was also seeking to establish weapons training and self-defence units, helmed by a former Indian Army colonel, to train Hindus.

Sandeep was slowly piecing together his dream project—of training Hindus in shaastra and shastra.

But his efforts have come at a cost. BJP supporters, who had been steadfast in their loyalty to him as long as he took down rivals, are now abandoning him. Views on his YouTube channel are dipping—from over three million a month to just over a million now. As a result, his earnings from YouTube have dropped, too, he said—it has halved from the earlier monthly earnings of $3,000.

Yet, Sandeep was going to continue fighting Modi and the BJP. Abrahamic religions, but especially Judaism, were out to destroy Hinduism, he told his followers. In their conspiracy, they had managed to co-opt the RSS and the BJP, 'just like they had co-opted Raja Ram Mohan and Mohandas Karamchand Gandhi,' he added. All this had only led him to conclude that Modi had to be defeated. Hindus had to be saved.

~

A lot has changed over the five years that it took to report and write this book.

Weeks after I sent this manuscript off, a film called *The Kerala Story* released across the country.

I tracked the reception to the film closely. The film, whose existence was shrouded in lies and, likely, deceit, received a rousing response from audiences. Audiences in cinema halls broke into spontaneous sloganeering against Muslims;[2] many stepped out of theatres seeking violence against them. Hindu nationalist groups booked movie theatres out and ensured free screenings for large groups of people.

In Mumbai, I found some of these groups going into slum localities and offering free movie tickets to women, especially. A well-oiled network of sympathizers seemed to have opened their coffers for the movie to be disseminated widely.

They realized the power it wielded.

I witnessed this power first-hand. A fourteen-year-old girl, the daughter of an acquaintance, living in a slum not far from the Mumbai airport, was offered a free ticket by a Hindutva group. They told her it was a film about self-defence, in case she ever finds herself harrassed.

For days after watching the movie, she refused to leave home, petrified that she might suffer brutality the way the Hindu women in the movie suffer after they join ISIS. It took many days of convincing by her parents for her to step out of her home.

In other parts of the country, the film was sparking violent clashes.

The attempts to weave propaganda into popular culture have only grown more brazen; its effects have only become more insidious. The riches this film earned, even as it further polarized an already-fragmented society, are sure to lure others to make such films—being a Hindutva cheerleader is an even more financially lucrative proposition now.

Communalism, in everyday life, has been normalized and made so commonplace that it no longer elicits outrage or disapproval for the most part. From Uttarakhand, where Hindus were identifying Muslim properties with 'X' marks, to Haryana, to Manipur, to my home state of Maharashtra, where a new right-wing organization emerged overnight and has held over fifty rallies peddling hate speech and Islamophobic rhetoric, communalism is now the mainstay of India's politics. Days after its inauguration, hate had now started ringing in the new Parliament, without any action or censure.[3]

Yet, as we have seen, no recognized political leader is identified with any of these movements. Instead, mobilization of masses and execution of violence are now outsourced to non-state actors, seemingly independent but tied with an invisible umbilical cord to the Hindu right.

The role of propaganda will become even more crucial, and so will the role of cheerleaders.

Grimmer days are upon us.

Acknowledgements

In 2020, I went on a ten-day silent meditation retreat, nestled in the Dhauladhar mountains. Of the many learnings from the course, one is particularly relevant to invoke here.

Each object that existed owed its existence to the efforts of an invisible chain of people. A coffee mug, for instance, existed because of the labour of many, not just the potter—everyone, from those who gathered the clay to those who transported the raw materials, to those who shaped it and those who finally sold it.

In the same manner, this book might carry my name, but it has been made possible by the efforts and kindness of a vast number of people.

Swati Chopra, whose belief in the book made this possible. Without you, this book might not exist, Swati.

Kamal, Kavi and Sandeep, for letting me into their lives and allowing me to tell their stories. To their families, especially Ramkesh, for patiently answering my questions. To Kamal's late father, Ashok Varma, for his warmth and gregariousness.

Samar Halarnkar, an editor who constantly inspires me, for sending me on long reporting trips to document hate crimes in the countryside, one of which led to this book. Madhur Singh and Alison Saldanha, for all the support in shaping some of the earliest reports.

To Bhavya Dore, for her jokes and her painstakingly detailed feedback. To Sukhada Tatke, for her patient edits. Mohamed Thaver, more a brother than a friend, for always being around. Erika Broers, for her friendship and her comments on early drafts that helped shape the book. Anahita Mukherji, for her detailed feedback and encouraging words. Reetu, for the enthusiasm, thank you.

Puja Changoiwala, for a lot, but especially the loud laughs and the mid-afternoon pep talks. Thank you also to Sangeeta Chakravorty, for the detailed comments and questions; Sadaf Modak, for all the afternoon chais; to Subir Sinha and Rohit Chopra, for their work and their comments. To Shivam Srivastav, for lending books and forgetting about them. To Rahul Fernandes, for his support.

To Rajdeep Sardesai and Ramachandra Guha, for being so gracious and supportive. Karishma Mehrotra, for her ever-welcoming hospitality. Navtej Purewal, for always having my back and inspiring me. Shakuntala Banaji, for her input and solidarity. Saunskruti Kher, for inviting me to Utopia, a quaint and serene farm stay that magically cracked open a woeful writer's block. Uttara and Adwait Kher, for their warmth and hospitality. Thank you to the staff at Buland, the site of another similar writing trip. Tanima Saha, for her sharp edits and patience.

To Jayesh Acharya, for being such a pillar of support. To Sapna Nair and Jugal Purohit, for allowing me to mooch off them on every Delhi visit I made, for their comments on the drafts and for their company. Jugal, for always inspiring me to do better. To Sandeep and Sheila Deshpande, for their constant support.

To Mom, Alka Purohit, who puts up with so much and asks for so little. You mean the world to me, Ma.

And finally, to Sejal. For enduring all that it took to make this happen. For everything, always.

Notes

Scan this QR code to access the detailed notes

About the Author

Kunal Purohit has been a journalist for nearly two decades, writing on issues of development, politics, inequality, gender and the intersections between them. He is an independent journalist and has, in the recent past, reported closely on hate crimes and the rise of Hindu nationalism across the country. He has worked in the newsrooms of *Hindustan Times* and *The Free Press Journal* in Mumbai. He is an alumnus of the School of Oriental and African Studies, University of London, from where, as a Felix Scholar, he earned an MSc in Development Studies with distinction in 2017. Kunal received the Ramnath Goenka Award for Excellence in Civic Journalism in 2012, the Statesman Award for Rural Reporting in 2014 and the UNFPA-Laadli Media Award for Gender Sensitive Reporting in 2014 and 2019. He has also received various fellowships and journalism grants. His work can be found in Al Jazeera, ProPublica, *The Times of India*, *Foreign Policy*, *Hindustan Times*, *South China Morning Post*, Deutsche Welle and The Wire, among others.

HarperCollins *Publishers* India

At HarperCollins India, we believe in telling the best stories and finding the widest readership for our books in every format possible. We started publishing in 1992; a great deal has changed since then, but what has remained constant is the passion with which our authors write their books, the love with which readers receive them, and the sheer joy and excitement that we as publishers feel in being a part of the publishing process.

Over the years, we've had the pleasure of publishing some of the finest writing from the subcontinent and around the world, including several award-winning titles and some of the biggest bestsellers in India's publishing history. But nothing has meant more to us than the fact that millions of people have read the books we published, and that somewhere, a book of ours might have made a difference.

As we look to the future, we go back to that one word—a word which has been a driving force for us all these years.

Read.

Harper
Collins

HARPER
PERENNIAL

HARPER
BUSINESS

HARPER
BLACK

हार्पर
हिन्दी

HarperCollins
Children'sBooks

HARPER
DESIGN

HARPER
VANTAGE

Harper
Sport